Hans G. Hoffmann
Marion Hoffmann

Power-Wortschatz
Englisch

Wortschatztraining leicht gemacht

Hueber Verlag

Wenn Sie Fragen zum englischen Sprachgebrauch oder Kommentare zum Inhalt dieses Buches haben, besuchen Sie uns bitte auf unserer Website www.englishmaster.de. Dort finden Sie auch Informationen zu Grammatik, Wortschatz, Sprachgebrauch und Landeskunde sowie Übungen und Hinweise auf nützliche Lernhilfen.

Hans G. Hoffmann, Marion Hoffmann

| 3. | 2. | 1. | | Die letzten Ziffern |
| 2013 | 12 | 11 | 10 | 09 | bezeichnen Zahl und Jahr des Druckes. |

Alle Drucke dieser Auflage können, da unverändert,
nebeneinander benutzt werden.
1. Auflage
© 2009 Hueber Verlag, 85737 Ismaning, Deutschland
Umschlaggestaltung: Parzhuber und Partner, München
Fotogestaltung Cover: wentzlaff | pfaff | güldenpfennig kommunikation gmbH, München
Coverfoto: © gettyimages / Photodisc
Zeichnungen: Martin Guhl, Stein am Rhein, Schweiz (www.cartoonexpress.ch)
Redaktion: Valerio Vial u. Stephanie Pfeiffer, Hueber Verlag, Ismaning
Layout: Cihan Kursuner, Hueber Verlag, Ismaning
DTP: Satz+Layout Fruth GmbH, München
Druck und Bindung: Ludwig Auer GmbH, Donauwörth
Printed in Germany
ISBN 978-3-19-107909-3

Vorwort

Dieses Buch hilft Ihnen, die wichtigsten englischen Wörter richtig zu gebrauchen. Hält man sich vor Augen, dass mit den 100 häufigsten Wörtern bereits über 50 Prozent eines jeden beliebigen Textes erfasst sind, so wird einem deutlich, wie wichtig es ist, gerade diese 100 Wörter intensiv zu üben. Dieses Buch übt aber nicht nur die 100 häufigsten Wörter, sondern etwa 1 000 Wörter, die erstens für die Kommunikation wichtig sind und zweitens in der Anwendung Schwierigkeiten bereiten.

Je häufiger ein Wort ist, desto höher ist die Zahl seiner Verwendungen; desto größer ist in der Regel auch die Menge der Fehlerquellen, die das Wort dem Lernenden bietet. Denken Sie an die Präpositionen *of*, *in* und *to*. Sie gehören zu den 10 am häufigsten gebrauchten Wörtern. Es ist also extrem wichtig, Fügungen zu üben, in denen diese Präpositionen anders als ihre deutschen Entsprechungen gebraucht werden: *typical of* („typisch für"), *in the British Isles* („auf den Britischen Inseln"), *welcome to London* („willkommen in London")!

Dieses Buch behandelt die häufigsten dieser Sprachfallen, wobei manchmal vom deutschen, manchmal vom englischen Wort ausgegangen wird. Welche Fehlerquellen lauern doch bei den englischen Entsprechungen für „fahren", „machen", „sollen", „als" oder „sicher", und wie leicht verwechselt man *street* und *road*, *lose* und *loose*, *bring* und *take*, *human* und *humane*!

In diesen Zusammenhang gehören auch die *false friends*, denen es in der Sprache (wie im Leben!) aus dem Weg zu gehen gilt. Nach Durcharbeitung dieses Buches wissen Sie natürlich, dass „aktuell" nicht *actual*, „blamieren" nicht *blame* und „eventuell" nicht *eventual* ist und dass Sie sich vor dem Falschgebrauch von *handy* und *backside* hüten müssen.

Das Verhindern typischer Fehler ist aber nur eine der Aufgaben, die sich dieses Buch stellt. Sie lernen idiomatische Redensarten kennen, mit denen Sie Ihrem Englisch Würze verleihen können: *the jury is still out on it* – was für eine plastische, aktuelle Art auszudrücken, dass über eine Sache das letzte Wort noch nicht gesprochen ist! Sie finden in diesem Buch u. a. auch Sprichwörter, beschönigende Formulierungen (Euphemismen) oder die im Englischen so wichtigen *phrasal verbs*.

Bekannterweise kann man im Englischen oft nicht von der Schreibung auf die Aussprache schließen. Dies führt zu typischen Aussprachefehlern, auch bei häufig gebrauchten Wörtern. Die meisten dieser Fälle finden Sie hier in Übungen zusammengefasst, sodass Sie am Ende wissen, dass *bury* sich mit *berry* reimt, *gone* mit *on* und *comb* mit *home*.

Dieses Buch soll nicht nur informativ, sondern auch unterhaltsam sein. Aus diesem Grund wechseln sich unterschiedliche Übungs- und Testformen ab. Sie finden Übersetzungs-, Einsetz- und Zuordnungsübungen, Texte und Antwortauswahltests in bunter Folge, die – jeweils in Kapiteln gebündelt – von einem Kreuzworträtsel abgeschlossen werden. Falls Sie die Übungen in einer anderen Reihenfolge durcharbeiten wollen, können Sie sich orientieren entweder anhand der Inhaltsübersicht nach Themen (S. 6–7) oder mit Hilfe des Registers (ab S. 218), das Ihnen auf Anhieb sagt, wo Sie etwa eine Übung zu *while – during*, *since – for*, „können" oder „werden" finden.

Beachten Sie für ein erfolgreiches Lernen die folgenden Empfehlungen:

– Lernen bzw. üben Sie in der Regel keine Einzelwörter! Wer Einzelwörter lernt, wird später Fehler bei der Bildung von Kollokationen und Sätzen machen. Kollokationen sind typische Wortkombinationen wie zum Beispiel *take a walk* = „einen Spaziergang machen". Lernen Sie also in diesem Fall das Verb *take* mit dem Nomen *walk* gleich mit; dann machen Sie später nicht den Fehler, *make a walk* zu sagen. Dieses Buch ermuntert Sie, in Kollokationen und Sätzen zu denken. Die Übungssätze sind alle authentisch und realistisch; d. h., sie wurden von Muttersprachlern in einer realen Situation in dieser Form gesprochen oder geschrieben und sind von hoher Gebrauchshäufigkeit.

– Üben Sie nicht nur mündlich, sondern auch schriftlich; d. h., schreiben Sie Ihre Lösung auf und korrigieren Sie sie auch schriftlich anhand des Schlüssels.

– Wiederholen Sie eine Übung, wenn Sie zu viele Fehler gemacht haben.

– Lernen bzw. üben Sie nicht zu lange an einem Stück! Eine Übung pro Arbeitssitzung ist genug. Sehen Sie in Ihrer Wochenplanung regelmäßige Englischsitzungen vor.

Last but not least: Wenn Ihnen mal nicht einsichtig ist, warum das Buch Ihnen eine bestimmte Lösung anbietet; wenn Sie wissen wollen, ob Ihre abweichende Lösung nicht doch vielleicht ebenfalls richtig ist (oder warum sie falsch ist); oder wenn Sie sonst eine Frage zum Englischlernen haben, besuchen Sie unsere Website <u>englishmaster.de</u>. Von dort können Sie über den *Contact us*-Link eine E-Mail mit Ihrer Frage an uns senden. Sie erhalten dann kostenlos eine persönliche Antwort.

Wir wünschen Ihnen viel Spaß und Erfolg beim Englischlernen.

Hans G. Hoffmann, Marion Hoffmann

Inhaltsübersicht nach Themen

Die Zahlenangaben beziehen sich auf die durchnummerierten Übungen.

Deutsche Verben, die es englisch in sich haben
bekommen 6; besuchen 115; brauchen 105; bringen 107; dürfen 36, 53;
erhöhen, steigen, senken, sinken 56; erreichen 108; fahren 57, 125;
gehen 125; halten 26; kommen 99; können 25, 36; lassen 71; laufen 10;
liegen – legen 91; machen 89; müssen 36, 88; sagen 93; sollen 30, 36;
sprechen, reden 117; stehen – stellen 68; verbessern – verschlechtern 69;
werden 15; wollen 37

Kleine deutsche Wörter – große englische Probleme
als 1; alle 2; alles 3; am 35; an 35; auch 86; auf 35; aus 109; erst 121;
es 43; in 123; mich 111; mir 111; schon 58; seit 129; sich 66; sie 97; so 103;
uns 52; unter 118; von 64; wie 82; zu 95

Deutsche Adjektive, die nicht ganz leicht zu übersetzen sind
böse 104; eigen 11; einzig 20; falsch 67; gern 113; groß 112; leicht –
schwer 12; leise – laut 27; nächste – letzte 46; schlecht – schlimm 75;
schnell 84; sicher 21

Deutsche Nomen mit englischem Fragezeichen
Ärger(nis) 104; Besuch 115; Fehler 67; Null 118; Platz 72; Preis, Gebühr,
Kosten 73; Problem, Thema, Frage 22; Rand 100; Stelle 118; -ung- und
-keit-Wörter 17

Englische Wörter mit Pfiff
be + Adjektiv 59; bring – take 107; do 38, 89; have 54; it 42; jump 78;
know 119; lie – lay 91; lose – loose 79; make – do 89, 102; remember –
remind 102; run 122; say – tell 93; since – for 129; street – road 8; take 89;
want 32, while – during 83

Tests stärken Ihr sprachliches Immunsystem
5; 18; 28; 34; 45; 55; 63; 76; 87; 98; 106; 114; 124; 129

***Idioms* würzen Ihr Englisch**
4; 31; 40; 49; 50; 77; 78; 93; 106; 119; 122

Proverbs sind geballte Volksweisheiten
16; 117; 120

Euphemismen sagen's durch die Blume
94

Slang sagt's im Blaumann
113; 116

Präpositionen verlieren ihre Schrecken
9; 35; 41; 51; 65; 74; 81; 96; 127

Falsche Freunde haben keine Chance
48; 61; 90; 110; 128

Phrasal verbs geben den *authentic touch*
7

Grammatik ermöglicht guten Wortgebrauch
23; 24; 62; 101; 111; 129

Kollokationen: wer mit wem kann und wer nicht
13; 60

Aussprache: ganz einfach, wenn man's weiß
33; 47; 85

Antonyme: Adjektive und ihr Gegenteil
19; 80

Minidialoge: für jeden Pott ein passender Deckel
44

Crosswords
10; 19; 29; 40; 50; 60; 70; 80; 90; 100; 110; 120; 130

Stories
14; 39; 92; 126

Inhalt nach Kapiteln

Seite

Kapitel 1

1	„Als" ist längst nicht immer *as*	13
2	„Alle" heißt längst nicht immer *all*	14
3	„Alles": Ende gut, alles gut	16
4	*Idioms:* Wenn jemand den Speck nach Hause bringt	17
5	*Multiple choice:* Ähnliche Wörter und andere falsche Freunde	19
6	„Bekommen": Mit *get* liegen Sie meistens richtig	20
7	*Phrasal verbs:* Verben, wie der Engländer sie mag	22
8	*Street* oder *road*? Die *Oxford Street* führt nicht nach Oxford	23
9	Präpositionen – die endlose Fehlerquelle	24
10	*„Laufen" Crossword*	26

Kapitel 2

11	„Eigen": ein Stolperstein besonderer Art	27
12	„Leicht" – „schwer": *The right word is sometimes hard to find*	28
13	Kollokationen: *Colourless green ideas sleep furiously*	30
14	*News in the silly season*	31
15	„Werden" – Ich dachte, ich werd' nicht mehr ...	32
16	Sprichwörter: Wenn man Omelettes macht, fallen Späne	34
17	Wie man „-ung"- und „-keit"-Wörter übersetzt	36
18	*Multiple choice:* Wörter, die man leicht verwechselt	38
19	*Antonym Crossword*	40

Kapitel 3

20	„Einzig" – „Einzel-" – „einzeln" – „für sich"	41
21	„Sicher" – Eines ist sicher ...	42
22	„Problem" – „Thema" – „Frage": *Global warming is the big issue*	43
23	Singular oder Plural – das ist hier die Frage	45
24	Mit oder ohne *-ly*? – *He is wise. He talks wisely.*	46
25	„Können": *can, could, be able to, may, might*	48
26	„Halten" ist nicht immer *hold*	49
27	„Leise" – „laut": Das kannst du laut sagen!	50
28	*Multiple choice:* Wörter, die man leicht verwechselt	52
29	*Illness Crossword*	54

Kapitel 4

30 „Sollen": *a difficult word to translate* 55
31 *Idioms:* Wenn Leute das Fett kauen 56
32 *Want – a dangerous friend* 58
33 *A donkey and a monkey eating their dessert in the desert* 59
34 *Multiple choice:* Wörter, die oft verwechselt werden 61
35 Präpositionen: „an", „am", „auf" 62
36 „Können", „müssen", „sollen", „dürfen", „wollen" 63
37 „Wollen" ist nicht immer *want* 64
38 *Do – the heavy-duty verb*, das Hochleistungsverb 65
39 *Another news story* 67
40 *Idioms Crossword:* Von Geldleuten und Bettgenossen 68

Kapitel 5

41 Präpositionen sind Glückssache – *a matter of luck* 69
42 *It* – wenn es nicht „es" heißt 70
43 „Es" – wenn „es" nicht *it* heißt 72
44 Minidialoge: *"I'm afraid I can't come." – "Congratulations!"* 73
45 *Dual choice: Two men stole a bank (or did they?)* 75
46 „Nächste" – „letzte": *The next train from the nearest station* 76
47 Aussprache: *The liquor-drinking vicar getting sicker* 78
48 *False friends: With friends like these ...* 79
49 *Idioms:* Wenn man am falschen Baum hochbellt 81
50 *Fruitcake Crossword* 82

Kapitel 6

51 Präpositionen: *You pay the cabby but pay for things bought* 83
52 „Uns" ist nicht immer *us* 84
53 „Dürfen" – *If I may make a suggestion ...* 86
54 *Have: another heavy-duty verb* 87
55 *Multiple choice: Looking incredulously at incredible targets* 88
56 „Erhöhen", „steigen", „senken", „sinken", „fallen" etc. 90
57 „Fahren": *PRETTY GIRLS DON'T RIDE THE SUBWAY* 91
58 „Schon": *Has she left yet? Has she left already?* 92
59 Deutsch: Verb + Nomen – Englisch: *be* + Adjektiv 94
60 *Collocations Crossword* 96

Kapitel 7

61 *False friends are worse than open enemies* 97
62 Nomen, die im Gegensatz zum Deutschen ohne Artikel stehen . . . 98
63 *Multiple choice: Confusables and other nuisances* 99
64 „Von": *Of Mice and Men* „Von Mäusen und Menschen" 101
65 *Prepositions for pleasure* 102
66 „Sich": *-self, each other* oder unübersetzt 104
67 „Falsch" – „Fehler": *Don't pull at your false beard.* 106
68 „Stehen" – „stellen" 107
69 „Verbessern" und „verschlechtern": *Making it better or worse* 108
70 *Occupations Crossword* 110

Kapitel 8

71 „Lassen" – *a pain in the translator's neck* 111
72 „Platz": Häufig ist *place* fehl am Platz 112
73 „Preis", „Gebühr", „Kosten" etc. – *Everything has its price* 114
74 Präpositionen: *best boxer in the world – champion of the world* . . 115
75 „Schlecht", „schlimm": manchmal schlecht auszudrücken 117
76 *Don't lose the loose dress you're carrying in your bag* 119
77 Von den Knien der Bienen: wieder ein paar *idioms* 120
78 *Jump: Getting jumpy when jumping the queue or a red light* 121
79 *You can lose your head only if it's already loose* 123
80 *Another Antonym Crossword* 124

Kapitel 9

81 Präpositionen: *Some more hard nuts to crack* 125
82 „Wie": *Is as strong as an ox; looks like an ox; but isn't an ox* 126
83 „Während": *while* oder *during*? 127
84 „Schnell": *He quickly got a fast car and drove too fast* 129
85 *What a worm does in a storm – and other pronunciation problems* . 130
86 „Auch": *There's more to it than "too" and "also"* 132
87 *Dual choice: Be sensitive and make a sensible choice* 133
88 „Müssen": Kein Mensch muss müssen 135
89 „Machen": *make, do, take (or drive)?* 136
90 *False Friend Crossword* 138

Kapitel 10

91 „Liegen" – „legen": Wie man sich bettet, so liegt man 139
92 *Opportunity makes a thief* – „Gelegenheit macht Diebe" 141
93 „Sagen" – *There's a lot to be said for "tell"* 142
94 Euphemismen: *Excuse me, where's the euphemism, please?* 143
95 „Zu": *Too good to be true?* 144
96 *Prepositions: You're good at them!* 146
97 „Sie": *she, her, they, them, it, you* 147
98 *Dual choice: A live coward is better than a dead hero* 149
99 „Kommen": *Coming down is easier than going up* 150
100 *„Rand" Crossword* 152

Kapitel 11

101 Deutsch: Adverb – Englisch: Verb 153
102 *I remember reminding you to make tea before doing your homework* 154
103 So ist es nun mal – *That's the way it is* 155
104 „Ärger", „Ärgernis", „ärgerlich", „verärgert", „böse", „wütend" .. 157
105 „Brauchen": *Do you have what it takes?* 158
106 *Multiple choice: If the shoe doesn't fit, don't wear it* 160
107 „Bringen": *Bring it here and take it there* 161
108 *Translating „sein" – not always easy to achieve* 163
109 „Aus": *Out of sight, out of mind* 164
110 *Advanced Learner's Crossword* 166

Kapitel 12

111 Andersartige Konstruktionen im Deutschen und Englischen 167
112 „Groß": *Big fish eat little fish* 168
113 „Gern": „Der kann mich mal gern haben!" 169
114 *Dual choice: The jury was convinced and convicted the defendant* .. 171
115 „Besuchen" – „Besuch": *Short visits make long friends* 172
116 *The F-word* 174
117 „Sprechen", „reden": *Talk less, listen more* 175
118 Ein deutsches Wort – mehrere englische Entsprechungen 177
119 *Idioms* mit *know: Knowing which side your bread is buttered* 178
120 *Proverb Crossword* 180

Kapitel 13

121 „Erst": Oft anders zu übersetzen, als man denkt 181

122 *A good run is better than a bad stand* 182

123 „In": *Are you in the picture?* 184

124 *Dual choice: The age of miracles is past* 185

125 „Gehen", „fahren": *If you want a thing done, go; if not, send* 187

126 *No news is good news* 188

127 Präpositionen: *Surprises never cease* 190

128 *Let me see that tattoo on your backside* 191

129 *Make your choice: How good is your grammar?* 192

130 *Superpower Crossword: The United States of America* 194

Lösungen 195

Register 218

1 „Als" ist längst nicht immer *as*

Als Entsprechungen für deutsch „als" kommen vor allem die folgenden Wörter in Frage:

as, but, from, than, when

Hauptfehler, die hier gemacht werden, sind:
1. Gebrauch von *as* (statt des meist richtigeren *when*) zur Einleitung von Nebensätzen der Zeit.
2. Gebrauch von *as* oder *then* (statt des richtigen *than*) nach Steigerungsformen wie *better*, *younger* etc.

Setzen Sie die passenden Entsprechungen für „als" ein.

a _____ she last saw him, he was still a child.

b She surprised the hell out of him _____ she said yes.

c One morning, just _____ she was about to leave, there was a scratch at the door and in walked two cats.

d In his youth he was employed _____ a gardener at Gordon Castle.

e I regard you _____ my friend.

f She's three years older _____ her brother.

g Research shows that vegetarians are more intelligent _____ meat eaters.

h I can't do more _____ try.

i I'd rather die _____ give a speech in public.

j He's different _____ most of the other kids at his school.

k It looks _____ if you're right.

l I've had nothing _____ trouble with this car since I got it.

m This incident should be taken _____ a warning.

surprise the hell out of someone	jemand verdammt überraschen
be about to do something	im Begriff sein, etwas zu tun
a scratch [skrætʃ] **at the door**	ein Kratzen an der Tür
research [rɪ'sɜːtʃ] **shows**	Forschungen haben ergeben
I'd rather die [daɪ]	ich würde lieber sterben
give a speech in public ['pʌblɪk]	öffentlich eine Rede halten
incident ['ɪnsɪdənt]	Vorfall

2 „Alle" heißt längst nicht immer *all*

Wesentliche Entsprechungen für deutsch „alle" sind *all, everyone / everybody* und *every*.

Bei *all* muss man gelegentlich unterscheiden zwischen einer Konstruktion mit *the* (z. B. *all the dogs*) oder ohne *the* (z. B. *all dogs*):
all dogs = „alle Hunde schlechthin";
all the dogs = „alle Hunde aus einer begrenzten Anzahl".

Übersetzen Sie.

a   Alle Leute lieben ihn.

b   Wir alle lieben ihn.

c   Ich kenne sie nicht alle.

d   Ich kenne sie alle nicht.

e   Es reicht nicht für alle.

f   Dieses Buch ist für alle, die ihr Englisch verbessern wollen.

g   Sie ist ein Vorbild für uns alle.

h   Wie wir alle wissen, hat der Kunde immer Recht.

i   Alle Kinder haben ein Recht auf Bildung.

j   Alle Kinder des Dorfes wurden geimpft.

k   Sie kennt alle Schüler, und alle Schüler kennen sie.

l   Alle Bürger sind vor dem Gesetz gleich.

m   Sie buchstabierte alle Wörter richtig.

n   Bei Nacht sind alle Katzen grau.

o   Alle Straßen führen nach Rom.

p   Er kommt alle vierzehn Tage.

q   Er kommt alle halbe Jahre.

improve [ɪmˈpruːv]	verbessern (→ Übung 69)
be an example [ɪgˈzɑːmpl] **to someone**	für jemand ein Vorbild sein
customer [ˈkʌstəmə]	Kunde, Kundin
be right [raɪt]	Recht haben
be entitled [ɪnˈtaɪtld] **to something**	ein Recht auf etwas haben
education [edjuˈkeɪʃn]	Bildung
village [ˈvɪlɪdʒ]	Dorf
vaccinate [ˈvæksɪneɪt]	impfen
citizen [ˈsɪtɪzən]	Bürger(in)
before the law [lɔː]	vor dem Gesetz
spell (– spelled/spelt – spelled/spelt)	buchstabieren
by / at night	bei Nacht

3 „Alles": Ende gut, alles gut

All's well that ends well ist das entsprechende englische Sprichwort. Shakespeare (1564–1616) hat es so gefallen, dass er eine seiner Komödien danach benannt hat.

Aber *all* ist nicht die einzige Entsprechung für „alles"; es gibt auch noch *everything* und *anything* – das letztere vor allem in der Bedeutung „alles / jedes x-beliebige".

Übersetzen Sie.

a   Hast du denn alles vergessen?

b   Ich sagte ihr alles, was ich wusste.

c   Geld ist nicht alles.

d   Alles hat seine Zeit.

e   Alles, was sie sagt, stimmt.

f   Ich habe dir alles gesagt, was ich weiß.

g   Das ist alles, was ich weiß.

h   Ist das alles, was Sie an Gepäck haben?

i   Bei eBay kann man alles kaufen oder verkaufen.

j   Ich würde alles für dich tun.

k   Diese Leute sind zu allem fähig.

l   Ich liebe dich über alles.

m   Er ist alles, nur kein Held.

n   Alles in allem bin ich mit der Qualität dieses Druckers sehr zufrieden.

o   Es ist nicht alles Gold, was glänzt.

forget – forgot – forgotten	vergessen – vergaß – vergessen
know [nəʊ] **– knew** [njuː] **– known** [nəʊn]	wissen – wusste – gewusst
it's true [truː]	es stimmt
luggage ['lʌgɪdʒ] / **baggage** ['bægɪdʒ]	Gepäck
buy [baɪ] **or sell** [sel]	kaufen oder verkaufen
be capable ['keɪpəbl] **of something**	einer Sache fähig sein
hero ['hɪərəʊ]	Held
quality ['kwɒləti]	Qualität
printer ['prɪntə]	Drucker
be pleased [pliːzd] **with something**	mit etwas zufrieden sein
glitter ['glɪtə]	glitzern

He who denies all confesses all. (Proverb)
Wer alles leugnet, gesteht alles. (Sprichwort)

4 *Idioms:* Wenn jemand den Speck nach Hause bringt

Ein *idiom* ist eine bildhafte Redensart, deren Gesamtbedeutung nicht der
Summe der Bedeutungen der einzelnen Wörter entspricht: *If you take the bull
by the horns*, wenn Sie also den Stier bei den Hörnern packen, dann ist in
Wirklichkeit gar kein Stier mit Hörnern da, sondern ein Problem, dem Sie sich
direkt, ohne Umschweife und mutig stellen. Und wenn man sagt: *Everything
in the garden is lovely*, dann zitiert man unbewusst eine zum *idiom* gewordene
Zeile aus einem uralten Schlager und meint damit: „Es ist alles in bester
Ordnung."
Hier nun einige geläufige *idioms*.

Ordnen Sie dem *idiom* in der linken Spalte jeweils die passende Erklärung zu.

a   She brings home the bacon.

b   She easily flies off the handle.

c   She has both feet on the ground.

d   She hasn't got a leg to stand on.

e   She keeps a low profile.

f   She keeps her own counsel.

g   She rubs me up the wrong way.

h   She runs a tight ship.

i   She runs rings around him.

j   She's not going to set the world on fire.

k   She's thrown her hat in the ring.

a   She avoids attracting attention.

b   She can't prove that what she says is right.

c   She doesn't say what she thinks.

d   She manages things strictly and effectively.

e   She often loses her temper.

f   She says things that annoy me.

g   She's a candidate.

h   She's much better than him.

i   She's not particularly good.

j   She's practical and sensible.

k   She's the breadwinner.

bacon ['beɪkən]	Speck
avoid [ə'vɔɪd] **doing something**	es vermeiden, etwas zu tun
attract attention [ə'trækt ə'tenʃn]	die Aufmerksamkeit auf sich lenken
fly off the handle ['hændl]	„vom Griff wegfliegen"
prove [pruːv]	beweisen
strict(ly) and effective(ly) [ɪ'fektɪv(li)]	streng und effektiv
lose [luːz] **one's temper**	die Beherrschung verlieren
counsel ['kaʊnsəl]	Rat
annoy [ə'nɔɪ]	ärgern
rub [rʌb]	reiben
run a tight ship ['taɪt 'ʃɪp]	ein Schiff streng führen
not particularly [pə'tɪkjʊləli] **good**	nicht besonders gut
set something on fire	etwas in Brand setzen
sensible ['sensəbl]	vernünftig ⚠
throw [əʊ] **– threw** [uː] **– thrown** [əʊ]	werfen – warf – geworfen
breadwinner ['bredwɪnə]	Ernährer(in) (*der Familie etc.*)

5 *Multiple choice:* Ähnliche Wörter und andere falsche Freunde

Multiple choice tests – also Antwortauswahl-Tests – sind besonders an amerikanischen Schulen beliebt. Für uns sind sie hier eher ein etwas leichterer Zeitvertreib, bei dem Sie mit vier ähnlich klingenden oder mitunter falsch gebrauchten Wörtern in Fehlerversuchung geführt werden und im Endeffekt vielleicht ein paar nützliche Wörter hinzulernen.

Wählen Sie das richtige Wort aus.

a   He was _____ of murder and sentenced to life imprisonment.
    converted · convicted · convinced · persuaded

b   The police were _____ that he had committed the murder.
    confirmed · converted · convinced · induced

c   They _____ a walk in the woods.
    did · made · took · went

d   Sorry, I can't talk about it right now – I have a bus to _____.
    catch · drive · get · take

e   I must have _____ a cold while waiting at the bus stop.
    caught · fetched · got · taken

f   The committee _____ the view that no changes needed to be made.
    came to · constituted · represented · took

g   They _____ about the problem of global warming.
    discussed · spoke · talked · told

h   We need to _____ a lifestyle that's in harmony with our natural surroundings.
    abide · adapt · adept · adopt

i   Rising health care costs _____ all of us.
    affect · effect · prefer · refer

j   Global warming is going to have an _____ on all of us.
    affect · effect · issue · outcome

convict [kən'vɪkt] **someone of murder**	jemand des Mordes schuldig sprechen
sentence someone to life imprisonment [ɪm'prɪznmənt]	jemand zu einer lebenslangen Freiheitsstrafe verurteilen
commit [kə'mɪt] **a murder**	einen Mord begehen
committee [kə'mɪti]	Ausschuss; Komitee
take the view [vjuː] **that ...**	die Ansicht vertreten, dass ...
global warming [gləʊbl 'wɔːmɪŋ]	(die) Erderwärmung
our natural surroundings [sə'raʊndɪŋz]	unsere natürliche Umgebung
affect [ə'fekt] **someone**	jemand betreffen / schaden

6 „Bekommen": Mit *get* liegen Sie meistens richtig

Das ist eines der ersten Dinge, die man lernt: „bekommen" ist nicht *become*. Trotzdem schleicht sich dieser total falsche Freund immer wieder mal ein (*she became a baby*), und überhaupt ist es nützlich, zu sehen, wie das häufig gebrauchte Verb „bekommen" im Englischen ausgedrückt wird – meistens (aber nicht immer!) mit *get*!

Übersetzen Sie.

a Wo haben Sie das bekommen?

_____

b Ich habe neulich einen Brief von ihr bekommen.

_____

c Was hast du denn zum Geburtstag bekommen?

_____

d Arbeit ist hier schwer zu bekommen.

_____

e Ich kann ihn nicht dazu bekommen, morgens etwas zu essen.

_____

f Wir mussten ihn aus dem Wasser herausbekommen.

_____

g   Sie bekommt ein Kind.

h   Du wirst eine Erkältung bekommen, wenn du da sitzt.

i   Du bekommst noch 50 Euro von mir.

j   Ich bekomme langsam Hunger.

k   Die Kinder bekamen Angst und rannten weg.

l   Schließlich bekamen sie Heimweh und kehrten zurück nach Irland.

m   Milch bekommt mir nicht.

the other day [ði ʌðə ˈdeɪ]	neulich
birthday [ˈbɜːθdeɪ]	Geburtstag
in the morning [ˈmɔːnɪŋ]	am Morgen; morgens
have a baby [ˈbeɪbi]	ein Kind bekommen
catch (a) cold	eine Erkältung bekommen
sit – sat – sat	sitzen – saß – gesessen
get hungry [ˈhʌŋgri]	Hunger bekommen
child [tʃaɪld] **– children** [ˈtʃɪldrən]	Kind – Kinder
get scared [skeəd]	Angst bekommen
run away [rʌn əˈweɪ]	wegrennen
eventually [ɪˈventʃuəli]	schließlich
get homesick [ˈhəʊmsɪk]	Heimweh bekommen
return [rɪˈtɜːn] **to**	zurückkehren nach
Ireland [ˈaɪələnd]	Irland
pork doesn't agree [əˈgriː] **with me**	Schweinefleisch bekommt mir nicht

7 *Phrasal verbs:* Verben, wie der Engländer sie mag

Ja, zusammengesetzte Verben wie *drop by* (= vorbeikommen) oder *put off* (= aufschieben) sind im Englischen außerordentlich häufig und beliebt. Für Muttersprachler sind sie elegant, modern, lässig, einfach zu gebrauchen – aber das letztere sind sie gerade für Ausländer nicht, die tun sich leichter mit „Einwortverben" wie *visit* oder *postpone*.

Wir können hier nicht alle *phrasal verbs* auflisten, geschweige denn üben – dafür brauchten wir ein Buch von tausend Seiten. Aber die nachstehende Übung kann Ihnen die *phrasal verbs* ein wenig näher bringen.

Ersetzen Sie die *phrasal verbs* in den folgenden Sätzen durch Ausdrücke aus der nachstehenden Liste in der korrekten Form.

address	discover	invent	overcharge	rise
be about	extinguish	like	reduce	tolerate
bully	happen to find	obtain	return	visit

a   Their salesman <u>calls on</u> us twice a month.

b   I don't <u>care for</u> this band and their songs.

c   As I cleared out my cupboards, I <u>came across</u> some old photos.

d   How did you <u>come by</u> this beautiful picture?

e   We'll have to <u>cut back on</u> our spending.

f   The article <u>deals with</u> the role of women in Egyptian society.

g   We <u>went back</u> to the cave the next day.

h   Prices are <u>going up</u> at an alarming rate.

i   The government thinks it has <u>hit on</u> the best way to
    promote growth and reduce poverty.

j   I <u>made up</u> a story about two lions walking along Broadway
    in New York.

k   Smaller children are often <u>pushed around</u> by the bigger ones.

l   Firefighters quickly <u>put out</u> the fire.

m   I don't think I would have <u>put up with</u> such behaviour.

n   In many tourist spots the local people make a living by
    <u>ripping off</u> tourists.

o   There are a lot of difficult issues that have to be <u>sorted out</u>.

clear out cupboards ['kʌbədz]	Schränke ausräumen
cut back on our spending	unsere Ausgaben einschränken
deal with the role of women ['wɪmɪn]	die Rolle der Frauen behandeln
cave [keɪv]	Höhle
at an alarming [ə'lɑːmɪŋ] rate	in alarmierender Weise
promote growth [prəməʊt 'grəʊθ]	das Wachstum fördern
rip off tourists ['tʊərɪsts]	Touristen abzocken

8 *Street* oder *road*? Die *Oxford Street* führt nicht nach Oxford

Streets sind in der Stadt, zwischen Häusern – sie haben Bürgersteige
(*pavements* BE / AE *sidewalks*), Geschäfte etc.:
We live in / on Russell Street.

Der deutschen „Hauptstraße" entspricht BE *High Street* (*the shoe shop in the
High Street*) und AE *Main Street* (*the shoe store on Main Street*).

Roads hingegen sind Verkehrswege, die irgendwo hinführen:
the Dover road (= die Straße nach Dover).

Viele *roads*, die sich ursprünglich zwischen Orten befanden, sind heute durch
die Ausbreitung der Städte mitten in der Stadt. *Edgware Road* (= die Straße
nach Edgware) z. B. ist heute ein Londoner Straßenname:
Her office is in / on Edgware Road. (Londoner sagen auch: *in / on the Edgware
Road*).

Setzen Sie *street(s)* oder *road(s)* ein.

a What we need is not more _____ but fewer cars.
b Our car broke down on the _____ to Kimberley.
c There's no place to park on the _____ where we live.
d There are many quaint old houses on our _____.
e A shower drove us to take shelter in a farmhouse by the _____.
f The sight of children playing in the _____ has become rare in our
cities.

g I feel safe walking the _____ of my neighbourhood alone after dark.
h Despite impressive average incomes, Asian immigrants are by no means living on easy _____.
i (*Proverb:*) The _____ to hell is paved with good intentions.
j (*Proverb:*) Better have a friend on the _____ than gold or silver in your purse.

break down (– broke – broken)	eine Panne haben
quaint old houses ['haʊzɪz]	malerische alte Häuser
take shelter ['ʃeltə]	sich unterstellen
impressive [ɪm'presɪv]	eindrucksvoll; beachtlich
average income [ævərɪdʒ 'ɪnkʌm]	Durchschnittseinkommen
by no means [miːnz]	keineswegs; durchaus nicht
live on easy street ['iːzi striːt]	ein leichtes Leben haben
paved [peɪvd] **with good intentions**	mit guten Absichten gepflastert

9 Präpositionen – die endlose Fehlerquelle

Präpositionen werden im Englischen häufig anders gebraucht als im Deutschen. Dieses Buch enthält zahlreiche Präpositionsübungen, in denen die meisten kritischen Fälle erfasst sind. Am besten schreiben Sie sich besonders fehleranfällige und für Sie wichtige Fügungen heraus, also zum Beispiel: *in a low voice* = „**mit** leiser Stimme".

Beachten Sie auch, dass in Frage- und Relativsätzen die Präposition umgangssprachlich **nach**gestellt wird:
*Who does the book you are reading **from** belong **to**?* (= Wem gehört das Buch, aus dem du vorliest?) Sehr unnatürlich wäre hier die Voranstellung der Präpositionen: *To whom does the book from which you are reading belong?*
Berühmt ist der spöttisch-unidiomatisch formulierte Satz, den Churchill (1874–1965) an den Rand eines Manuskripts schrieb, in dem ihm ein pedantischer Korrektor die Präpositionen umgestellt hatte: *This is a kind of nonsense up **with** which I will not put.* Normal wäre gewesen: *This is a kind of nonsense I won't up **with**.* (= Dies ist eine Art von Unfug, die ich mir nicht gefallen lasse.)

Setzen Sie jeweils eine der folgenden Präpositionen ein.

at	by	for	from	in	on	with

a Columbus discovered America _____ accident.

b We learn _____ experience.

c The house is _____ fire!

d We're going _____ holiday next week.

e When she heard the good news, she wept _____ joy.

f He dropped out of college _____ lack of money.

g The issue was discussed _____ length.

h She played the sonata _____ memory.

i Police officers are suspicious _____ nature.

j He studies during the day and works _____ night.

k She's a teacher _____ profession.

l Some of the wounded were screaming _____ pain.

m Louis won the fight _____ points.

n God knows how many died while the dictator was _____ power.

o They say they didn't shoot him _____ purpose.

p Our flight arrived _____ schedule.

by accident [ˈæksɪdənt]	durch Zufall; zufällig
discover [dɪˈskʌvə]	entdecken
experience [ɪkˈspɪəriəns]	Erfahrung
weep – wept – wept	weinen – weinte – geweint
drop out of college [ˈkɒlɪdʒ]	das Studium abbrechen
lack of money [ˈmʌni]	Geldmangel
issue [ˈɪʃuː]	Thema; Frage; Problem (→ Übung 22)
suspicious [səˈspɪʃəs]	misstrauisch
the wounded [ˈwuːndɪd] ⚠	die Verwundeten
scream [skriːm]	schreien
on purpose [ˈpɜːpəs]	mit Absicht
on schedule [ˈʃedjuːl]	planmäßig

10 „Laufen" Crossword

In den folgenden Sätzen fehlen die Wörter, die eine Form von „laufen"
ausdrücken.

Beispiel:
Last year, she _____ her first marathon in 5 hours and 37 minutes.
Hier fehlt das Wort *ran*, das Sie also an der betreffenden Stelle im *Crossword*
einsetzen.

Across

1 This product _____ well
   in the United States.
3 Everything is _____ well.
5 The program doesn't _____
   on my computer.
6 Time _____ and we can
   do nothing to stop it.
7 He _____ like the wind.
9 The water is _____ into
   my shoes.
11 After _____ half the
   distance we stopped to rest.

Down

1 At which cinema is the film _____?
2 Everything _____ according to plan.
4 We'll have to wait and see how things _____.
5 She jumped up and _____ out of the room.
7 My nose was _____ like a faucet.
8 You can't just let things _____.
10 You can _____ to the station.

11 „Eigen": ein Stolperstein besonderer Art

Im Englischen besteht grammatisch ein gewaltiger Unterschied zwischen „ihr eigenes Haus" (*their own house*) und „ein eigenes Haus" (*a house of their own*). Nach einem Nomen mit vorangehendem *a(n)* muss also die Konstruktion *of my / your / his / her / its / our / their own* stehen!

Beachten Sie das bei der Übersetzung der folgenden Beispiele.

a   Es war meine eigene Schuld.

b   Er ist ein Opfer seines eigenen Erfolgs.

c   Ich ziehe es vor, in meinem eigenen Bett zu schlafen.

d   Kümmere dich um deine eigenen Angelegenheiten!

e   Wir sahen mit eigenen Augen, was da passierte.

f   Sie bezahlten alles aus eigener Tasche.

g   Dies ist mein eigener Computer.

h   Ich habe einen eigenen Computer.

i   Sie hat ihre eigenen Talente.

j   Sie hat eigene Talente.

k   Bis zum Alter von 105 Jahren lebte sie in ihrer eigenen Wohnung.

l   Sie hatte genug Geld gespart, um in eine eigene Wohnung zu ziehen.

m   Unsere Katze ist sehr eigen mit ihrem Futter.

it's my fault [fɔːlt]	es ist meine Schuld
victim [ˈvɪktɪm]	Opfer
prefer [prɪˈfɜː] **to do something**	es vorziehen, etwas zu tun
mind one's own business	sich um seine eigenen Angelegen-
[ˈbɪznɪs]	heiten kümmern
what has happened?	was ist passiert?
pay for something ⚠	eine Sache bezahlen
up to the age [eɪdʒ] **of 105**	bis zum Alter von 105 Jahren
save money [ˈmʌni]	Geld sparen
move [muːv] **into a flat**	in eine Wohnung ziehen
be particular about	mit etwas eigen sein; es sehr
something	genau mit etwas nehmen
the cat's food [fuːd] ⚠	das Futter der Katze

▸ Aussprache der Buchstabenverbindung *ove*: *love* [ʌ] (= Liebe),
▸ *drove* [əʊ] (= fuhr), *move* [uː] (= bewegen), *novel* [ɒ] (= Roman).

Die Übung enthält noch einige weitere Fehlerversuchungen, so etwa die
Aussprache von *fault* (wie in *all*, nicht wie in *oh*!), *business* (zwei-, nicht
dreisilbig!) und *food* (langes uh – *foot* dagegen mit kurzem u!), die Beachtung
des Unterschieds zwischen *victim* (Opfer z. B. eines Verbrechens) und *sacrifice*
(Opfer, das man den Göttern darbringt oder für seine Kinder auf sich nimmt)
und zwischen *pay* (*you **pay** the taxi driver, you **pay** a price*) und *pay for* (*you
pay for something you buy – a drink, a meal, a ticket, etc.*).

12 „Leicht" – „schwer": *The right word is sometimes hard to find*

Der Linguist stellt die Frage so: Welche Kollokationen sind hier die geläufigsten?
Mit anderen Worten: Kann man von *a serious bag* oder *an easy delay* sprechen?
Nein, normalerweise nicht. Es gibt eben Wortverbindungen, die häufig verwendet werden (Kollokationen), und solche, die nur ein Dichter oder ein Spaßvogel
benutzt, so wie etwa Shakespeare von *loving hate* („liebender Hass") oder
heavy lightness („schwere Leichtheit") spricht. Da wäre also *a serious bag* und
an easy delay durchaus erlaubt, nicht aber bei uns normalen Sprachbenutzern,
die wir uns bemühen, das Englische konventionell-richtig zu gebrauchen.

Was also ist „leicht" oder „schwer" in den folgenden Kollokationen? Wählen Sie aus:

| easy / easily   light(ly)   slight(ly)   scanty / scantily |
| difficult   grave   hard   heavy / heavily   serious(ly)   severe(ly) |

a eine leichte Tasche
b eine leichte Aufgabe
c eine leichte Lektüre
d eine leichte Verzögerung
e leichte Kopfschmerzen
f leichter Regen
g leicht zu verstehen
h leicht getan
i leichter gesagt als getan
j leicht verletzt
k leicht bekleidet

l eine schwere Tasche
m eine schwere Aufgabe
n schwere Zeiten
o eine schwere Krankheit
p ein schwerer Fehler
q ein schwerer Schlag
r schwer zu sagen
s schwer arbeiten
t schwer bewaffnet
u schwer verletzt

bag [bæg]	Tasche
task [tɑːsk]	Aufgabe
reading [ˈriːdɪŋ]	Lektüre
delay [dɪˈleɪ]	Verzögerung
a headache [ˈhedeɪk]	Kopfschmerzen
injured [ˈɪndʒəd]	verletzt
clad [klæd] / **dressed** [drest]	bekleidet
illness [ˈɪlnəs]	Krankheit
mistake [mɪˈsteɪk]	Fehler
blow [bləʊ]	Schlag
armed [ɑːmd]	bewaffnet

13 Kollokationen: *Colourless green ideas sleep furiously*

Was Kollokationen sind, haben wir gerade in der Übung 12 erfahren. In der Überschrift zitieren wir einen berühmten Satz des Linguisten Chomsky (*1928), mit dem er veranschaulicht, dass eine Formulierung zwar grammatisch richtig, dabei aber logisch und kollokativ unsinnig sein kann: „Farblose grüne Ideen schlafen wütend." Wir aber haben es nicht mit „wütend schlafenden farblos-grünen Ideen", sondern wollen in den folgenden Sätzen jeweils das zum Bezugswort am besten passende Verb einsetzen.

Setzen Sie das jeweils passendste Verb in der richtigen Form ein.

| give   have   keep   make   play   run   suffer   take   take out |

a Everyone needs to stop and _____ a break every now and then.
b It's very difficult to _____ a living by freelance writing.
c Every time I book a trip, the travel agent recommends that I _____ travel insurance.
d I _____ A levels in History, Art and English and studied History at Stirling University.
e They have until the 15th of April to _____ us their decision.
f What sports did you _____ in high school?
g Professional sport _____ enormous demands on the body.
h He lived in the wilderness with only a dog to _____ him company.
i I like to cook but I don't think I'd be any good at _____ a restaurant.
j She _____ a number of operations as a child.
k She's not a woman who _____ fools gladly.

everyone ['evriwʌn]	jeder
needs [niːdz] **to stop**	muss mal innehalten
break [breɪk]	Pause
every now and then	ab und zu; hin und wieder
living ['lɪvɪŋ]	Lebensunterhalt
freelance ['friːlɑːns] **writing**	freiberufliches Schreiben
the travel agent ['trævl eɪdʒənt]	das Reisebüro
recommend [rekə'mend]	empfehlen

travel insurance [ɪnˈʃʊərəns]	(eine) Reiseversicherung
A levels [ˈeɪ levlz]	*BE* ≈ Abitur
decision [dɪˈsɪʒn]	Entscheidung
enormous [ɪˈnɔːməs]	enorme
demands [dɪˈmɑːndz]	Anforderungen
she doesn't suffer fools gladly	sie kann Dummköpfe nicht vertragen

14 *News in the silly season*

The silly season, „die alberne Jahreszeit" nennt man in England die Ferienzeit im Sommer, wenn alle Leute im Urlaub sind und sich nichts Wichtiges ereignet – die Saure-Gurken-Zeit. Die Zeitungen müssen trotzdem ihre Seiten füllen, und das tun sie dann mit *human interest stories* wie der folgenden.

Ersetzen Sie die unterstrichenen Verben durch andere mit ähnlicher Bedeutung (und in der passenden Form!) aus der folgenden Liste.

deposit disappear inform load make pack remove	
renovate take	

Dustmen <u>dump</u> bride's presents

BRIDE EMILY BELL WAS SHATTERED WHEN HER
WEDDING PRESENTS WERE <u>CARTED</u> AWAY – BY DUSTMEN

EMILY, 23, and her husband, Oliver, had stored the gifts in their yard while they <u>decorated</u> their new home. They had carefully <u>placed</u> about £2,000 worth of cutlery, crockery and glasses in cartons.

But when they went out to bring them back in, the boxes had <u>gone</u>.

Heartbroken, Emily said last night: "A neighbour told us she saw the refuse collectors <u>taking</u> them. We <u>put in</u> a claim for compensation, but the council's insurers more or less <u>told</u> us the cartons shouldn't have been <u>left</u> near the dustbin."

31

dustman [ˈdʌstmən]	*BE* Müllmann
(*Pl.* **-men** [mən])	
dump [dʌmp]	abladen; (*hier:*) zur Müllkippe mitnehmen
present [ˈpreznt] / **gift** [gɪft]	Geschenk
shattered [ˈʃætəd]	am Boden zerstört
wedding [ˈwedɪŋ]	Hochzeit
cart away [kɑːt əˈweɪ]	abtransportieren
store something [stɔː]	etwas lagern
yard [jɑːd]	*BE* Hof
decorate [ˈdekəreɪt]	*BE* streichen und tapezieren
place in cartons [ˈkɑːtnz]	in Kartons verstauen
cutlery [ˈkʌtləri]	*BE* Besteck
crockery [ˈkrɒkəri]	Geschirr
the boxes had gone [gɒn] ⚠	die Kartons waren weg
the refuse [ˈrefjuːs] **collectors**	*BE* die Leute von der Müllabfuhr
put in a claim for compensation	Schadenersatz beantragen
the council's insurers [ɪnˈʃʊərəz]	die Versicherung der Stadtverwaltung
dustbin [ˈdʌstbɪn]	*BE* Mülltonne

15 „Werden" – Ich dachte, ich werd' nicht mehr …

Das Verb „werden" gehört zu den 30 häufigsten der deutschen Sprache; wir gebrauchen es mit Nomen, Adjektiven und Verben (und gelegentlich salopp-idiomatisch, wie in der Überschrift). Wir machen uns kaum Gedanken, wann und wie wir „werden" benutzen, aber im Englischen müssen wir es, da es eine ganze Reihe von Entsprechungen gibt: vor Nomen oft *become*; vor Adjektiven oft *get*, aber auch *become*; für allmähliches Werden oft *grow*; für plötzliches vielleicht *turn*; im Passiv eine Form von *be* (*am, is, are, was, were, have been* etc.) Darüber hinaus gibt es auch ein paar idiomatische Fügungen wie zum Beispiel *go crazy* und *go mad*, aber so ein deutsches *idiom* wie „ich dachte, ich werd' nicht mehr" hat überhaupt keine direkte Entsprechung; man müsste es mit einem anderen Bild ausdrücken, etwa so: *You could have knocked me down with a feather.*

Übersetzen Sie.

a   Ihr Sohn wurde ein berühmter Musiker.

b   Was willst du werden, wenn du erwachsen bist?

c   Er wurde sehr böse.

d   Ich konnte sehen, dass er böse wurde.

e   Wir gehen besser. Es wird spät.

f   Die wirtschaftliche Lage ist sehr schwierig geworden.

g   Dein Tee wird kalt.

h   Es wird täglich schlimmer.

i   Alle Systeme werden zweimal jährlich überprüft.

j   Der Mann wird zur Zeit von der Polizei verhört.

k   Das Buch wurde in mehrere Sprachen übersetzt.

l   Er ist zu fünf Monaten Gefängnis verurteilt worden.

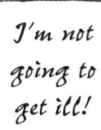

m   Ich werde langsam müde.

n   Bist du verrückt geworden?

o   Sie wird nächstes Jahr 80.

p   Sie ist gerade 20 geworden.

q   Ich werde nicht krank werden!

a famous musician [mju'zɪʃn]	ein berühmter Musiker
he was very angry ['æŋgri]	er war sehr böse / wütend
the economic situation [sɪtjʊ'eɪʃn]	die wirtschaftliche Lage
worse [wɜːs]	schlimmer; schlechter
check the systems ['sɪstəmz]	die Systeme überprüfen
question ['kwestʃən] **someone**	jemand verhören
translate into several languages	in mehrere Sprachen übersetzen
sentence to five months	zu fünf Monaten Gefängnis
in prison ['prɪzn]	verurteilen

16 Sprichwörter: Wenn man Omelettes macht, fallen Späne

Sprichwörter (= *proverbs* ['prɒvɜːbz]) sind Lebensweisheiten, die zumeist seit
Jahrhunderten, vielleicht Jahrtausenden, in einer Kultur weitergegeben werden.
Oft werden sie in Bildern, also metaphorisch, ausgedrückt: *Too many cooks spoil
the broth* (= Zu viele Köche verderben die Brühe bzw. Suppe). Was gesagt
werden soll, gilt ja nicht nur in der Küche, sondern überhaupt im Leben: *The
quality of work does not necessarily increase with the number of people doing it.*
Im Fall der zu vielen Köche hat das deutsche Sprichwort fast das gleiche Bild
wie das englische, nur die Brühe ist durch Brei ersetzt: „Viele Köche verderben
den Brei."

Es gibt aber auch englische Sprichwörter, die eine Lebenserfahrung in ein ganz
anderes Bild kleiden als das entsprechende deutsche Sprichwort: *You cannot
make an omelette without breaking eggs* (≈ Wo gehobelt wird, fallen Späne).
Nicht alle Sprichwörter sind so alt wie das von den Köchen oder Spänen. Jede
Generation gewinnt neue Erfahrungen, die – prägnant formuliert – ebenfalls
zu Sprichwörtern werden, in unserer Zeit zum Beispiel die aus der Datenver-
arbeitung stammende Einsicht *Garbage in, garbage out* (= Wenn man in den
Computer Müll, also Unsinn, eingibt, kommt auch Unsinn heraus).

Im Folgenden finden Sie zwei Listen:
1. links alphabetisch geordnet eine Liste **englischer** Sprichwörter,
2. rechts alphabetisch geordnet eine Liste **deutscher** Sprichwörter.
Einem englischen Sprichwort entspricht jeweils ein deutsches mit anderem
Bild, aber etwa gleicher Aussage.

Ordnen Sie die Sprichwörter einander zu.

1	A bird in the hand is worth two in the bush.	1	Alles hat seinen Preis.
2	Birds of a feather flock together.	2	Der Spatz in der Hand ist besser als die Schwalbe auf dem Dach.
3	Charity begins at home.	3	Der Zweck heiligt die Mittel.
4	Dog does not eat dog.	4	Ehre wem Ehre gebührt.
5	Don't count your chickens before they are hatched.	5	Ein Unglück kommt selten allein.
6	Don't put all your eggs in one basket.	6	Eine Krähe hackt der anderen kein Auge aus.
7	Easy come, easy go.	7	Gleich und gleich gesellt sich gern.
8	Every man is the architect of his own fortune.	8	Jeder ist seines Glückes Schmied.
9	Fine feathers make fine birds.	9	Jeder ist sich selbst der Nächste.
10	Give credit where credit is due.	10	Kleider machen Leute.
11	It never rains but it pours.	11	Man soll den Tag nicht vor dem Abend loben.
12	It's too late to shut the stable door after the horse has bolted.	12	Man soll nicht alles auf eine Karte setzen.
13	Like father, like son.	13	Morgenstund' hat Gold im Mund.
14	The early bird catches the worm.	14	Probieren geht über Studieren.
15	The end justifies the means.	15	Wenn das Kind in den Brunnen gefallen ist, deckt man ihn zu.
16	The proof of the pudding is in the eating.	16	Wie der Herr, so's Gescherr.
17	There's no such thing as a free lunch.	17	Wie gewonnen, so zerronnen.

worth [wɜ:θ]	wert
bush [bʊʃ] ⚠	Busch; Strauch; Gebüsch
birds of a feather ['feðə]	(etwa:) Vögel mit gleichem Federkleid
flock together [tə'geðə]	sich scharenweise zusammenfinden
charity ['tʃærəti]	Mildtätigkeit; (tätige) Nächstenliebe
hatch [hætʃ]	ausschlüpfen; ausbrüten
basket ['bɑ:skɪt]	Korb
architect ['ɑ:kɪtekt]	Architekt(in)
fortune ['fɔ:tʃən]	Glück; Schicksal; Geschick
credit ['kredɪt]	Anerkennung
be due (to someone)	(jemandem) zustehen
pour [pɔ:]	gießen
stable ['steɪbl]	(Pferde-)Stall
bolt [bəʊlt]	weglaufen; (Pferd:) durchgehen
catch [kætʃ] – caught [ɔ:] – caught	fangen – fing – gefangen
worm [wɜ:m] ⚠	Wurm; Made
end [end]	Zweck; Ziel
the means [mi:nz]	das / die Mittel
proof [pru:f]	Beweis
pudding ['pʊdɪŋ] ⚠	(BE) warme, süße Nachspeise
free [fri:]	kostenlos
lunch [lʌntʃ]	(Mittag-)Essen

17 Wie man „-ung"- und „-keit"-Wörter übersetzt

Deutschen Nomen auf „-ung" oder „-keit" entspricht im Englischen oft eine verbale Konstruktion:

| Eine kommerzielle **Nutzung** des Materials ist nicht zulässig. | *The material **may not be used** for commercial purposes.* |
| Leichte **Lesbarkeit** der Texte ist von großer Wichtigkeit. | *It is very important that the texts **are easy to read**.* |

Versuchen Sie bei der Übersetzung der folgenden Sätze statt des fett gedruckten Nomens ein Verb zu benutzen.

a   Für die **Beantwortung** der Fragen stehen Ihnen 60 Minuten zur **Verfügung**.

b   Die Dinge haben eine völlig unerwartete **Entwicklung** genommen.

c   Wie ist die **Entscheidung** ausgefallen?

d   Das ist keine **Erklärung** für sein Verhalten.

e   Ich bin der **Meinung**, dass es sich hier um ein Missverständnis handelt.

f   Wir haben die **Erfahrung** gemacht, dass viele Kunden diese Art von Service begrüßen.

g   Diese Chemikalien finden oft zur **Herstellung** von Bomben **Verwendung**.

h   Die Behörden arbeiten an einer **Lösung** dieses Problems.

i   Diese Gebäude lassen sich nicht für die **Unterbringung** von Gefangenen nutzen.

j   Wir setzten uns sofort mit der Bank in **Verbindung**.

k   Die **Verständigung** mit diesen Patienten ist oft schwierig.

l   Er betonte die **Wichtigkeit** von Verhandlungen.

develop [dɪˈveləp] **in an unexpected way**	eine unerwartete Entwicklung nehmen
explain someone's behaviour [bɪˈheɪvjə]	jemandes Verhalten erklären
misunderstanding [mɪsʌndəˈstændɪŋ]	Missverständnis

we have found [faʊnd]	wir haben die Erfahrung gemacht
welcome / appreciate [əˈpriːʃieɪt] something	etwas begrüßen
chemical [ˈkemɪkl]	Chemikalie
build bombs [bɪld ˈbɒmz] ⚠	Bomben herstellen
the authorities [ɔːˈθɒrətiz]	die Behörden
solve a problem [ˈprɒbləm]	ein Problem lösen
house [haʊz] ⚠ prisoners [ˈprɪznəz]	Gefangene unterbringen
contact [ˈkɒntækt] someone	sich mit jemand in Verbindung setzen
communicate with someone	sich mit jemand verständigen
negotiate [nɪˈgəʊʃieɪt]	verhandeln

18 *Multiple choice:* Wörter, die man leicht verwechselt

Nur eine der jeweils vier Möglichkeiten macht Sinn.

Welches Wort passt?

a She's the _____ owner of the company.
alone · lonely · single · sole

b You can't leave the child _____ at home.
alone · lonely · single · sole

c It's tough being a _____ parent.
alone · lonely · single · sole

d Her husband's illness left her _____ and despairing at times.
alone · lonely · single · sole

e If the backpack is too _____, it can lead to injuries to the back and shoulders.
difficult · heavily · heavy · tough

f If the task is too _____, the child will give up.
   difficult · hardly · heavily · heavy

g Diphtheria is a very _____ disease.
   earnest · heavy · series · serious

h Most people are much too _____ to believe such nonsense.
   sensible · sensibly · sensitive · sensitively

i If you have _____ skin, you should avoid the sun whenever possible.
   sensible · sensibly · sensitive · sensitively

single ['sɪŋgl]	einzige(r, s); alleinerziehend
sole [səʊl]	einzig; alleinig
it's tough [tʌf]	es ist hart / schwierig
parent ['peərənt]	Elternteil
despairing [dɪ'speərɪŋ]	verzweifelt
at times [ət 'taɪmz]	manchmal
backpack ['bækpæk]	Rucksack
injuries ['ɪndʒəriz] **to the back**	Verletzungen am Rücken
tough [tʌf]	hart; zäh
task [tɑːsk]	Aufgabe
diphtheria [dɪf'θɪəriə]	Diphtherie
disease [dɪ'ziːz]	(*eine bestimmte*) Krankheit
sensible ['sensəbl]	vernünftig
sensitive ['sensətɪv]	sensibel; empfindlich
avoid [ə'vɔɪd] **the sun**	die Sonne meiden

19 *Antonym Crossword*

Antonyms ['æntənɪmz] sind Gegensatzwörter wie zum Beispiel *black – white, father – mother* etc.

Tragen Sie in das *Crossword* jeweils das Antonym des unterstrichenen Wortes ein.

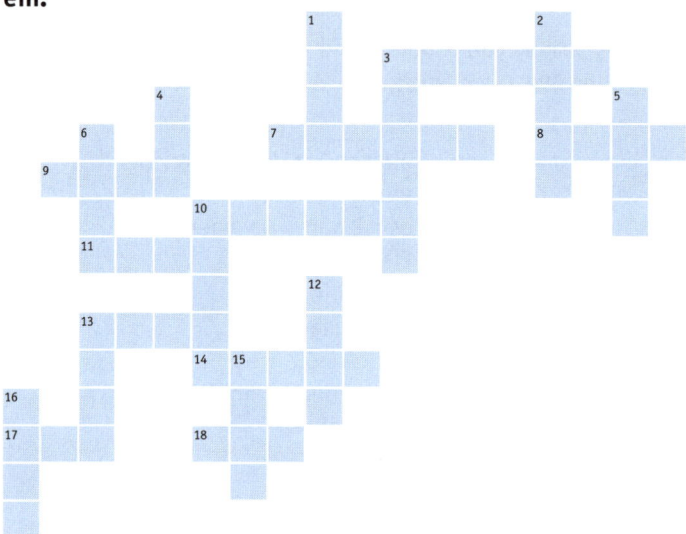

Across

3 a <u>clever</u> remark
7 a <u>weak</u> argument
8 a <u>short</u> person
9 an <u>industrious</u> student
10 a <u>dim</u> light
11 an <u>interesting</u> book
13 <u>fat</u> meat
14 <u>soft</u> treatment
17 a <u>young</u> man
18 an <u>old</u> shirt

Down

1 a <u>rough</u> skin
2 <u>clean</u> clothes
3 a <u>rough</u> surface
4 a <u>wet</u> surface
5 a <u>fast</u> car
6 a <u>soft</u> drink
10 a <u>sharp</u> knife
12 a <u>low</u> wall
13 a <u>soft</u> voice
15 a <u>closed</u> door
16 a <u>good</u> example

20 „Einzig" – „Einzel-" – „einzeln" – „für sich"

Übersetzen Sie.

a   Eric war ihr einziges Kind.

b   Eric war ein Einzelkind.

c   Eric ist immer ein Einzelgänger gewesen.

d   Geld ist nicht unsere einzige Sorge.

e   Es ist das Einzige, was wir tun können.

f   Wir sind nicht die Einzigen, die das denken.

g   Es fehlte kein einziges Stück.

h   Ich erinnere mich an jedes einzelne Wort.

i   Die Kinder kamen einzeln herein.

j   Der Einzelne ist machtlos.

k   Ich möchte mit jedem Mitglied einzeln sprechen.

l   Teile des Pakets können nicht einzeln verkauft werden.

m   Er verbrachte über 11 Jahre in Einzelhaft.

n   Leider ist das kein Einzelfall.

o   Wir prüfen jeden Einzelfall.

p   Wir betrachten jeden Fall für sich.

their only child [tʃaɪld]	ihr einziges Kind
loner [ˈləʊnə]	Einzelgänger(in)
it's a great worry [ˈwʌri]	es ist eine große Sorge
be missing [ˈmɪsɪŋ]	fehlen
remember [rɪˈmembə] **something**	sich an etwas erinnern
	(→ Übung 102)
the individual [ɪndɪˈvɪdʒuəl]	der Einzelne
powerless [ˈpaʊələs]	machtlos
talk to a member [ˈmembə]	mit einem Mitglied sprechen
part / component [kəmˈpəʊnənt]	(Bestand-)Teil
package [ˈpækɪdʒ]	(z. B. Software-)Paket
spend – spent – spent	verbringen – verbrachte – verbracht
solitary (confinement	Einzelhaft
[kənˈfaɪnmənt]**)**	
unfortunately [ʌnˈfɔːtʃənətli]	unglücklicherweise; leider
look at a case [keɪs]	einen Fall betrachten / prüfen

21 „Sicher" – Eines ist sicher ...

... *yes, one thing is for sure: there's more than one word for "sicher" in English.*
Es kommen vor allem diese Entsprechungen in Frage:

certain(ly), safe(ly), secure(ly), sure(ly)

Setzen Sie eine passende Entsprechung für „sicher" ein.

a   He saved me from _____ death.

b   I'm _____ you've heard this joke before.

c   It is unwise to be too _____ of one's own wisdom.

d   It's not _____ that property prices will rise.

e   Very little is known for _____ about Shakespeare's private life.

f   _____ you don't mean to say that I'm too old to start something new.

g   This statement is quite _____ true.

h   Important documents should be kept in a _____ place.

i   Many women don't feel _____ walking the streets alone at night.

j   The mice realized that they would never be _____ from the cat unless they tied a bell to her leg to tell them when she was coming.

k   The plane carrying 107 people landed _____ and there were no injuries.

l   When people are confident their jobs are _____, they tend to spend freely.

m   You can easily pay for your shopping via the internet using your credit card but you should always check that your card details are kept _____.

n   Electronic privacy is achieved by using a _____ server, removing the data as soon as possible, and storing electronic files in _____ locations.

save someone from death [deθ]	jemand vor dem Tod bewahren
wisdom ['wɪzdəm]	Weisheit; Klugheit
property prices ['prɒpəti praɪsɪz]	(die) Grundstückspreise
you don't mean to say	du willst doch nicht sagen
statement ['steɪtmənt]	Darstellung; Behauptung; Aussage
the mice realized ['rɪəlaɪzd]	die Mäuse erkannten
tie a bell to her leg	ihr ein Glöckchen ans Bein binden
privacy ['prɪvəsi]	Schutz der Intimsphäre; Datenschutz
remove the data [rɪ'muːv ðə 'deɪtə]	die Daten entfernen / löschen

22   „Problem" – „Thema" – „Frage": *Global warming is the big issue*

Ein Wort, dessen Gebrauchshäufigkeit in den letzten Jahren enorm zugenommen hat, ist *issue* ['ɪʃuː] in der Bedeutung *problem*.

Genau genommen bedeutet *issue* eher *topic*, also „Thema", in dem Sinn: *an important topic for debate or discussion*.
Aber ein wichtiges „Diskussionsthema" ist eben meistens ein „Problem", und es sind nicht zuletzt die Politiker, die gern auf das leicht beschönigende Wort *issue* ausweichen, wenn sie eine Aussage abschwächen wollen.

Bei der Übersetzung der nachstehenden Kollokationen helfen Ihnen die folgenden Wörter und Ausdrücke:

address an issue [əˈdres]	solve [sɒlv] / resolve [rɪˈzɒlv]
make an issue [ˈɪʃuː] of something	solution [səˈluːʃn]

a   ein Problem angehen

b   sich mit dem Thema häusliche
    Gewalt auseinandersetzen

c   die Korruption zum Thema machen

d   ein Problem lösen

e   eine Lösung des Problems

f   Geld ist kein Thema

g   ein umstrittenes Thema

h   ein großes Problem

i   ein brennendes Problem

j   eine entscheidende Frage

k   ein ungelöstes Problem

l   ein globales Problem

m   Umweltprobleme

Money isn't an issue.

global warming [ɡləʊbl ˈwɔːmɪŋ]	(die) Erderwärmung
domestic violence [ˈvaɪələns]	häusliche Gewalt
controversial [kɒntrəˈvɜːʃl]	umstritten; kontrovers
crucial [ˈkruːʃl]	entscheidend; äußerst wichtig
unresolved [ʌnrɪˈzɒlvd]	ungelöst
global [ˈɡləʊbl]	global; weltweit; Erd-
environmental [ɪnvaɪrənˈmentl]	Umwelt-

23 Singular oder Plural – das ist hier die Frage

Auf dieser Seite haben wir für Sie einige häufig gebrauchte Nomen zusammengestellt, bei denen der Numerus im Deutschen und Englischen nicht übereinstimmt.

Übersetzen Sie.

a   Die Möbel sind schön.

b   Die Abendnachrichten waren deprimierend.

c   Diese Informationen sind sehr wertvoll.

d   Die Fortschritte, die wir gemacht haben, sind höchst ermutigend.

e   Viele seiner Ratschläge sind gut.

f   Einige der Hausaufgaben waren ziemlich schwierig.

g   Meine Französischkenntnisse haben sich verbessert.

h   Die Vereinigten Staaten sind ein Land der Gegensätze.

i   Die Treppe ist ziemlich steil.

j   Dies ist meine beste Brille.

k   Diese Hose ist ein bisschen eng.

l   Die Umgebung ist schön.

m   Der Inhalt dieser Schachtel ist ein Vermögen wert.

n   Die Polizei ist auf der richtigen Spur.

o   Das amerikanische Volk ist sehr religiös.

the furniture ['fɜːnɪtʃə]	die Möbel
the evening news ['iːvnɪŋ njuːz]	die Abendnachrichten
depressing [dɪ'presɪŋ]	deprimierend
valuable ['væljʊbl]	wertvoll
make progress ['prəʊgres]	Fortschritte machen
most encouraging [ɪn'kʌrɪdʒɪŋ]	höchst ermutigend
my knowledge ['nɒlɪdʒ] of French	meine Französischkenntnisse
advice [əd'vaɪs]	Rat(schläge)
contrast ['kɒntrɑːst]	Gegensatz
steep stairs ['stiːp 'steəz]	eine steile Treppe
tight trousers ['taɪt 'traʊzəz]	eine enge Hose
the surroundings [sə'raʊndɪŋz]	die Umgebung
the contents ['kɒntents] of this box	der Inhalt dieser Schachtel
worth a fortune [wɜːθ ə 'fɔːtʃən]	ein Vermögen wert
on the right track [træk]	auf der richtigen Spur
religious [rɪ'lɪdʒəs]	religiös

24 Mit oder ohne -ly? – *He is wise. He talks wisely.*

Viele häufig gebrauchte Wörter gibt es in zwei Varianten:
- ohne die Endung -*ly*, also als Adjektiv,
- mit der Endung -*ly*, also als Adverb.

Entscheiden Sie bei den eingeklammerten Wörtern, ob die Form ohne oder mit -*ly* angebracht ist.

Die einfachste Regel ist eine negative:
Benutzen Sie **nicht** die -*ly*-Form, wenn sich das Wort auf ein **Nomen** (= Substantiv, Hauptwort), **Pronomen** (= Fürwort) oder einen **Namen** bezieht.

Man kann die Regel aber auch positiv formulieren:
Benutzen Sie die -*ly*-Form, wenn sich das Wort auf ein **Verb**, **Adjektiv** (= Eigenschaftswort), **Adverb** (= Umstandswort) oder einen **Satz** bezieht.

Setzen Sie die richtige Form ein.

a Fast cars are a (real) _____ danger on our roads.
b Drunk drivers are (real) _____ a danger on our roads.
c The driver was (obvious) _____ drunk.
d It was (obvious) _____ that the driver was drunk.
e It's (obvious) _____ safer to drive (slow) _____.
f Accidents are (frequent) _____ here.
g Accidents are (frequent) _____ caused by drunken drivers.
h Was she (serious) _____ injured? – No, her injuries were not (serious) _____.
i (Unfortunate) _____ I didn't have my mobile with me.
j (Unfortunate) _____ my battery is (extreme) _____ low.
k The battery (normal) _____ lasts about two years.
l Under (normal) _____ conditions the battery will last several years.
m For a child, a sting in the throat is (extreme) _____ (dangerous) _____.
n His political views are (dangerous) _____ (extreme) _____ .
o We should remove graffiti as (quick) _____ as possible.
p All graffiti will be (quick) _____ removed.
q (Quick) _____ removal of graffiti is the best way to discourage taggers.

danger ['deɪnʒə]	Gefahr
drunk(en) drivers [drʌŋk(n) 'draɪvəz]	betrunkene Autofahrer
obvious(ly) ['ɒbviəs(li)]	offensichtlich
frequent(ly) ['fri:kwənt(li)]	häufig
cause an accident ['æksɪdənt]	einen Unfall verursachen
injured ['ɪnʒəd] – **injuries** ['ɪnʒəriz]	verletzt – Verletzungen
the battery lasts two years	die Batterie hält zwei Jahre
a sting in the throat [θrəʊt]	ein Insektenstich im Hals
political views [pə'lɪtɪkl vju:z]	politische Ansichten
remove graffiti [rɪ'mu:v grə'fi:ti]	Schmierereien beseitigen
discourage [dɪs'kʌrɪdʒ] **taggers**	Sprayer vom Sprayen abhalten

25 „Können": *can, could, be able to, may, might*

„Können" in der Bedeutung „fähig sein", „beherrschen" ist *can* bzw. *could*.
Gebrauchen Sie *could* nur dann in der Bedeutung „konnte", wenn es nicht mit
„könnte" verwechselt werden kann, also wenn aus dem Zusammenhang hervor-
geht, dass „konnte" (nicht „könnte") gemeint ist. Benutzen Sie in allen
anderen Fällen *be able to*, also in der Vergangenheit ohne Zeitangabe, in der
Zukunft, nach *to* etc.
„Können" in der Bedeutung „es ist möglich, dass" ist *may* (= „kann") bzw.
might (= „könnte").
Um Erlaubnis wird mit *Can I / we* ... bzw. förmlicher *May I / we* ... gebeten.

Beachten Sie das bei der Übersetzung dieser Sätze.

a   Kannst du Schach spielen?

b   Wir können ja eine Partie Schach spielen.

c   Ich kann Englisch.

d   Ich kann dir nicht helfen.

e   Wir werden diesen Leuten nicht helfen können.

f   Es gab nicht viel, was der Präsident tun konnte.

g   Ich konnte den Schaden selbst beheben.

h   Mozart konnte schon mit vier Jahren Klavier spielen.

i   Es muss herrlich sein, Klavier spielen zu können.

j   Das kann die richtige Methode sein.

k   Das kann nicht die richtige Methode sein.

l   Es kann zu einem Bürgerkrieg kommen.

m Es könnte zu Schwierigkeiten kommen.

n Kann ich Ihnen helfen?

o Kann ich ein weiteres Exemplar haben?

It must be wonderful to be able to play the piano.

a game of chess [tʃes]	eine Partie Schach
repair [rɪˈpeə] **the damage** ['dæmɪdʒ]	den Schaden beheben
at the age [eɪdʒ] **of four**	mit vier Jahren
play the △ piano [piˈænəʊ]	Klavier spielen
wonderful ['wʌndəfl]	wunderbar; herrlich
the right method ['meθəd]	die richtige Methode
civil war [sɪvl 'wɔ:]	Bürgerkrieg
difficulty ['dɪfɪkəlti]	Schwierigkeit
another copy ['kɒpi]	ein weiteres Exemplar

26 „Halten" ist nicht immer *hold*

Etwas mit der Hand „halten" ist *hold*, etwas in einem Zustand „halten" ist *keep*, „anhalten" ist *stop*, eine Rede „halten" ist *give* oder *make*, ein Tor „halten" ist *save*, und wenn etwas eine Zeit lang „hält", dann sagt man *last*. Das ist es *in a nutshell*, aber außerhalb der Nussschale gibt es noch manche andere Entsprechungen für „halten", die wir hier nicht erklären können. Versuchen Sie sich an den folgenden Sätzen.

Setzen Sie die richtige Form des passenden Verbs ein.

a He was _____ a gun in his right hand.

b Can you _____ the ladder so that it's steady?

c There is little optimism that the truce will _____ for long.

d If you make a promise, you've got to _____ it.

e The internet makes it so easy to _____ in touch with family and friends.

f "Teaching the young _____ me young," says the 90-year-old professor.

g The milk won't _____ long in this heat.

h In 1946 Winston Churchill _____ a speech in Zurich calling for a "kind of United States of Europe".

i We were told that the bus _____ just outside the hotel.

j The Liverpool goalkeeper _____ two penalties and the trophy was Liverpool's.

k The battery in my cell phone _____ about a week.

l A good friendship _____ a lifetime.

m I'm sure he's a nice guy and all, but I wouldn't _____ him a friend.

n What do you _____ me for?

o It's important to _____ to the rules.

truce [tru:s]	Waffenstillstand
make a promise ['prɒmɪs]	ein Versprechen geben
call [kɔ:l] **for something**	zu etwas aufrufen
outside the hotel [həʊ'tel]	vor dem Hotel
penalty ['penəlti]	Elfmeter
cell phone ['sel fəʊn] *AE*	Mobiltelefon; Handy

27 „Leise" – „laut": Das kannst du laut sagen!

Diese beiden einfachen deutschen Wörter haben im Englischen eine ganze Reihe differenzierter Entsprechungen. So „kollokiert" z. B. *loud* mit *voice*, nicht aber mit *road*, und es besteht ein Unterschied zwischen *reading a poem aloud* (d. h. nicht still vor sich hin) und *reading a poem loudly* (d. h. mit lauter Stimme), ganz davon abgesehen, dass „mit lauter Stimme" im Englischen **in** *a loud voice* ist.

Übersetzen Sie.

a Er sprach leise.

b Der Typ am Nachbartisch redete laut von einem Videospiel, das er gerade spielte.

c Er sprach mit leiser Stimme.

d Könnten Sie bitte ein bisschen leiser sprechen?

e Könnten Sie bitte ein bisschen lauter sprechen?

f Ich höre Sie laut und deutlich.

g Sie klagte laut darüber, dass alles so teuer sei.

h Ich meine, sie sollte dies ein bisschen leiser singen.

i Aus dem Nachbarhaus kam leise Musik.

j Wir hörten das leise Murmeln eines Baches.

k Das Hotel ist in einer sehr lauten Straße.

l Was ich am meisten hasse, sind laute Nachbarn.

m Kannst du das Radio nicht ein wenig leiser / lauter stellen?

n Ein leiser Duft von Parfüm hing in der Luft.

o Ich hatte nicht die leiseste Ahnung.

p Könnten Sie uns das Gedicht mal laut vorlesen?

q „Das ist doch hier reine Abzocke!" – „Das kannst du laut sagen!"

at the next table ['nekst teɪbl]	am Nachbartisch
the guy [gaɪ] **over there**	der Typ da drüben
play a video ['vɪdɪəʊ] **game**	ein Videospiel spielen
voice [vɔɪs]	Stimme
complain about something	über etwas klagen; sich über etwas beklagen
expensive [ɪk'spensɪv]	teuer
I think [θɪŋk]	ich meine / glaube / denke
the house next door [nekst 'dɔː]	das Nachbarhaus
music ['mjuːzɪk]	Musik
the murmur ['mɜːmə] **of a brook** [brʊk]	das Murmeln eines Baches
what I hate most [məʊst]	was ich am meisten hasse
neighbour ['neɪbə]	Nachbar(in)
the smell of perfume ['pɜːfjuːm]	der Duft von Parfüm
have no idea [aɪ'dɪə]	keine Ahnung haben
it's just a rip-off ['rɪp ɒf]	es ist reine Abzocke
rip someone off	jemand abzocken

28 *Multiple choice:* Wörter, die man leicht verwechselt

In diesem *Multiple Choice* geht es um notorische Fehlerverursacher wie die Unterscheidung zwischen *human* und *humane*, *industrial* und *industrious*. Um die Sache noch etwas spannender zu machen, haben wir auch die *-ly*-Formen hinzugenommen – Sie müssen also auch beachten, worauf sich das Wort jeweils bezieht, um hier die richtige Entscheidung zu treffen.

Welches Wort passt?

a The group campaigns for the _____ treatment of laboratory animals.
human · humane · humanitarian · humanly

b The company had done all that was _____ possible to prevent the accident.
human · humane · humanitarian · humanly

c The organization provides _____ aid to Third World countries.
   human · humane · humanitarian · humanly

d It's _____ to make mistakes.
   human · humane · humanitarian · humanly

e Prisoners should be treated _____ and in accordance with
   international law.
   human · humane · humanely · humanly

f The Kingswood _____ area is located north of the railway line.
   industrial · industrially · industrious · industriously

g The town, once important _____, is now just a holiday resort.
   industrial · industrially · industrious · industriously

h Being _____ doesn't mean you're going to be financially successful.
   industrial · industrially · industrious · industriously

i She studied _____ and graduated in 2002.
   industrial · industrially · industrious · industriously

human ['hjuːmən]	menschlich (= *Menschen betreffend*)
humane [hjuː'meɪn]	human; menschenwürdig
campaign [kæm'peɪn] **for something**	sich für etwas einsetzen
do all that's humanly possible ['pɒsəbl]	alles Menschenmögliche tun
prevent [prɪ'vent] **an accident** ['æksɪdənt]	einen Unfall verhindern
provide aid [prəvaɪd 'eɪd]	Hilfe leisten
in accordance with international law	gemäß dem Völkerrecht
graduate ['grædʒueɪt]	einen Hochschulabschluss machen
industrious(ly) [ɪn'dʌstriəs(li)]	fleißig

29 *Illness Crossword*

Hier nun wieder ein kleines *Crossword*. Diesmal geht es um Verben, die im Zusammenhang mit Krankheitsbezeichnungen oder Medikamenten gebraucht werden.

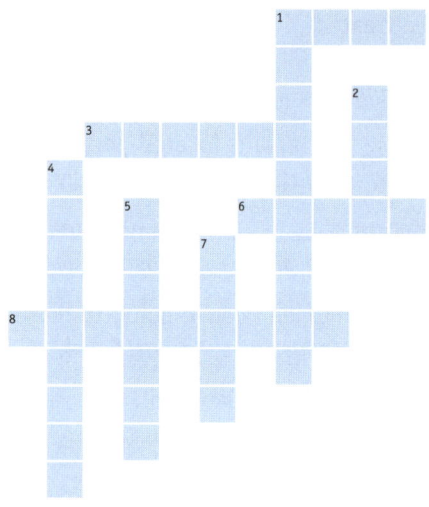

Across

1 Two hours after eating a chicken sandwich she _____ down with food poisoning.

3 I must have _____ a cold while sitting in the garden yesterday.

6 He sees a psychiatrist and _____ medication, but he doesn't seem to be getting better.

8 When he _____ heart trouble last August, he went to London for treatment.

Down

1 Paul _____ AIDS through a contaminated blood transfusion a couple of years ago.

2 She had a stroke six months ago but has _____ a good recovery.

4 The president is reported in serious condition after _____ a heart attack.

5 She had to _____ surgery to have her gallbladder removed.

7 When I was three years old, I _____ out in a rash from eating strawberries.

30 „Sollen": *a difficult word to translate*

„Sollen" ist im Englischen schwer auszudrücken. *Shall* heißt es nur bei Vorschlägen (*Shall I ...? Shall we ...?*) oder in biblischen Geboten (*Thou shalt not ... / You shall not ...*). In den meisten anderen Fällen liegt man mit *be (supposed) to* in der Regel richtig. Darüber hinaus weisen die Übungssätze noch ein paar andere Möglichkeiten auf.

Übersetzen Sie.

a   Sollen wir ein Taxi nehmen?

b   Soll ich den Hund füttern?

c   Was soll ich tun – ihr die Meinung sagen oder sie einfach ignorieren?

d   Du sollst nicht denken, dass ich dich nicht liebe.

e   Du sollst mich nicht so verwöhnen.

f   Wir sollen vor dem Bahnhof warten.

g   Sollen wir diese Sätze alle übersetzen?

h   Du weißt doch, dass du das nicht tun sollst.

i   Soll das ein Witz sein?

j   Was soll denn das heißen?

k   Der Präsident soll davon nichts gewusst haben.

l   Er soll sehr reich sein.

m   Er soll früher mal reich gewesen sein.

n   Du solltest Chinesisch lernen – da liegt die Zukunft.

o   Du solltest diesen Leuten dankbar sein.

p   Ich hätte mir Notizen machen sollen.

q   Das hätte ich früher wissen sollen.

r   Man sagte mir, ich solle in einer Woche wiederkommen.

s   Du sollst nicht stehlen.

feed – fed – fed	füttern – fütterte – gefüttert
give someone a piece of your mind	jemand die Meinung sagen
ignore someone [ɪgˈnɔː]	jemand ignorieren
spoil [spɔɪl] **someone**	jemand verwöhnen
outside the station [ˈsteɪʃn]	vor dem Bahnhof
translate [trænsˈleɪt] **sentences**	Sätze übersetzen
Chinese [tʃaɪˈniːz]	Chinesisch
be grateful [ˈgreɪtfl] **to someone**	jemand dankbar sein
before [bɪˈfɔː] **/ earlier** [ˈɜːliə]	früher
take notes (– took – taken)	sich Notizen machen
steal – stole – stolen	stehlen – stahl – gestohlen

31   *Idioms:* Wenn Leute das Fett kauen

Was ein *idiom* [ˈɪdiəm] ist, wissen wir bereits (→ Übung 4): eine Wortgruppe, die als Ganzes eine andere Bedeutung hat als die Wörter, die sie ausmachen. Ein Radiokommentator fragt: *But are they all singing from the same hymn sheet?* Auch das ein *idiom*, und wie wunderbar anschaulich (= *graphic*)! Es ging um die Teilnehmer an einer internationalen Konferenz, die eben nicht alle nach den gleichen (Gesangbuch-)Noten singen, d. h. recht unterschiedlicher Meinung über die anstehenden Probleme sind.

Hier nun erhalten Sie Sätze, in denen eine Wortgruppe unterstrichen ist, für die es ein hübsches *idiom* gibt.

Welches *idiom* passt in welchen Satz?

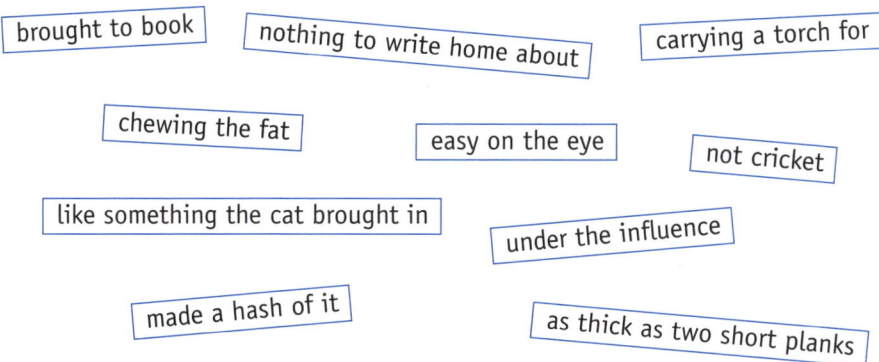

brought to book

nothing to write home about

carrying a torch for

chewing the fat

easy on the eye

not cricket

like something the cat brought in

under the influence

made a hash of it

as thick as two short planks

a The food was <u>not particularly good</u>.
b I know it's <u>unfair</u> to attack an opponent from behind.
c He's <u>very stupid</u>.
d She can act and she's <u>pleasant to look at</u>.
e The driver was clearly <u>drunk</u>.
f Well, you've really <u>done it very badly</u>, haven't you?
g What's happened is unacceptable, and the culprits must be <u>punished</u>.
h Does she know he's <u>in love with</u> her?
i Gee, what's happened? You look <u>dirty and untidy</u>.
j The old men just sat there <u>chatting in a leisurely way</u>.

hymn [hɪm] **– hymn sheet** ['hɪm ʃiːt]	Kirchenlied – Notenblatt
torch [tɔːtʃ]	Fackel
chew [tʃuː]	kauen
hash [hæʃ]	*Gericht aus Hackfleisch und Kartoffeln*
plank [plæŋk]	(*langes, schmales*) Brett
influence ['ɪnfluəns]	Einfluss
particularly [pə'tɪkjələli]	besonders
opponent [ə'pəʊnənt]	Gegner(in)
culprit ['kʌlprɪt]	(Übel-)Täter(in); Schuldige(r)
gee! [dʒiː]	(*AE Ausruf:*) Mensch!

32 *Want – a dangerous friend*

Want wird zum Teil anders konstruiert als das deutsche „wollen":
*I want **to go**.* = Ich will **gehen**.
*I want **you to go**.* = Ich will, **dass du gehst**.
Bei verneintem *want* und mit einem „Unterton von Verlaufsform" geht auch:
*I don't want **you going*** (around making a fool of yourself).

Übersetzen Sie nun die folgenden Sätze mit *want*.

a   Willst du wirklich nach Hause gehen?

_____

b   Willst du wirklich, dass ich nach Hause gehe?

_____

c   Sie wollte die Wahrheit sagen.

_____

d   Sie wollte, dass ich die Wahrheit sage.

_____

e   Sie wollte, dass man ihr die Wahrheit sagt.

_____

f   Sie wollte, dass die Wahrheit gesagt wird.

_____

g   Ich will keinen Kaffee kochen.

_____

h   Ich will nicht, dass du Kaffee kochst.

_____

i   Ich will nicht, dass du dir diesen Film ansiehst.

_____

j   Meinst du nicht, dass deine Haare mal geschnitten werden müssten?

_____

k   Ich will nicht, dass du mir die Haare schneidest.

_____

l   Ich möchte meine Haare kurz geschnitten haben.

_____

m   Meine Mutter will, dass mir die Haare wirklich kurz geschnitten werden.

_____

n   Ich möchte nicht, dass du enttäuscht bist.

o   Ich möchte nicht, dass du mich enttäuschst.

p   Ich weiß, du willst nicht, dass ich darüber Witze mache.

q   Sie hätte bleiben können, wenn sie es gewollt hätte.

r   Ich bat sie zu bleiben, aber sie wollte nicht.

go home [gəʊ ˈhəʊm]	nach Hause gehen
tell the truth [truːθ]	die Wahrheit sagen
make coffee [ˈkɒfi]	Kaffee kochen
watch a film / movie [ˈmuːvi]	sich einen Film ansehen
cut someone's hair [heə]	jemand die Haare schneiden
real(ly) [ˈrɪəl(i)]	wirklich
disappointed [dɪsəˈpɔɪntɪd]	enttäuscht
disappoint [dɪsəˈpɔɪnt] **someone**	jemand enttäuschen
make jokes about something	Witze über etwas machen
stay [steɪ]	bleiben (→ Übung 45)
ask someone to do something	jemand bitten, etwas zu tun

33 *A donkey and a monkey eating their dessert in the desert*

Bei den folgenden Wortpaaren verführt die Ähnlichkeit oder Gleichheit der Schreibung häufig zu fehlerhafter Aussprache.

Sprechen Sie die Wortpaare laut und achten Sie dabei auf die Lautschrift.

leaf [liːf] – **deaf** [def]   *Blatt – taub*
ever [ˈevə] – **fever** [ˈfiːvə]   *jemals – Fieber*
devil [ˈdevl] – **evil** [ˈiːvl]   *Teufel – böse*
cloth [klɒθ] – **clothes** [kləʊðz]   *Tuch – Kleidung*
bomb [bɒm] – **comb** [kəʊm]   *Bombe – Kamm*

love [lʌv] – **grove** [grəʊv]	*Liebe – Wäldchen*
dove [dʌv] – **move** [muːv]	*Taube – bewegen*
golf [gɒlf] – **wolf** [wʊlf]	*Golf – Wolf*
dull [dʌl] – **bull** [bʊl]	*trübe – Bulle*
done [dʌn] – **gone** [gɒn]	*getan – gegangen*
rough [rʌf] – **cough** [kɒf]	*grob – husten*
school [skuːl] – **wool** [wʊl]	*Schule – Wolle*

stranger ['streɪndʒə] – **anger** ['æŋgə]	*Fremder – Zorn*
wildness ['waɪldnəs] – **wilderness** ['wɪldənəs]	*Wildheit – Wildnis*
climber ['klaɪmə] – **timber** ['tɪmbə]	*Kletterer – (Bau-)Holz*
pint [paɪnt] – **hint** [hɪnt]	*(ca. ¹/₂ Liter) – Andeutung*
bow [bəʊ] – **bow** [baʊ]	*Bogen – Verbeugung*
suit [suːt] – **suite** [swiːt]	*Anzug – Suite*
storm [stɔːm] – **worm** [wɜːm]	*Sturm – Wurm*
donkey ['dɒŋki] – **monkey** ['mʌŋki]	*Esel – Affe*

hero ['hɪərəʊ] – **heroine** ['herəʊɪn]	*Held – Heldin*
lumber ['lʌmbə] – **plumber** ['plʌmə]	*Gerümpel – Installateur*
iron ['aɪən] – **irony** ['aɪrəni]	*Eisen – Ironie*
business ['bɪznəs] – **busyness** ['bɪzinəs]	*Geschäft – Geschäftigkeit*
discount ['dɪskaʊnt] – **viscount** ['vaɪkaʊnt]	*Preisnachlass – (Adelstitel)*

desert ['dezət] – **dessert** [dɪ'zɜːt]	*Wüste – Nachtisch / Dessert*
heroism ['herəʊɪzm] – **heroic** [hə'rəʊrɪk]	*Heldentum – heldenhaft*
liquor ['lɪkə] – **liqueur** [lɪ'kjʊə]	*Schnaps – Likör*
petrol ['petrəl] – **patrol** [pə'trəʊl]	*Benzin – Patrouille / Streife*
recipe ['resəpi] – **receipt** [rɪ'siːt]	*(Koch-)Rezept – Quittung*
vomit ['vɒmɪt] – **omit** [ə'mɪt]	*(sich) erbrechen – auslassen*

Beachten Sie außerdem, dass bei *gn-* und *kn-* am Wortanfang das *g* bzw. *k* immer stumm ist:
You get bitten by gnats [næts] (= von Mücken gestochen), *gnash* [næʃ] *your teeth* (= knirschen mit den Zähnen), *have gnomes* [nəʊmz] (= Gartenzwerge) *in your front garden, and eat gnocchi* ['nɒki] *at the Italian eatery, go down on your knees* [niːz] (= Knie), *and eat your knackwurst* ['nækwɜːst] *with a knife* [naɪf].

34 *Multiple choice:* Wörter, die oft verwechselt werden

Wählen Sie das passende Wort aus.

a We can't _____ your salary; you're already overpaid.
grow · heighten · raise · rise

b If prices _____, people will buy less.
higher · raise · rise · up

c The _____ situation has improved.
economic · economical · economically · economics

d Bringing peace to the Middle East would be a _____ achievement.
historian · historic · historical · history

e The film is only partly based on _____ events.
historian · historic · historical · history

f Only 20 per cent of Afghan women are _____.
literal · literally · literary · literate

g A _____ translation is the opposite of a free translation.
literal · literally · literary · literate

h It _____ broke my heart to see him do such a stupid thing.
literal · literally · literary · literate

i Dickens was one of the _____ giants of Victorian England.
literal · literally · literary · literate

salary ['sæləri]	(Monats-/Jahres-)Gehalt
heighten ['haɪtn] (*e.g.* interest)	(*z. B. das Interesse*) erhöhen
raise [reɪz] **taxes**	die Steuern erhöhen
prices rise [raɪz]	die Preise steigen
economic [iːkə'nɒmɪk]	wirtschaftlich; Wirtschafts-
economical [iːkə'nɒmɪkl]	sparsam
economics [iːkə'nɒmɪks]	(Volks-)Wirtschaftslehre
historian [hɪ'stɔːriən]	Historiker(in)
historic [hɪ'stɒrɪk]	historisch (bedeutsam)
a historical [hɪ'stɒrɪkl] **fact**	eine geschichtliche Tatsache

history ['hɪstri]	(die) Geschichte
literal ['lɪtərəl]	wörtlich
literally ['lɪtərəli]	wörtlich; buchstäblich
literary ['lɪtərəri]	literarisch; Literatur-
they're literate ['lɪtərət]	sie können lesen und schreiben

35 Präpositionen: „an", „am", „auf"

Setzen Sie die dem deutschen „an", „am" und „auf" entsprechenden Präpositionen ein.

a There's a fly _____ the wall.

b He was standing _____ the wall looking _____ the fly.

c They have a charming little cottage _____ the sea.

d She died _____ the morning.

e She died _____ the morning of March 6.

f He died _____ cancer.

g He died _____ his injuries several hours after the accident.

h She never thinks _____ herself.

i Vienna is _____ the Danube.

j Someone saw him down _____ the river.

k A holiday _____ the seaside would be the right thing.

l You can come _____ Saturday.

m At midnight he was still _____ work.

n The city doesn't have much to offer _____ entertainment.

o She sat down _____ the only chair in the room _____ the big table _____ the window.

p Nearly 2500 species of moths have been found _____ the British Isles.

q We don't have much money _____ the bank.

r He's deaf _____ one ear.

s She put the vase _____ the windowsill.

t Last year we went _____ the Isle of Man.

u The meeting has been postponed _____ Thursday morning.

v In the UK there is one doctor _____ every 434 people.

w We walked _____ and down the roads of this pretty town.

cottage ['kɒtɪdʒ]	Häuschen
injuries ['ɪnʒəriz]	Verletzungen
the Danube ['dænjuːb]	die Donau
entertainment [entə'teɪnmənt]	Unterhaltung
species ['spiːʃiːz]	Art(en); Spezies
moth [mɒθ]	Nachtfalter; Motte
deaf [def]	taub
windowsill ['wɪndəʊsɪl]	Fensterbrett; Fensterbank
the Isle of Man [aɪl əv 'mæn] is an island ['aɪlənd] in the Irish Sea	die Insel Man ist eine Insel in der Irischen See
postpone [pəʊst'pəʊn] a meeting	eine Besprechung verschieben

36 „Können", „müssen", „sollen", „dürfen", „wollen"

Im Deutschen benutzen wir diese Hilfsverben manchmal allein, d. h. nicht in Verbindung mit einem Vollverb. Im Englischen ist das in der Regel nicht möglich.

Bei der Übersetzung der folgenden Sätze müssen Sie also immer ein Vollverb ergänzen.

a Kann sie das? _____

b Ich kann nicht mehr. _____

c Ich kann kein Französisch. _____

d Ich muss jetzt weg. _____

e Ich muss mal. _____

f Das sollst du nicht. _____

g Was soll das? _____

h Wann dürfen wir ins Wasser? _____

i „Darf der das?" – „Der darf das!" _____

j Wir wollen noch nicht nach Hause. _____

k Ich will zum Bahnhof. _____

l Wir wollen da rein. _____

37 „Wollen" ist nicht immer *want*

In den folgenden Sätzen lässt sich „wollen" nicht immer mit *want* ausdrücken.

a   Sie will Architektin werden.

_____

b   Sie will Chinesisch lernen.

_____

c   Sie will, dass ich Chinesisch lerne.

_____

d   Sie will unbedingt die Rechnung bezahlen.

_____

e   Das Auto wollte nicht anspringen.

_____

f   Sie will gesehen haben, wie er das Geld nahm.

_____

g   Der Präsident will davon nichts gewusst haben.

_____

h   Ich will lieber zu Hause bleiben.

_____

The bloody car wouldn't start.

i Wir wollten gerade gehen.

_____

j Wollen Sie sich nicht setzen?

_____

k Wollen wir zu mir gehen?

_____

pay the bill [peɪ ðə 'bɪl]	die Rechnung bezahlen
start [staːt]	(*Auto:*) anspringen
know [nəʊ] **nothing about it**	nichts davon wissen
stay at home [ət 'həʊm]	zu Hause bleiben
go to my / your place	zu mir / dir gehen

38 *Do – the heavy-duty verb*, das Hochleistungsverb

Do gehört zu den 10 wichtigsten Verben der englischen Sprache. Häufig gebraucht man dieses *all-round verb*, um Dinge auszudrücken, für die es auch „spezialisierte" Verben gibt.

Ersetzen Sie in den folgenden Sätzen die unterstrichenen Formen von *do* durch solche „Spezialisten".

a I've done the first three chapters.
b Have you done your essay yet?
c She has done biographies of Nixon and Eisenhower.
d He has done several successful musicals.
e You've done me a great service.
f She's doing well at college.
g She did a history degree at University College, Dublin.
h In most cases, one drop will do.
i Each room was done in a different colour.
j You've been done.
k His brother did him out of his inheritance.
l Most of Europe did away with capital punishment decades ago.

To be or not to be: that is the question.

He's doing Hamlet.

m He has <u>done</u> Hamlet and other Shakespearean heroes.
n We have <u>done away with</u> the old system and replaced it with one that's completely computer-based.
o This box will have to <u>do for</u> a table until the furniture arrives.
p I couldn't <u>do</u> without my computer.
q One more failed crop and we're <u>done for</u>.
r The long walk to the lake <u>did me in</u>.
s When he's not working, Jack is busy <u>doing up</u> the house.

do someone a service ['sɜ:vɪs]	jemand einen Dienst erweisen
do well [du: 'wel]	gut zurechtkommen
do a history degree [dɪ'gri:]	einen Universitätsabschluss in Geschichte machen
one drop will do	ein Tropfen genügt
inheritance [ɪn'herɪtəns]	Erbe; Erbschaft
do away with capital punishment	die Todesstrafe abschaffen
Shakespearean heroes ['hɪərəʊz]	Shakespeare-Helden
replace something with something	etwas durch etwas ersetzen
failed crop [feɪld 'krɒp]	Missernte
we're done for ['dʌn fɔ:]	wir sind erledigt
the long walk did me in	die Wanderung hat mich geschafft
do up the house [haʊs]	das Haus herrichten / renovieren

39 *Another news story*

Hier ist eine Meldung aus einer amerikanischen Lokalzeitung. Schreiben Sie sie ab, und setzen Sie dabei die folgenden Verben in der richtigen Form an passender Stelle ein.

> drive   hit   lose   realize   reduce   release
> stop   suffer   swerve   treat   wear

TWO MEN HURT IN CAR CRASH

TWO MEN were ▭ at St. Francis Medical Center Monday for injuries they ▭ in a collision at the junction of Illinois Route 89 and Rutland Road in Marshall County. Both were ▭ after treatment.

Terry Hufford, 35, of Toluca, was ▭ north on Route 89 when his car was ▭ by a camper ▭ by Byron Jenkins, 73, of Texas. Jenkins, who was headed south, ▭ too late that a car in front of him had ▭ to make a left turn. Jenkins ▭ control when he braked and ▭ into the northbound lane, state police said.

Hufford was ticketed for not ▭ his seat belt. Jenkins was ticketed for failure to ▭ speed and using the wrong lane, state police said.

hit another car	in ein anderes Auto hineinfahren
release [rɪˈliːs]	(z. B. aus dem Krankenhaus) entlassen
suffer [ˈsʌfə]	erleiden; (sich Verletzungen) zuziehen
swerve [swɜːv]	schwenken; eine Schwenkung machen
wear a / one's seat belt	angeschnallt sein
car crash [ˈkɑː kræʃ]	Autounfall; Zusammenstoß
injuries [ˈɪnʒəriz]	Verletzungen
junction [ˈdʒʌŋkʃn]	Kreuzung
treatment [ˈtriːtmənt]	Behandlung
camper [ˈkæmpə]	Wohnwagen; Wohnmobil
headed south [hedɪd ˈsaʊθ]	nach Süden unterwegs
make a left turn [left ˈtɜːn]	nach links abbiegen
brake [breɪk]	Bremse; bremsen
the northbound lane	die Fahrspur nach Norden
he was ticketed	er erhielt einen Bußgeldbescheid

40 *Idioms Crossword:* Von Geldleuten und Bettgenossen

Die *clues* enthalten einige idiomatische Redensarten.

Setzen Sie die fehlenden Wörter in das *Crossword* ein.

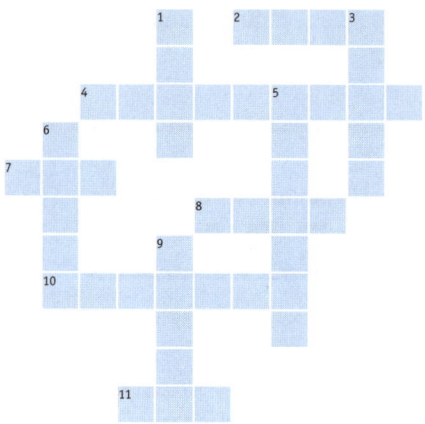

Across

2 He knew who'd done it but he _____ his mouth shut.

4 From the moment we arrived to the moment we left everything ran like _____.

7 His first meal in prison was a far _____ from the luxurious meals he had been used to.

8 A football club should be run by football people, not money men out to make a fast _____.

10 We all know that politics makes _____ bedfellows.

11 Let them sue us. They can't prove anything. They don't have a _____ to stand on.

Down

1 I tell you what, this fight is not over – not by a long _____.

3 I'm sick and _____ of you sulking when something upsets you.

5 A _____ pot never boils.

6 Some people get so caught up in small details that they can't see the wood for the _____.

9 By and _____ he's a great guy and he really knows how to throw a party.

41 Präpositionen sind Glückssache – *a matter of luck ...*

... aber den Leuten, die 1963 anlässlich von Präsident Kennedys Besuch in Deutschland eine offizielle Gedenkmünze schufen, war das Glück nicht hold: Drei englische Wörter prägten sie auf die Münze und dachten wohl, da könne nichts schiefgehen: *Welcome in Germany*. Die Präposition wurde ihnen zum Verhängnis: *Welcome to Germany* hätte es heißen müssen.

Wenn Sie alle Präpositionen in den folgenden Sätzen richtig einsetzen, sind Ihre Englischkenntnisse „echt geil" bzw. *cool* oder geradezu *wicked* ['wɪkɪd]. Und: in drei Sätzen sollten Sie besser gar keine Präposition einsetzen.

Setzen Sie – wo nötig – passende Präpositionen ein.

a   I heard the news the minute I arrived _____ the office.

b   I heard the news the minute I arrived _____ home.

c   When we arrived _____ London it was raining.

d   She died _____ cancer.

e   Was he killed or did he die _____ a natural death?

f   You're more likely to die _____ natural causes than _____ an accident.

g   She died _____ suicide.

h   He died _____ his own hand.

i   I don't envy him _____ his job.

j   She jumped _____ the fence.

k   Thankfully I'm still living _____ my parents so I don't pay rent.

l   He lives _____ his parents' money and spends his days boozing with his buddies.

m   The family lives _____ less than a dollar a day in a mud hut without electricity or running water.

n   We live _____ selling our skills and experience.

o   He survived _____ eating insects.

suicide ['suːɪsaɪd]	Selbstmord
envy ['envi] **someone something**	jemand um etwas beneiden
boozing ['buːzɪŋ] **with his buddies**	saufend mit seinen Kumpeln
mud hut ['mʌd hʌt]	Lehmhütte
skills and experience [ɪk'spɪəriəns]	Können und Erfahrung

42 *It* – wenn es nicht „es" heißt

It gebraucht man mit Bezug auf Nichtlebewesen und Tiere; die deutsche Entsprechung kann dann außer „es" (*the house – it*) auch „er" (*the table – it*) oder „sie" (*the door – it*) sein.

Darüber hinaus steht *it* aber auch in Fällen, wo das Deutsche statt einem Ausdruck mit „es", „er", „sie" eine ganz andere Konstruktion aufweist.

Wie zum Beispiel übersetzt man die folgenden Sätze ins Deutsche?

a   It took me an hour.

b   It was hoped that a compromise could be reached.

c   As it turned out, the material was not waterproof.

d   The cheek of it!

e   Who is it? – Frank.

f   It wasn't us, it was the others.

g   It's the poor who are going to suffer.

h   It was for your sake that I came back.

The car's had it.

i   Why is it always me who has to do the dirty work?

j   If it hadn't been for you, I would have died.

k   The car's had it.

l   Our marriage has had it.

m   If I don't pay up, I've had it.

n   Let him have it!

o   Rumour has it that the two banks are going to merge.

p   I think we should have it out.

q   I take it that you'll finish today.

r   The old woman is still very much with it.

s   He thinks he's really it. (Vgl. Übung 77, Satz i)

reach a compromise ['kɒmprəmaɪz]	einen Kompromiss erzielen
as it turned out [tɜːnd 'aʊt]	wie sich erwies
material [məˈtɪəriəl]	Material; Stoff
waterproof ['wɔːtəpruːf]	wasserdicht; wasserfest
cheek [tʃiːk]	Frechheit; Dreistigkeit
suffer ['sʌfə]	leiden
for your sake [fə 'jɔː seɪk]	um deinetwillen
do the dirty work ['dɜːti wɜːk]	die Drecksarbeit machen
our marriage ['mærɪdʒ]	unsere Ehe
if I don't pay up [peɪ 'ʌp]	wenn ich nicht zahle
rumour ['ruːmə]	Gerücht
merge [mɜːdʒ]	fusionieren

43 „Es" – wenn „es" nicht *it* heißt

Hier nun haben wir den umgekehrten Fall: Dem deutschen Ausdruck mit „es"
entspricht ein englischer ohne *it*.

Übersetzen Sie.

a   Das Volk hungert – es braucht Hilfe.

b   Es gibt viele Menschen, die sich nicht selber helfen können.

c   Es ist jemand an der Tür.

d   Es war einmal ein König, der eine wunderschöne Tochter hatte.

e   Es lebe die Königin!

f   Es gefällt dir hier wohl?

g   Es tut mir leid, dass ich dir nicht helfen kann.

h   Es freut mich zu sehen, dass es dir so gut geht.

i   In diesem Schloss spukt es.

j   Ich meine es gut mit dir.

k   „Wird er wieder gesund werden?" – „Ich hoffe es."

l   „Wohnt sie immer noch dort?" – „Ich weiß es nicht."

the people ['piːpl] (*Plural!*)	das Volk
starve [stɑːv]	hungern
need help [niːd 'help]	Hilfe brauchen
many / lots of people ['piːpl]	viele Menschen

at the door [ət ðə ˈdɔː]	an der Tür
king [kɪŋ] **– queen** [kwiːn]	König – Königin
a beautiful [ˈbjuːtəfl] **daughter**	eine (wunder)schöne Tochter
a haunted castle [ˈhɔːntɪd ˈkɑːsl]	ein Schloss, in dem es spukt
recover [rɪˈkʌvə]	wieder gesund werden
live [lɪv]	leben; wohnen

 Sprichwörter wiederum beginnen oft mit *it*. Beispiele:

It ain't the things you don't know that make you ignorant as much as the things you know that ain't so.
It is a bold mouse that breeds in the cat's ear.
It is a sad house where the hen crows louder than the cock.
It is a wise boy that knows that he isn't.
It is comparison that makes men miserable.
It is easier to praise poverty than to bear it.
It is easy to be brave from a safe distance.
It is impossible to defeat an ignorant man in argument.
It is only the ignorant that despise education.
It's better to be an old man's sweetheart than a young man's slave.

44 Minidialoge: *"I'm afraid I can't come." – "Congratulations!"*

Sie merken natürlich: In der Überschrift passt etwas nicht zusammen. Mitunter formuliert man schon die Frage falsch. So riet man einem deutschen Freund, nicht allzu direkt nach der Toilette zu fragen. *Excuse me, where can I wash my hands?* sei eine angemessen umwundene Frage. Er wurde prompt in einen Raum geführt, wo zwar ein Waschbecken, aber keine Toilette war. Gut, die Amerikaner nennen „das Örtchen" fast immer *the bathroom*, gerade auch im Restaurant, wo man zuletzt daran denken würde, ein Bad zu nehmen. Kurzum: nicht immer weiß man die richtige Frage; nicht immer gibt man die richtige Antwort.

Im Folgenden finden Sie links eine Reihe von konventionellen Fragen und *statements*; versuchen Sie, ihnen aus den angebotenen Antworten jeweils eine passende zuzuordnen.

a   Can I get you a drink?
b   Can I help you?
c   Did you have a good trip?
d   He says he loves her.
e   Hello, is that Lucy Tyler?
f   Hello. May I join you?
g   How are you?
h   I'm afraid I can't come.
i   Lovely day, isn't it?
j   New bike, Jack?
k   Sorry I'm late.
l   Take care.
m   Well, I must be off now.
n   What are you doing tonight?
o   What does she do?
p   What time do you finish work?
q   What took you so long?
r   Why don't you have a car?
s   You own this house, do you?

Nothing much.

No, it's rented.

That's all right.

Oh, what a pity!

Can't afford one.

I will.

Had to go to the loo.

Yes, speaking.

No thanks. I'm just having a look round.

Cheerio, then. Have a good trip.

She's an architect.

Well, let's hope it lasts.

I should be through by five.

Yes, not too bad, thanks.

Thought I'd cycle to the gym. Not much point in driving there.

Fine, thanks.

Yes, please do.

Men say a lot of things.

Maybe some water.

I can't afford [ə'fɔːd] **it**	ich kann es mir nicht leisten
the loo [luː]	das Klo
may I join [dʒɔɪn] **you?**	darf ich mich zu Ihnen setzen?
cycle to the gym	mit dem Rad zum Fitnesscenter fahren

45 *Dual choice: Two men stole a bank (or did they?)*

Welches Wort passt?

a The shipment must be _____ against loss and damage.
ensured · insured

b The safety of civilians must be _____.
ensured · insured

c The missing boy's body was _____ in a field not far from his home.
found · founded

d The company was _____ in 2002.
found · founded

e Thieves broke into the house and _____ my digital camera.
robbed · stole

f The man put a gun to his head and _____ him of cash and his mobile phone.
robbed · stole

g Police are searching for two men who _____ a bank in Gambrills yesterday.
robbed · stole

h Police are searching for two men who _____ a car in Gambrills yesterday.
robbed · stole

i How long are you going to _____?
remain · stay

j Not much _____ of the once thriving settlement except the parish church.
remains · stays

k The country's higher education system _____ the envy of the world.
remains · stays

l They invited me to _____ the night.
remain · stay

shipment [ˈʃɪpmənt]	Lieferung
insure [ɪnˈʃʊə]	versichern
ensure [ɪnˈʃɔː]	sichern; gewährleisten
loss and damage [ˈdæmɪdʒ]	Verlust und Beschädigung
the safety of	die Sicherheit von Zivilisten /
civilians [səˈvɪliənz]	Zivilpersonen
found [faʊnd]	gründen
search [sɜːtʃ] **for**	suchen nach
the once thriving [ˈθraɪvɪŋ]	die einst blühende
settlement	Siedlung
parish church [pærɪʃ ˈtʃɜːtʃ]	Pfarrkirche
the higher education system [ˈsɪstəm]	das höhere Schulwesen
the envy [ˈenvi] **of the world**	„der Neid der Welt"

46 „Nächste" – „letzte": *The next train from the nearest station*

Das räumlich Nächste ist *the nearest*; das in der Reihenfolge als nächstes Kommende ist *the next*.

The last bezeichnet das Letzte, nach dem nichts mehr kommt; „letzte" in der Bedeutung „neueste" ist dagegen *latest*. Also *his **latest** novel* bei einem noch lebenden Schriftsteller, dagegen *"The Tempest" was Shakespeare's **last** play*.

Besonders zu beachten das Hinzusetzen von *few* bei:
„in den nächsten Tagen / Wochen" etc.   *in the next **few** days / weeks* etc.
„in den letzten Tagen / Wochen" etc.   *in the last **few** days / weeks* etc.
„In letzter Zeit" ist nicht etwa ~~*in the last time*~~, sondern schlicht *recently*.

Übersetzen Sie.

a   Wo ist das nächste Internetcafé?

b   Ich steige an der nächsten Haltestelle aus.

c   Wer wird der nächste Präsident der Vereinigten Staaten?

d   Der nächste Stern ist 4,2 Lichtjahre entfernt.

e   Der Nächste bitte!

f   In Australien ist dein nächster Nachbar vielleicht 50 Meilen entfernt.

g   Die Energiekosten werden in den nächsten Jahren enorm steigen.

h   In den letzten Wochen ist viel passiert.

i   Während der letzten Monate hat die Venus ihren Abstand zur Sonne ständig vergrößert.

j   Wir haben gerade noch den letzten Bus geschafft.

k   Sie kämpften bis zum letzten Mann.

l   Sie gab ihm ihr letztes Geld.

m   Wir kamen als Letzte (an).

n   Der Kapitän verließ als Letzter das Schiff.

o   Die letzten Nachrichten sind nicht sehr ermutigend.

p   Er hat sich in letzter Zeit sehr gebessert.

4.2 light years ['laɪt jɪəz] **away**	4,2 Lichtjahre entfernt
energy costs ['enədʒi kɒsts] ⚠	(die) Energiekosten
rise enormously [ɪ'nɔːməsli]	enorm (an)steigen
a lot has happened ['hæpənd]	es ist viel passiert
increase [ɪn'kriːs] **steadily**	ständig vergrößern
distance ['dɪstəns] **from the Sun**	Abstand zur Sonne
encouraging [ɪn'kʌrɪdʒɪŋ]	ermutigend
improve [ɪm'pruːv]	sich bessern (→ Übung 69)

47 Aussprache: *The liquor-drinking vicar getting sicker*

**Unter den folgenden Wörtern reimen sich jeweils zwei miteinander.
Schreiben Sie diese Wortpaare heraus.**

ache	choose	front	juice	off	says
air	climber	gone	limb	on	sicker
aren't	comb	got	loose	out	slim
aunt	cough	heart	lord	put	start
berry	dizzy	height	lose	red	sword
blood	done	heir	meant	rent	timer
Britain	doubt	hen	men	right	vicar
bury	fez	home	mood	run	written
busy	food	hunt	mud	said	yacht
cake	foot				

_____

_____

_____

_____

_____

_____

_____

_____

_____

_____

_____

liquor ['lɪkə]	Schnaps
vicar ['vɪkə]	Pfarrer(in)
get sick [sɪk]	krank werden
ache [eɪk]	Schmerzen; wehtun
berry ['beri]	Beere
bury ['beri]	begraben
busy ['bɪzi]	beschäftigt
climber ['klaɪmə]	Bergsteiger(in)
comb [kəʊm]	Kamm; kämmen

cough [kɒf]	Husten; husten
dizzy ['dɪzi]	schwindlig
doubt [daʊt]	Zweifel; zweifeln
fez [fez]	Fes (= rote Filzkappe der Muslime)
height [haɪt]	Höhe
heir [eə]	Erbe, Erbin
limb [lɪm]	Glied
loose [luːs]	lose
lose [luːz] – **lost** – **lost**	verlieren – verlor – verloren
mud [mʌd]	Schlamm; Matsch
slim [slɪm]	schlank
sword [sɔːd]	Schwert

48 *False friends: With friends like these ...*

... *who needs enemies?* „Wer braucht Feinde, wenn er solche Freunde hat?" Eine herrlich unterkühlte, resignierende Art auszudrücken, dass einem Freunde zum Problem werden können.

Wir nun haben es im Englischen mit echt gefährlichen falschen Freunden zu tun, die uns sprachlich in des Teufels Küche (*into a hell of a mess*) bringen können.

Hier ist die erste Hälfte unserer „Fahndungsliste"; die zweite finden Sie in Übung 61. (Vergleichen Sie zu *false friends* auch noch die Übungen 90 und 128.)

Versuchen Sie (richtig) zu übersetzen.

a in der **aktuellen** Situation _____

b die **aktuelle** Mode _____

c ein Thema von **aktuellem** Interesse _____

d einen **Beamer** einsetzen _____

e ein Baby **bekommen** _____

f ich will mich nicht **blamieren** _____

g sei schön **brav**! _____

h der **Chef** von Airbus _____

You must be brave.

i	die Geschäfte in der **City**
j	ein **cleverer** Geschäftsmann
k	der Kölner **Dom**
l	ein **engagierter** Umweltschützer
m	politisch **engagierte** Bürger
n	ein **eventueller** Nachfolger
o	eine Schokoladen**fabrik**
p	ein **famoser** Kerl
q	eine **blühende Fantasie**
r	ein berühmter **Fotograf**
s	ein **genialer** Schachzug
t	für Hunde ist Schokolade **Gift**
u	wo ist mein **Handy**?
v	das wäre nicht **human**
w	das Schild **irritiert** die Autofahrer
x	eine **konsequente** Herangehensweise
y	**konsequent** handeln
z	Fahrkarten **kontrollieren**
aa	multinationale **Konzerne**
bb	**Kritik** ernst nehmen
cc	es ist eine interessante **Lektüre**

49 *Idioms:* Wenn man am falschen Baum hochbellt

Die englischen Sätze enthalten häufig gebrauchte Redensarten.
Ordnen Sie sie den deutschen Entsprechungen zu.

a   I don't know what you're on about.

b   I think you're barking up the wrong tree.

c   I'm all at sea with this problem.

d   I'm dying for her to come back.

e   She thinks nothing of phoning you in the middle of the night.

f   She's the spitting image of her mother.

g   She's used to having things her own way.

h   The ball is in your court now.

i   The jury is still out on this question.

j   This program is the best thing since sliced bread.

k   We're beginning to get on top of this problem.

l   You can't walk out on me like this.

a   Bei dieser Aufgabe blicke ich nicht mehr durch.

b   Da bist du wohl auf dem Holzweg.

c   Darüber ist das letzte Wort noch nicht gesprochen.

d   Dieses Programm ist einfach toll.

e   Du kannst mich doch nicht einfach so sitzen lassen.

f   Ich sehne mich danach, dass sie zurückkommt.

g   Ich weiß nicht, wovon du redest.

h   Jetzt bist du am Zug.

i   Sie findet nichts dabei, einen mitten in der Nacht anzurufen.

j   Sie ist es gewohnt, ihren Willen durchzusetzen.

k   Sie ist ihrer Mutter wie aus dem Gesicht geschnitten.

l   Wir kriegen dieses Problem allmählich in den Griff.

---

be on about something

be dying for something to happen

be the spitting image [spɪtɪŋ ˈɪmɪdʒ] **of someone**

the jury [ˈdʒʊəri] **is still out**

get on top of something

walk out on someone

(in ermüdender Weise) von etwas reden

unbedingt wollen, dass etwas geschieht

jemand wie aus dem Gesicht geschnitten sein

„die Geschworenen beraten noch"

etwas in den Griff bekommen

jemand verlassen / sitzen lassen

50 *Fruitcake Crossword*

Für „verrückt" gibt es im Englischen unendlich viele, zum Teil reizend bildhafte Ausdrucksmöglichkeiten: *mad as a hatter* („wie ein Hutmacher"), *mad as a March hare* („wie ein Märzhase"), *round the bend* („um die Kurve"), *out to lunch* („weg zum Mittagessen") und eben auch: *nutty as a fruitcake*. Inzwischen ist *fruitcake* selbst zu einem Synonym für *lunatic* [ˈluːnətɪk], *madman*, *madwoman* geworden.

He's (as) nutty as a fruitcake ist also ein bildhafter Ausdruck für „er ist total verrückt". Wir haben nichts Entsprechendes, wohl aber Ausdrücke wie „dumm wie Bohnenstroh", „klar wie Kloßbrühe" oder „blau wie ein Veilchen". Das Englische hat sehr viel mehr solcher Vergleiche als das Deutsche.

Versuchen Sie im *Crossword* jeweils das passende Vergleichswort einzusetzen.

Across

1 as cheap as _____
5 as proud as a _____
6 as good as _____
7 as fit as a _____
9 as cool as a _____
11 as drunk as a _____
12 as busy as a _____
13 as dull as _____
14 as brave as a _____
16 as light as a _____
17 as strong as an _____

Down

2 as hard as a _____
3 as clear as _____
4 as black as _____
5 as flat as a _____
7 as nutty as a _____

8 as dead as a _____
10 as blind as a _____
15 as cold as _____
16 as cunning as a _____

51 Präpositionen: *You pay the cabby but pay for things bought*

Beachten Sie das vom Deutschen abweichende *for: You pay **for** your groceries, you pay **for** tickets, **for** your evening paper, etc., but you pay the taxi driver, the electrician, your taxes.* Also:

die Medikamente bezahlen = *pay **for** the drugs*
die Behandlung bezahlen = *pay **for** the treatment*
das Arzthonorar bezahlen = *pay the doctor's fee*
den Arzt bezahlen = *pay the doctor*

Setzen Sie – wo nötig – passende Präpositionen ein.

a Under torture people often confess _____ crimes they never committed.
b The shop deals _____ rare books and manuscripts.
c The shop specializes _____ fine 19th century French antiques.
d Global warming is a problem all governments have to deal _____.
e They all laughed _____ Christopher Columbus when he said the world was round.
f We left the dog _____ a neighbour when we went _____ holiday.
g The chair is made _____ nickel-plated steel.
h Most butter is made _____ cow's milk.
i What do you mean _____ that?
j Our attempts to settle the matter amicably didn't meet _____ success.
k He was operated _____ _____ a hernia.
l If you cancel and have already paid _____ the goods, you will receive a full refund.
m Many manufacturing jobs have been replaced _____ machines or robots.
n The wounded man was screaming _____ pain.
o The whole place smelled _____ disinfectant, and the wine tasted _____ it.
p Hello, this is Bill Clark. Can I speak _____ Ms Lindsay, please?
q He was wounded _____ the leg.

6
KAPITEL

commit [kə'mɪt] **a crime**	ein Verbrechen begehen
century ['sentʃəri]	Jahrhundert
antiques [æn'tiːks]	Antiquitäten
global warming [gləʊbl 'wɔːmɪŋ]	(die) Erderwärmung
deal with a problem ['prɒbləm]	sich mit einem Problem befassen
settle a matter amicably ['æmɪkəbli]	eine Sache gütlich beilegen / regeln
meet with success [sək'ses]	Erfolg haben
operated on for a hernia ['hɜːniə]	wegen eines Leistenbruchs operiert
cancel ['kænsl] **an order**	einen Auftrag stornieren
refund ['riːfʌnd]	Rückzahlung; Rückerstattung

52 „Uns" ist nicht immer *us*

Entsprechungen für „uns" können sein: *us, ourselves, ours, each other* oder *one another*. Vielfach bleibt „uns" unübersetzt.

Übersetzen Sie.

a Unsere Eltern lieben uns bedingungslos.

b Die Bibel sagt, wir sollen andere lieben, wie wir uns selbst lieben.

c Wir lieben uns, aber wir streiten uns auch viel.

d Wir wollen uns nichts vormachen.

e Eine Freundin von uns ist Ärztin.

f Wenn wir anderen schaden, schaden wir uns selbst.

g Wir werden uns eine Insel im Südpazifik kaufen.

h Wir fürchten uns vor uns selbst.

i   Uns war beiden kalt.

j   Wir haben uns alle verändert.

k   Wir treffen uns alle 14 Tage.

l   Wir sollten uns bei ihr entschuldigen.

m   Wir können es uns nicht leisten, zu wenig für unser Bildungswesen auszugeben.

parents ['peərənts]	Eltern
unconditional(ly) [ʌnkən'dɪʃnəl(i)]	bedingungslos
the Bible ['baɪbl]	die Bibel
fight [faɪt] / **quarrel** ['kwɒrəl] / **argue** ['ɑːgjuː]	sich streiten
delude [dɪ'luːd] **oneself**	sich etwas vormachen
harm [hɑːm] **someone**	jemand schaden
buy [baɪ] **(oneself) something**	(sich) etwas kaufen
island ['aɪlənd]	Insel
the South Pacific [pə'sɪfɪk]	der Südpazifik
be afraid [ə'freɪd] **of someone**	sich vor jemand fürchten
I'm cold [kəʊld]	mir ist kalt
change [tʃeɪndʒ]	(sich) verändern
meet [miːt]	sich treffen
every two weeks [wiːks]	alle 14 Tage
apologize [ə'pɒlədʒaɪz]	sich entschuldigen
we cannot afford [ə'fɔːd] **to do that**	wir können es uns nicht leisten, das zu tun
spend money ['mʌni] **on something**	Geld für etwas ausgeben
education [edju'keɪʃn]	(die) Bildung; (das) Bildungswesen

53 „Dürfen" – *If I may make a suggestion ...*

„Wenn ich einen Vorschlag machen darf ...", schauen Sie sich diese Sätze (und ihre Übersetzungen) genau an. „Dürfen" drückt wichtige Nuancen aus, und es ist nicht immer leicht, die passende englische Entsprechung zu finden:

> may   can (*auch wenn Puristen manchmal Einwände erheben*)
> be allowed to   mustn't ['mʌsnt]   should   shouldn't

Übersetzen Sie.

a   Dürfen wir ein Wörterbuch benutzen?

b   Ja, Sie dürfen ein Wörterbuch benutzen.

c   Werden wir ein Wörterbuch benutzen dürfen?

d   Leider durften wir kein Wörterbuch benutzen.

e   Ich weiß nicht, ob ich ihn hätte besuchen dürfen.

f   Du darfst nicht so viel Zucker essen.

g   Du darfst die Hoffnung nicht verlieren.

h   Der Hund weiß, dass er hier nicht bellen darf.

i   So etwas dürfte ein Lehrer nicht sagen.

j   Das hättest du nicht sagen dürfen.

k   Diese Änderungen dürften leicht durchzuführen sein.

l   Es dürfte nicht allzu schwierig sein, ein Zimmer zu finden.

m   Das dürfte eigentlich keinen Unterschied machen.

use a dictionary ['dɪkʃənəri]	ein Wörterbuch benutzen
unfortunately [ʌn'fɔːtʃənətli]	leider
visit ['vɪzɪt] **someone**	jemand besuchen
sugar ['ʃʊgə]	Zucker
lose [luːz] **hope** ⚠	die Hoffnung verlieren
bark [bɑːk]	bellen
make changes ['tʃeɪndʒɪz]	Änderungen durchführen
easy ['iːzi] **to make**	leicht zu machen / durchzuführen
difficult ['dɪfɪkəlt]	schwierig
difference ['dɪfrəns]	Unterschied

54 *Have: another heavy-duty verb*

Have ist nach *be* (*is, was*) das zweithäufigste englische Verb und wird in einer Vielzahl von Kollokationen verwendet, in denen statt *have* auch ein anderes Verb stehen könnte. Oft ist die Variante mit *have* besonders geläufig und idiomatisch.

Ersetzen Sie *have* durch ein anderes Verb mit etwa gleicher Bedeutung.

a I <u>had</u> a look at the room and it was very nice.

b During the hottest part of the day they <u>had</u> a rest to recharge their batteries.

c Before dinner we <u>had</u> a walk in the park and made the acquaintance of a donkey.

d She <u>has</u> arthritis.

We made the acquaintance of a donkey.

e   The book <u>had</u> considerable success.

f   The company <u>has</u> an excellent reputation.

g   I <u>have</u> little Latin and no Greek.

h   I <u>had</u> a letter from her just a few weeks ago.

i   I won't <u>have</u> this sort of behaviour in my class.

j   We've been <u>had</u>.

k   He'd <u>had</u> three whiskies and was a bit drunk.

l   She <u>had</u> it copied for all the students.

m   She <u>had</u> twins.

n   Shall we <u>have</u> a game of chess?

o   She's <u>having</u> an affair with a colleague.

p   The cold-blooded dictator <u>had</u> no mercy for those
    who opposed him.

have a rest [rest]	sich ausruhen
recharge their batteries ['bætəriz]	neue Kräfte sammeln / tanken
acquaintance [ə'kweɪntəns]	Bekanntschaft
considerable [kən'sɪdərəbl] **success**	beträchtlicher Erfolg
an excellent ['eksələnt] **reputation**	ein ausgezeichneter Ruf
this sort of behaviour [bɪ'heɪvjə]	so ein Benehmen
she had it copied ['kɒpid]	sie ließ es kopieren
twins [twɪnz]	Zwillinge
have a game of chess [tʃes]	eine Partie Schach spielen
colleague ['kɒli:g] ⚠	Kollege, Kollegin
cold-blooded ['kəʊld blʌdɪd]	kaltblütig
have no mercy ['mɜːsi] **for someone**	kein Erbarmen mit jemand haben
oppose [ə'pəʊz] **someone**	sich jemand entgegenstellen

55 *Multiple choice: Looking incredulously at incredible targets*

In diesem Test geht es um ähnlich geschriebene und/oder gesprochene Wörter, die deshalb leicht verwechselt werden – übrigens manchmal auch von Mutter-sprachlern.

Welches Wort passt?

a Her colleagues were _____ when she told them she planned to become an actress.
   incredible · incredibly · incredulous · incredulously

b Her colleagues looked at her _____ when she said, "I've decided I'm going to be an actress."
   incredible · incredibly · incredulous · incredulously

c We all know that it is _____ difficult to become a movie star.
   incredible · incredibly · incredulous · incredulously

d She had to overcome _____ difficulties to become a successful actress.
   incredible · incredibly · incredulous · incredulously

e She has won everything, _____ Olympic gold.
   accept · except · excess · expect

f We _____ to win gold and anything less than gold would be a disappointment.
   accept · except · excess · expect

g We have to _____ that we can't win gold every time.
   accept · except · excess · expect

h There's an _____ of office space in this area.
   accept · except · excess · expect

colleague ['kɒliːg] ⚠	Kollege, Kollegin
incredible [ɪn'kredəbl]	unglaublich
incredulous [ɪn'kredjələs]	ungläubig; skeptisch
I've decided [dɪ'saɪdɪd]	ich habe beschlossen
overcome difficulties ['dɪfɪkəltiz]	Schwierigkeiten überwinden
accept [ək'sept]	akzeptieren; annehmen
except [ɪk'sept]	außer
an excess [ɪk'ses] **of**	ein Übermaß an
expect [ɪk'spekt]	erwarten
anything less than gold [gəʊld]	alles, was weniger als Gold ist
office space ['ɒfɪs speɪs]	Bürofläche(n)

56 „Erhöhen", „steigen", „senken", „sinken", „fallen" etc.

Hier ist vor allem der Unterschied zwischen *raise* (transitiv) und *rise* (intransitiv) zu beachten. Andererseits können *increase* und das sehr viel seltenere *decrease* sowohl transitiv als auch intransitiv verwendet werden, sind also relativ „sicher", wenn auch nicht immer die gängigste Ausdrucksform.

Verwenden Sie bei der Übersetzung die folgenden Verben.

climb	fall	heighten	put up	rise
decrease	go down	increase	raise	sink
drop	go up	lower	reduce	

a   Die Fahrpreise sind **erhöht** worden.

_____

b   Die Flugpreise sind um 12 Prozent **gestiegen**.

_____

c   Wir sind außerstande, unsere Preise zu **senken**.

_____

d   Wir haben unsere Kosten **senken** können.

_____

e   Im Moment **sinken** die Ölpreise.

_____

f   Die Musik **erhöht** die Spannung.

_____

g   Die Titanic **sank** am 15. April 1912.

_____

h   Er ist 85, aber **steigt** immer noch auf Bäume.

_____

i   Wenn die Temperaturen **sinken**, **steigen** die Heizkosten.

_____

j   Er **fiel** auf die Knie.

_____

k   Pass auf, dass du die Teller nicht **fallen** lässt.

_____

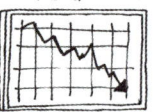

TEMPERATURES

HEATING COSTS

When temperatures fall, heating costs rise.

fare [feə]	Fahrpreis; Flugpreis
airfare ['eəfeə]	Flugpreis
be unable [ʌn'eɪbl]	außerstande sein
be able ['eɪbl] **to do something**	etwas tun können
costs [kɒsts] ⚠	Kosten
at the moment ['məʊmənt] ⚠	im Moment / Augenblick
tension ['tenʃn]	Spannung
temperature ['temprətʃə]	Temperatur
knee [niː]	Knie
make sure you ... [meɪk 'ʃʊə]	pass auf, dass du ...
plate [pleɪt]	Teller

 Wie man ein Datum spricht:
on the fifteenth of April, nineteen twelve
on April the fifteenth, nineteen twelve

57 „Fahren": *PRETTY GIRLS DON'T RIDE THE SUBWAY*

„Hübsche Mädchen fahren nicht mit der U-Bahn" – diesen blöden Slogan haben wir uns nicht ausgedacht, sondern er erschien mehrere Stunden lang auf einer elektronischen Anzeigetafel (= *electronic message board*) in einer New Yorker *subway station*. Ein elektronisch gewitzter Spaßvogel hatte ihn dort platziert, und es dauerte geraume Zeit, bis der unerwünschte Hinweis beseitigt war. Wir behandeln hier Entsprechungen für „fahren", um Ihnen deutlich zu machen, dass „fahren" längst nicht immer *drive* ist. *Drive* ist lediglich angebracht, wenn die Tätigkeit als „Fahrzeugführer" betont werden soll.

Setzen Sie das passende Wort für „fahren" in der richtigen Form ein.

a We're _____ on holiday next week.
b I'm _____ to Paris on business today and will be back next week.
c Why don't you _____ by train?
d More than 4.5 million people _____ the subway each day in New York.
e He was _____ about 90 mph when police stopped him.
f She _____ a nice car, eats at elegant restaurants, and wears beautiful clothes.

g   You really should _____ more carefully.
h   In the UK cars _____ on the left-hand side of the road.
i   The mothers in our group take turns _____ the children to school.
j   Can you _____ a bike?
k   The train only _____ on weekdays.
l   When does the next bus _____?

go on holiday [ˈhɒlədeɪ]	in Urlaub / in die Ferien fahren
on business [ˈbɪznəs]	geschäftlich
subway [ˈsʌbweɪ]	*AE* U-Bahn
90 mph [em piː ˈeɪtʃ]	(= 145 km/h)
(= miles per hour)	
when police [pəˈliːs]	als Polizisten ihn anhielten / die
stopped him	Polizei ihn anhielt (police *ist Plural!*)
restaurant [ˈrestərɒnt]	Restaurant
she wears [weəz] **beautiful**	sie trägt schöne
clothes [kləʊðz]	Sachen
(more) carefully [ˈkeəfəli]	vorsichtig(er)
take turns doing something	etwas abwechselnd tun
bike [baɪk] **/ bicycle** [ˈbaɪsɪkl]	Fahrrad

58   „Schon": *Has she left yet? Has she left already?*

Die englischen Entsprechungen für „schon" sind etwas für Fortgeschrittene.
Dass sowohl *yet* als auch *already* das Wort der Wahl sein kann, sehen wir
schon (!) in der Überschrift:
yet fragt nur sachlich, ob es schon passiert ist;
already drückt Erstaunen darüber aus, dass es schon passiert ist.
Darüber hinaus gibt es ein paar ungefähre idiomatische Entsprechungen (*as
early as, before*); mitunter bietet sich das **Perfekt** an („Wie lange kennst du ihn
schon?" = *How long have you known him?*) oder die **Verlaufsform** („Ich komm
ja schon." = *I'm coming.*); in vielen Fällen aber ist „schon" ein die Aussage
nuancierendes **Füllwort**, das im Englischen gar keinen Ausdruck findet („Es war
schon ein eigenartiges Gefühl." = It **was** a strange feeling.).

Übersetzen Sie.

a Als wir kamen, hatte die Show schon begonnen.

b Wir haben schon für nächstes Jahr gebucht.

c Musst du denn schon gehen?

d Sie konnte schon mit vier Jahren lesen und schreiben.

e Schimpansen haben schon in der Steinzeit Werkzeuge benutzt.

f Vielleicht sieht morgen alles schon wieder rosiger aus.

g Werden Sie schon bedient?

h Welche Frau würde mich schon heiraten wollen?

i Wir sind schon ein seltsames Paar, nicht?

j Schon bei dem bloßen Gedanken daran wird mir übel.

k Wie lange kennst du Judy schon?

l Sind Sie schon mal in Australien gewesen?

m Diesen Film habe ich schon mal gesehen.

n Ich war schon immer Pessimist.

o Ist sie schon gegangen?

p Sie hat es mir schon erzählt.

q Ich suche dich schon seit einer halben Stunde.

when she was four	mit vier Jahren
chimp / chimpanzee [tʃɪmpæn'ziː]	Schimpanse
the Stone Age ['stəʊn eɪdʒ]	die Steinzeit
look brighter ['braɪtə]	rosiger aussehen
an odd pair [ɒd 'peə]	ein seltsames Paar
the mere thought [mɪə 'θɔːt]	der bloße Gedanke

59 Deutsch: Verb + Nomen – Englisch: *be* + Adjektiv

In manchen Fällen entspricht
der deutschen Verbindung **Verb** (häufig: „haben") **+ Nomen**
im Englischen die Fügung ***be*** **+ Adjektiv:**

Angst haben	**be afraid**
Durst haben	**be thirsty**
eine Riesenwut haben	**be hopping mad**
Erfolg haben	**be successful**
Frust haben	**be frustrated**
Geduld haben	**be patient**
Glück haben	**be lucky**
Hunger haben	**be hungry**
keinen Erfolg haben	**be unsuccessful**
Pech haben	**be unlucky**
sich Sorgen machen	**be worried**
Wirkung zeigen	**be effective**
zur Verfügung stehen	**be available**

Benutzen Sie diese Ausdrücke nun bei der Übersetzung.

a   Hast du Angst vor mir?

b   Du hast Glück gehabt.

c   Wir hatten Pech mit dem Wetter.

*He's successful
with women.*

d   Die Kinder hatten großen Hunger.

_____

e   Ich habe keinen Durst.

_____

f   Er hat Erfolg bei Frauen.

_____

g   Diese Bemühungen hatten keinen Erfolg.

_____

h   Du musst Geduld mit ihm haben.

_____

i   Sie hat eine Riesenwut auf ihn.

_____

j   Ich habe Frust und ärgere mich über mich selber.

_____

k   Wir machen uns große Sorgen.

_____

l   Diese Formulare stehen online zur Verfügung.

_____

m   Diese Maßnahmen zeigten keine Wirkung.

_____

weather ['weðə]	Wetter
efforts ['efəts]	Bemühungen
be angry at / with someone	sich über jemand ärgern
form [fɔːm]	Formular
measures ['meʒəz]	Maßnahmen

60 *Collocations Crossword*

Setzen Sie im *Crossword* das jeweils passendste Verb in der richtigen Form ein:

ask	have	make	pay	serve	treat
bring	live	meet	reach	take	wage

Across

3 When my great-grandmother turned 100, the mayor _____ her a visit.

5 We do our best to _____ our customers' demands.

9 We are happy to field any questions you may wish to _____.

11 He was recently released after _____ six years for manslaughter.

12 They seem to have _____ the conclusion that talking is better than fighting.

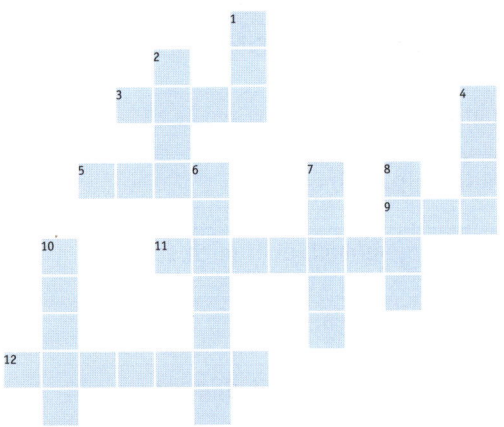

Down

1 I _____ a talk with my doctor and he advised me to give up smoking.

2 If you _____ a promise, you should do your best to keep it.

4 I can't really remember where I _____ this photo.

6 Last night, her sons _____ her to a fabulous Chinese dinner in Soho.

7 Money doesn't _____ happiness – nor does the lack of it.

8 The best use of an army is not to _____ war, but to keep the peace.

10 He jetted between five homes around the world and _____ a life of luxury.

61 *False friends are worse than open enemies*

Hier nun der „Fahndungsliste" zweiter Teil
(→ Übung 48; vergleichen Sie zu *false
friends* auch noch die Übungen 90 und 128).
Beachten Sie nicht zuletzt die
hinterhältigen „Scheinengländer in
unserer Mitte": Mobbing, Smoking
und Wellness.

Versuchen Sie (richtig) zu übersetzen.

Checking his documents.

a **Mobbing** am Arbeitsplatz

b den **Mörder** fangen

c sich **Notizen** machen

d eine **Novelle** von Hemingway

e das zweite Fernseh**programm**

f eine **Provision** von 20 Prozent

g jemandes Papiere **prüfen**

h einen Schüler **prüfen**

i die letzte **Rate** bezahlen

j eine **Rente** beziehen

k nur auf **Rezept** erhältlich

l einen kurzen **Rock** tragen

m die **Rückseite** des Hauses

n Finnlands unzählige **Seen**

o sein **selbstbewusstes** Auftreten

p Rundfunkprogramme **senden**

q ein **sensibler** Mensch

r ein **seriöser** Herr

s eine **seriöse** Firma

t einen **Smoking** tragen

u Geld **sparen**

v Geld **spenden**

w eine **sympathische** Frau

x das **Thema** wechseln

y ein Gesprächs**thema**

z eine Bemerkung (absichtlich) _____
   überhören _____
aa einen Fehler **übersehen** _____
bb **wandern** gehen _____
cc **Warenhäuser** wie Harrods in London _____
dd ein **Wellness**-Hotel _____
ee **wer** ist der beste Spieler? _____
ff **wo** sind die Schlüssel? _____

62 Nomen, die im Gegensatz zum Deutschen ohne Artikel stehen

Beachten Sie beim Übersetzen der folgenden Ausdrücke, dass die englischen Entsprechungen der fett gedruckten Nomen ohne *the* stehen.

a die Weisheit, die mit **dem Alter** kommt _____
b etwas gegen **die Arbeitslosigkeit** tun _____
c der Kampf gegen **die Armut** _____
d mehr Geld für **die Bildung** _____
e wir müssen **das Böse** bekämpfen _____
f die Vorteile **der Demokratie** _____
g Sex vor **der Ehe** _____
h für **die Freiheit** sterben _____
i was wir aus **der Geschichte** _____
   lernen können _____
j die Rolle der Frau in **der Gesellschaft** _____
k die Zunahme **der Gewalt** _____
l wem nützt **die Globalisierung**? _____
m in **der Industrie** arbeiten _____
n traumatische Erlebnisse in _____
   der Kindheit _____
o in **den Krieg** ziehen _____
p der Hund in **der Kunst** und **Literatur** _____
q **die Landwirtschaft** subventionieren _____
r sie liebte **das Leben** _____
s was **die Leute** über uns sagen _____
t in **der Liebe** ist alles möglich _____

u   Frauen an **der Macht**   _____
v   für **die Meinungsfreiheit** kämpfen   _____
w   aus **der Mode** kommen   _____
x   die Freuden **der Musik**   _____
y   die Schönheiten **der Natur**   _____
z   was in **der Politik** passiert   _____
aa sein Interesse an **der Religion**   _____
bb die Gefahren **der Technik**   _____
cc jemand vor **dem Tod** bewahren   _____
dd für **die Unabhängigkeit** kämpfen   _____
ee **das Wirtschaftswachstum** fördern   _____
ff wie doch **die Zeit** vergeht!   _____

the role of women ['wɪmɪn]	die Rolle der Frau
who benefits ['benɪfɪts] **(from it)?**	wem nützt es?
experiences [ɪk'spɪəriənsɪz]	Erlebnisse
subsidize ['sʌbsɪdaɪz]	subventionieren

63 *Multiple choice: Confusables and other nuisances*

Welches Wort passt?

a   The tranquilizer helped him to stay _____ and avoid panic.
calm · calmly · quiet · quietly

b   The child kept completely _____, never said a word.
calm · calmly · quiet · quietly

c   The financial markets reacted _____ to the election results.
calm · calmly · quiet · quietly

d   Excuse me, could you speak more _____, people are trying to work.
calm · calmly · quiet · quietly

e   Working _____ doesn't always guarantee success.
hard · hardly · heavy · heavily

f He learned his ideals from his _____-working parents and passed them on to his own children.
hard · hardly · heavy · heavily

g They lent me the money even though they _____ knew me.
hard · hardly · rare · rarely

h The shop deals in _____ books and manuscripts.
infrequent · rare · rarely · seldom

i We have to _____ to the environment to survive.
abide · adapt · adept · adopt

j We all have to _____ by the rules and regulations.
abide · adapt · adept · adopt

k As an exporting nation we have to be _____ at dealing with different cultures.
abide · adapt · adept · adopt

l If we want to save the planet, we have to _____ sustainable lifestyles and working practices.
abide · adapt · adept · adopt

confusables [kən'fjuːzəblz]	leicht zu verwechselnde Wörter
tranquilizer ['træŋkwəlaɪzə]	Beruhigungsmittel
calm(ly) ['kɑːm(li)]	ruhig (= *unaufgeregt*)
quiet(ly) ['kwaɪət(li)]	still, ruhig, leise (= *geräuscharm*)
guarantee [gærən'tiː] **success**	Erfolg garantieren
work hard – hard work	schwer arbeiten – schwere Arbeit
hardly ['hɑːdli]	kaum ⚠
abide [ə'baɪd] **by the law**	sich an das Gesetz halten
adapt [ə'dæpt] **to something**	sich an etwas anpassen
be adept [ə'dept] **(at something)**	geschickt / gut sein (in etwas)
sustainable [sə'steɪnəbl]	nachhaltig; umweltgerecht

64 „Von": *Of Mice and Men* „Von Mäusen und Menschen"

Of Mice and Men heißt der kleine, tragisch ausgehende Roman (1937) des Nobelpreisträgers John Steinbeck (1902–68). *Of* ist die häufigste Entsprechung für „von", aber *from* („von ... her") ist ebenfalls häufig, und *by* bezeichnet oft den „Urheber" der Handlung.

Übersetzen Sie.

a Ruth ist eine Freundin von ihr.

b Hast du ein Foto von ihr?

c Sie ist eine Frau von Charakter.

d Es war sehr nett von ihr.

e Der Ring ist ein Geschenk von ihm.

f Er stammt von der Küste.

g Sie zogen von Montrose nach Aberdeen.

h Montrose liegt südlich von Aberdeen.

i Es ist eine Entfernung von etwa 40 Meilen.

j Hier ist ein Bericht von unserem Korrespondenten in Moskau.

k Er ruft von Zeit zu Zeit an.

l Von hier an wird es leichter.

m Sie waren beide müde von der Arbeit.

n Ich sah, wie er von der Brücke sprang.

o Er verlor das Gleichgewicht und fiel von der Leiter.

p Er lieh sich Geld von ihr.

q Ich kaufte es von meinem Taschengeld.

r Sie wurde von ihm getäuscht.

s Von wem wurde das Radio erfunden?

t Ich habe gerade einen Roman von Steinbeck gelesen.

u Sie hat ein Kind von ihm.

v Von Beruf ist sie Psychologin.

move [muːv] **from Montrose to Aberdeen**	von Montrose nach Aberdeen ziehen
distance ['dɪstəns]	Entfernung
report [rɪ'pɔːt]	Bericht
lose one's balance (– lost – lost)	das Gleichgewicht verlieren
ladder ['lædə]	Leiter
borrow money ['mʌni]	(sich) Geld leihen / borgen
buy [baɪ] **– bought** [bɔːt] **– bought**	kaufen – kaufte – gekauft
deceive [dɪ'siːv] **someone**	jemand täuschen
invent [ɪn'vent] **something**	etwas erfinden
novel ['nɒvl]	Roman ⚠
psychologist [saɪ'kɒlədʒɪst]	Psychologe, Psychologin

65 *Prepositions for pleasure*

Die folgenden Sätze enthalten wieder ein paar unangenehme (aber hoffentlich lehrreiche) Überraschungen. Sie wissen ja: *prepositions are a prime source of error*.

Setzen Sie – wo nötig – passende Präpositionen ein.

a Welcome _____ London!

b Welcome _____ home!

c The editor sent me a cheque _____ £50 for my story and I was overjoyed.

d I only have 70 dollars _____ my account _____ the moment.

e If you already have an account _____ us, simply type in your name and password.

f We offer our customers a discount of 10 per cent _____ condition that they pay within four weeks.

g The islanders are living _____ fear of the next tsunami.

h Many old people don't go out after dark _____ fear of being robbed.

i When she heard that her son was alive, she wept _____ joy.

j The children laughed _____ joy and excitement.

k The last point, although very interesting, was not discussed _____ lack of time.

l Many people have trouble getting out of bed _____ the morning.

m _____ the morning of December 7, 1941, the Japanese navy made its surprise attack on Pearl Harbor.

n Do you know anyone _____ the name of Steve Holden?

o She wrote three books _____ the name of Sarah Culara.

p _____ my opinion he doesn't deserve to be described _____ a hero.

editor [ˈedɪtə]	Herausgeber(in); Redakteur(in)
overjoyed [əʊvəˈdʒɔɪd]	überglücklich
account [əˈkaʊnt]	Konto
discount [ˈdɪskaʊnt]	Skonto; Preisnachlass; Rabatt
islander [ˈaɪləndə]	Inselbewohner(in)
weep [wiːp] **– wept – wept**	weinen – weinte – geweint
joy and excitement [ɪkˈsaɪtmənt]	Freude und Aufregung
lack of time [læk əv ˈtaɪm]	Zeitmangel
he has trouble getting out of bed	es fällt ihm schwer, aus dem Bett zu kommen
surprise attack [səˈpraɪz ətæk]	Überraschungsangriff
deserve [dɪˈzɜːv]	es verdienen

66 „Sich": -self, each other oder unübersetzt

Die in der Überschrift genannten sind die Hauptentsprechungen. Lediglich die letzten vier Sätze erfordern eine andere Lösung.

Übersetzen Sie.

a Gönnen Sie sich eine Nacht im Ritz.

b Beschränken Sie sich bitte auf ein Gepäckstück pro Person.

c Er stellte sich vor.

d Sie hält sich für äußerst großzügig.

e Glücklicherweise gelang es dem Tier, sich zu befreien.

f Und diese Leute bezeichnen sich als Demokraten.

g Man muss sich selbst gegenüber ehrlich sein.

h Sie lieben sich und wollen heiraten.

i Die Kinder erzählten sich Geschichten und neckten sich.

j Sie sollten sich bei ihr entschuldigen.

k Sie hat sich sehr gut benommen.

l Die Welt verändert sich.

m Sie beschwerte sich beim Geschäftsführer.

n Sie vermieden es, sich anzusehen.

o Sie trafen sich in einem Pub in der Nähe des Bahnhofs.

p   Sie macht sich Sorgen um ihn.

q   Sie fürchtet sich vor Hunden.

r   Würden Sie bitte die Tür hinter sich zumachen.

s   Sie hat eine große Karriere vor sich.

t   Sie brach sich den rechten Arm.

u   Mehrere Gefangene nahmen sich das Leben.

She's afraid of dogs.

treat [triːt] **oneself to something**	sich etwas gönnen
restrict [rɪ'strɪkt] **oneself to something**	sich auf etwas beschränken
introduce [ɪntrə'djuːs] **oneself**	sich vorstellen
extremely generous ['dʒenərəs]	äußerst großzügig
honest ['ɒnɪst]	ehrlich
get married [get 'mærɪd]	heiraten
tease [tiːz] **someone**	jemand necken
apologize [ə'pɒlədʒaɪz] **to someone**	sich bei jemand entschuldigen
complain [kəm'pleɪn] **to someone**	sich bei jemand beschweren
avoid [ə'vɔɪd] **doing something**	es vermeiden, etwas zu tun
worry ['wʌri] **about someone**	sich um jemand Sorgen machen
prisoner ['prɪznə]	Gefangene(r)

67 „Falsch" – „Fehler": *Don't pull at your false beard.*

Setzen Sie ein passendes Wort für „falsch" ein: *false(ly)*, *incorrect(ly)* oder *wrong(ly)*.

a It was easy to see that he was wearing a(n) _____ beard.

b He was _____ accused of being a terrorist.

c She originally came to the US under a(n) _____ name.

d He pleaded guilty to giving _____ information to an immigration officer and faces deportation.

e We lost because we did everything _____ from the start.

f Some of the words were _____ spelled.

g I don't like people who spell my name _____.

h "Happyness" is a(n) _____ spelling of "happiness".

i The incident proved to be a(n) _____ alarm.

j "My watch says 4:17." – "Then your watch is _____."

k Police officials admitted they had arrested the _____ man.

„Fehler", „Fehleinschätzung", „Fehlschlag", „Versagen".
Setzen Sie die passende Form von einem der folgenden Nomen ein: *error*, *failure*, *fallacy*, *fault*, *flaw* oder *mistake*.

l The text contains a few grammatical _____.

m I know I have my _____, but I'm doing my best to correct them.

n The book has one serious _____ – it doesn't have an index.

o The accident was due to human _____.

p My decision was based on a(n) _____ of judgment.

q It's not my _____ if you don't read the instructions, is it?

r The mission was a complete _____.

s It's a popular _____ to believe that wicks must be made of flammable material.

originally [ə'rɪdʒənəli]	ursprünglich
plead guilty ['gɪlti] **to something**	sich einer Sache schuldig bekennen
he faces deportation [diːpɔː'teɪʃn]	ihm droht die Ausweisung
prove [pruːv] **to be**	sich erweisen als
was due [djuː] **to**	war zurückzuführen auf
wick [wɪk]	Docht

68 „Stehen" – „stellen"

Die englischen Entsprechungen von „stehen" und „stellen" bereiten manchmal Schwierigkeiten. Es besteht eben ein Unterschied zwischen „Auf dem Tisch steht ein leeres Weinglas" und „Auf dem Schild steht ZIMMER FREI".

Übersetzen Sie.

a   Die Freiheitsstatue steht seit 1886 an der Einfahrt zum New Yorker Hafen.

b   Ich stehe hier schon seit einer halben Stunde.

c   Das Klavier steht im Wohnzimmer.

d   Auf dem Tisch steht ein leeres Weinglas.

e   In der Zeitung steht nichts darüber.

f   Auf dem Schild steht ZIMMER FREI.

g   Wie steht es? – Eins zu null für Arsenal.

h   Das Kleid steht dir nicht.

i   Wie stehst du in der Schule?

j   Und wie steht es mit der Bezahlung?

k   Stell doch bitte die Weingläser auf den Tisch, ja?

l   Diese Lampe können wir ins Wohnzimmer stellen.

m   Darf ich Ihnen ein paar Fragen stellen?

n   Wie stellt man die Uhr?

o   Lass uns den Wecker auf 5 Uhr 30 stellen.

the Statue ['stætʃuː] of Liberty	die Freiheitsstatue
since 1886 (eighteen eighty-six)	seit 1886
the entrance ['entrəns] to the	die Einfahrt zum
harbour ['hɑːbə]	Hafen
for half an hour ['hɑːf ən 'aʊə]	seit einer halben Stunde
piano [pi'ænəʊ]	Klavier
living room ['lɪvɪŋ rʊm]	Wohnzimmer
an empty wine glass ['waɪn glɑːs]	ein leeres Weinglas
sign [saɪn]	Schild
vacancies ['veɪkənsiz]	Zimmer frei
score [skɔː]	(Spiel-)Stand
nil [nɪl]	(Fußball:) null
dress [dres]	Kleid
pay [peɪ]	Bezahlung
ask questions ['kwestʃənz]	Fragen stellen
alarm [ə'lɑːm] (clock)	Wecker

69 „Verbessern" und „verschlechtern": *Making it better or worse*

Wie so oft hat auch hier das Englische mehr Möglichkeiten der semantischen (= bedeutungsmäßigen) Differenzierung als das Deutsche.
Die Tabelle zeigt Ihnen die hauptsächlichen englischen Entsprechungen für „verbessern" und „verschlechtern" – mit ihren „Untertönen":

improve [ɪm'pruːv]	make (something) better	*verbessern*
improve	become better	*sich (ver)bessern*
worsen ['wɜːsn]	make (something) worse	*verschlechtern*
worsen	become worse	*sich verschlechtern*
deteriorate [dɪ'tɪəriəreɪt]	become worse	*sich verschlechtern*

enhance [ɪn'hɑ:ns]	make (something good) better	*verbessern*
exacerbate [ɪg'zæsəbeɪt]	make (something bad) worse	*verschlimmern*
aggravate ['ægrəveɪt]	make (something bad) worse	*verschlimmern*
ameliorate [ə'mi:liəreɪt]	make something bad more tolerable	*(sich) verbessern*

Vervollständigen Sie die Sätze durch Verben aus der Tabelle.

a   The reforms _____ the situation slightly but did not resolve all the problems.

b   During the last few days the situation in the flooded areas has _____ dramatically and has now reached crisis proportions.

c   Entire chapters have been revised or replaced, and chapters that were well done before have been _____.

d   Ethnic tensions were _____ by the murder, and civil disturbances appeared imminent.

e   The humanitarian crisis has been _____ in recent years by harvest failures and annual flooding.

resolve [rɪ'zɒlv] **all the problems**	alle Probleme lösen
during the last few [fju:] **days**	in den letzten Tagen
flooded areas [flʌdɪd 'eəriəz]	überschwemmte Gebiete
entire chapters [ɪntaɪə 'tʃæptəz]	ganze Kapitel
revise or replace [rɪ'pleɪs]	überarbeiten oder ersetzen
ethnic tensions [eθnɪk 'tenʃnz]	ethnische Spannungen
civil disturbances [dɪ'stɜ:bənsɪz]	Unruhen (in der Bevölkerung)
appeared imminent ['ɪmɪnənt]	schienen unmittelbar bevorzustehen
harvest failure ['hɑ:vɪst feɪljə]	Missernte

70 *Occupations Crossword*

Setzen Sie die Berufsbezeichnungen in das *Crossword* ein.

Down

2 a woman who performs on the stage, in films, etc.

3 someone who repairs machines and cars

4 someone who treats people who are ill

5 someone who prepares and sells medicines

6 someone who makes women's clothes

9 someone who prepares food

11 someone who makes men's clothes

12 someone who receives and pays out money in a bank

13 someone who writes books

Across

1 a priest in the Church of England

7 someone who helps people learn

8 someone who serves customers in a shop

10 someone who is elected to serve as a member of parliament, of the government, etc.

14 a man who serves customers in a restaurant

15 someone who writes plays for the theatre

16 someone who operates on people

17 someone who serves in the army

71 „Lassen" – *a pain in the translator's neck*

„Lassen" bereitet bei der Übertragung ins Englische außerordentliche Schwierigkeiten. Grob zu unterscheiden ist zwischen **let** („zulassen"), **leave** („in einem Zustand lassen"), **have / get** („eine Dienstleistung veranlassen") und **make** („durch Zwang veranlassen"). Darüber hinaus gibt es einige Sonderfälle wie **keep someone waiting** (= jemand warten lassen), **send for someone** (= jemand kommen lassen) und **divorce someone** (= sich von jemand scheiden lassen).

Übersetzen Sie.

a Lass mich gehen!

b Lass die Kinder ihren Spaß haben.

c Lass uns ein Taxi nehmen, ja?

d Du hättest ihn nicht ins Haus lassen dürfen.

e Du hättest den Hund im Haus lassen sollen.

f Du kannst alles so lassen, wie es ist.

g Lass mich in Ruhe!

h Sie wagte es nicht, das kranke Kind allein zu lassen.

i Dummerweise hatte ich mein Handy zu Hause gelassen.

j Ich lasse mir alle sechs Wochen die Haare schneiden.

k Sie ließ das Buch in rotem Leder binden.

l Ich habe drei Kopien machen lassen.

m Man kann sein Auto waschen lassen, während man einkauft oder Mittag isst.

n   Kannst du es nicht reinigen lassen?

o   Man ließ mich über eine Stunde warten.

p   Die Wachen ließen die Gefangenen stundenlang in der sengenden Hitze marschieren.

q   Wir mussten den Arzt kommen lassen.

r   Er lässt sich von seiner Frau scheiden.

unfortunately [ʌnˈfɔːtʃənətli]	dummerweise
have lunch [lʌntʃ]	(zu) Mittag essen
dry-clean [draɪ ˈkliːn] **something**	etwas (chemisch) reinigen
scorching [ˈskɔːtʃɪŋ] / **burning heat**	sengende Hitze

72 „Platz": Häufig ist *place* fehl am Platz

Unterscheiden Sie beim Übersetzen vor allem zwischen *place, room / space, square* und *seat*. Darüber hinaus sind hier noch einige Sonderfälle berücksichtigt.

Übersetzen Sie.

a   Dies ist ein guter Platz zum Parken.

b   Jeder will einen Platz an der Sonne.

c   So eine Methode wäre hier fehl am Platz.

d   In diesem Fall ist eine Entschuldigung am Platze.

e   Unsere Mannschaft kam auf den dritten Platz.

f   Im Kleiderschrank ist viel Platz.

g   Es ist nicht genug Platz für Bücher.

h   Im Kofferraum ist kein Platz mehr.

i   Dies Zeug nimmt viel Platz weg.

j   Berlins Gendarmenmarkt ist einer der schönsten Plätze Deutschlands.

k   Die Place de la Concorde ist der größte Platz von Paris.

l   Er verbringt die meiste Zeit auf dem Tennisplatz.

m   Zwei Spieler wurden vom Platz gestellt.

n   Ein junger Mann bot mir seinen Platz an.

o   Ich habe zwei Plätze im Piccadilly Theatre reservieren lassen.

p   Ist dieser Platz noch frei?

q   Bitte nehmen Sie Platz.

r   Direkt neben dem Hotel ist ein großer Parkplatz.

s   Die natürliche Fortpflanzung macht langsam der künstlichen Fortpflanzung Platz.

No room left in the boot.

method ['meθəd]	Methode
in this case [keɪs]	in diesem Fall
apology [ə'pɒlədʒi]	Entschuldigung
wardrobe ['wɔːdrəʊb]	Kleiderschrank
boot BE / AE trunk	Kofferraum (im Auto)
stuff [stʌf]	Zeug
spend – spent – spent	verbringen – verbrachte – verbracht
tennis court ['tenɪs kɔːt]	Tennisplatz
send a player off	einen Spieler vom Platz stellen
offer somebody something	jemand etwas anbieten
book / reserve [rɪ'zɜːv] seats	Plätze reservieren (lassen)
car park BE / AE parking lot	Parkplatz
reproduction [riːprə'dʌkʃn]	Fortpflanzung
artificial [ɑːtɪ'fɪʃl]	künstlich

73 „Preis", „Gebühr", „Kosten" etc. – *Everything has its price*

Setzen Sie jeweils eines der folgenden Wörter ein.

| amount | cost(s) | fare(s) | price(s) | sum |
| charge(s) | expense(s) | fee(s) | prize(s) | |

a There's a special offer available: four nights for the _____ of three.

b She won first _____ in a children's piano competition.

c I wouldn't do that at any _____ .

d Sheets and pillows are provided free of _____, woollen blankets and blanket covers can be borrowed for a small _____ .

e Hospital and doctors' _____ are high in Finland.

f Irish bank _____ are among the highest in Europe.

g The _____ of living has risen dramatically over the last 25 years.

h The rise in imports, coupled with mounting labour _____, crippled the US steel industry.

i We must do all we can to lower the _____ of health care.

j He lives at other people's _____ .

k The first _____ was a trip to New York, all _____ paid.

l On average, train _____ have risen by 4.3 per cent.
m The painting fetched the enormous _____ of £1.5 million.
n What happens if I cannot pay the full _____ of the Penalty Fare on the spot?

special offer [speʃl 'ɒfə]	Sonderangebot
be available [ə'veɪləbl]	vorhanden sein
piano competition [kɒmpə'tɪʃn]	Klavierwettbewerb
sheets and pillows ['pɪləʊz]	Betttücher und Kopfkissen
provide [prə'vaɪd]	(zur Verfügung) stellen
blanket cover ['blæŋkɪt kʌvə]	Bezug (*für die Bettdecke*)
rise [aɪ] **– rose – risen** ['rɪzn]	steigen – stieg – gestiegen
coupled ['kʌpld] with	verbunden mit
mounting ['maʊntɪŋ]	steigend
health care ['helθ keə]	Gesundheitswesen, -fürsorge
all expenses [ɪk'spensɪz] **paid**	alle Unkosten bezahlt; ohne Unkosten
on average ['ævərɪdʒ]	im Durchschnitt; durchschnittlich
painting ['peɪntɪŋ]	Gemälde; Bild
fetch an enormous [ɪ'nɔːməs] **price**	einen enormen Preis erzielen
penalty fare ['penəlti feə]	erhöhtes Beförderungsentgelt
on the spot [spɒt]	an Ort und Stelle

74 Präpositionen: *best boxer in the world – champion of the world*

Der Unterschied zwischen *in the world* und *of the world* wäre allein eine Übung wert; in den folgenden Sätzen kommt er nur beiläufig vor. Also:

in the world bezieht sich auf die Welt als „geographisches Gebilde", als „Ort"; *of the world* meint „von allen auf der Welt", also nicht „Ort", sondern „Zugehörigkeit":

*There are 20 million bloggers **in the world**.*
*Bloggers **of the world**, unite!*
*Sweden is one of the richest countries **in the world**.*
*Las Vegas is the gambling capital **of the world**.*

Setzen Sie – wo nötig – passende Präpositionen ein.

a   He buys houses, renovates them and sells them _____ a profit.

b   The car was going _____ a speed of about 30 miles an hour when it crashed into the bus.

c   Two men were detained _____ suspicion of aiding terrorists.

d   If the train arrives _____ time, we'll be _____ time for dinner.

e   The package includes a tour _____ Bollywood where you might just catch a glimpse _____ your favourite stars.

f   Our room has a wonderful view _____ the mountains and the ocean.

g   A visit _____ Hatfield House is always worthwhile.

h   There were some family photos _____ the wall, but I didn't recognize anyone _____ them.

i   _____ over 40 years, the Empire State Building was the tallest building _____ the world.

j   Joe Louis was heavyweight champion _____ the world _____ 11 years.

k   Orders _____ goods _____ stock are shipped the same day the order is received.

l   There's an old joke about an actor overly fond _____ talking about himself who ends one monologue _____ saying: "But enough _____ me; what do you think _____ my new play?"

detain [dɪ'teɪn] **someone**	jemand verhaften
suspicion [sə'spɪʃn]	Verdacht
Bollywood ['bɒliwʊd]	(*die indische Filmindustrie in Bombay*)
catch a glimpse [glɪmps] **of someone**	jemand kurz zu Gesicht bekommen
recognize ['rekəgnaɪz] **someone**	jemand erkennen
ship orders ['ɔːdəz]	Aufträge ausliefern
stock [stɒk]	Vorrat; Lager
the day the order is received [rɪ'siːvd]	am Tag des Auftragseingangs

75 „Schlecht", „schlimm": manchmal schlecht auszudrücken

Bad(ly) ist hier das Allerweltswort, *poor(ly)* eine mildere Alternative, mit der *less than adequate* bzw. *inferior* ausgedrückt wird. *Evil* ist „böse" im ethischen bzw. religiösen Sinn. „Schlechtes" erfordert im Englischen oft ein Stützwort, also *bad **things**, evil **things***.

Übersetzen Sie.

a   Der Film bekam viele schlechte Kritiken.

b   Das ist eine schlimme Nachricht.

c   Die Angst vor Schmerzen ist schlimmer als die Schmerzen selbst.

d   Ich habe nichts als Schlechtes über ihn gehört.

e   Viele erfolgreiche Menschen hatten in der Schule schlechte Noten.

f   Ich bin schlecht in Mathe(matik).

g   Er soll bei schlechter Gesundheit sein.

h   Vielleicht habe ich ein schlechtes Beispiel gewählt.

i   Die Bedienung war ziemlich schlecht.

j   Diese Steine sind von schlechterer Qualität.

k   Die Milch ist wieder schlecht geworden.

l   Mein Spanisch ist gut, aber mein Französisch ist ziemlich schlecht.

m   Es wird täglich schlimmer.

n   Danach war mir schlecht.

o   Sie war offensichtlich in schlechter Verfassung.

p   Auch ein schlechter Mensch tut nicht immer Böses.

q   Sie hat sich dir gegenüber schlecht benommen.

r   Die Nachmittagsvorstellung war schlecht besucht.

s   Das wird sich schlecht machen lassen.

t   Er kann seine Gefühle schlecht ausdrücken.

review [rɪ'vjuː]	(Film-, Theater-)Kritik
that's good news [njuːz]	das ist eine gute Nachricht
the fear of pain ['fɪər əv peɪn]	die Angst vor Schmerzen
bad / poor marks / grades	schlechte Noten
maths *BE / AE* **math**	Mathe(matik)
obvious(ly) ['ɒbvɪəs(li)]	offensichtlich
in good / bad shape [ʃeɪp]	in guter / schlechter Verfassung
afternoon performance / matinee ['mætɪneɪ]	Nachmittagsvorstellung
attend a performance [pə'fɔːməns]	eine Vorstellung besuchen
that can be arranged [ə'reɪndʒd]	das lässt sich machen
express [ɪk'spres] **one's feelings**	seine Gefühle ausdrücken

76 *Don't lose the loose dress you're carrying in your bag*

Hier geht es um die verschiedenen Entsprechungen für „tragen":
bear – bore – borne (Verantwortung, Kosten, Schuld, ein Gewicht tragen)
carry – carried – carried (mit sich führen, bei sich haben, transportieren)
wear – wore – worn (am Körper tragen)

Welches Wort passt?

a   I always _____ a loose dress when I travel.
    bear · carry · wear

b   I always _____ make-up when I go out.
    bear · carry · wear

c   He always _____ a loaded gun.
    bears · carries · wears

d   He always _____ a Rolex watch.
    bears · carries · wears

e   She always _____ glasses because she's short-sighted.
    bears · carries · wears

f   He _____ a cell phone twenty-four hours daily and was always on call.
    bore · carried · wore

g   Each truck _____ up to 9 cubic yards of concrete.
    bore · carried · wore

h   Who will _____ the cost?
    bear · carry · wear

i   We shared the risks and we _____ the responsibility together.
    bore · carried · wore

j   The ice was too thin to _____ his weight.
    bear · carry · wear

k   I never _____ much money on me.
    bear · carry · wear

l   She alone _____ the blame for the accident.
    bears · carries · wears

lose [luːz] **– lost – lost**	verlieren – verlor – verloren
a loose [luːs] **dress** ⚠	ein loses / locker sitzendes Kleid
a loaded gun [ˈləʊdɪd ˈɡʌn]	eine geladene Pistole
wear glasses [weə ˈɡlɑːsɪz]	eine Brille tragen
be on call [kɔːl]	telefonisch erreichbar sein
concrete [ˈkɒnkriːt]	Beton
share [ʃeə] **the risks**	die Risiken teilen / gemeinsam tragen
responsibility [rɪspɒnsəˈbɪləti]	Verantwortung
bear the blame for something	(die) Schuld an / für etwas tragen

77 Von den Knien der Bienen: wieder ein paar *idioms*

Ordnen Sie die Umschreibungen den unterstrichenen *idioms* zu.

annoys me | do what was expected of her | don't like | the greatest

enjoy each other's company | I'm sure it won't happen | doesn't impress

became suspicious | in short supply | is to blame | exactly what I need

avoid being punished | I don't believe you | very close | be too hasty

very suitable for me | do you think of | very easy

a Fat chance of that happening any time soon.
b Good schools are thin on the ground.
c His clever talk cuts no ice with me.
d His whining gets on my wick.
e I have no time for people like him.
f It's just what the doctor ordered.
g It's very important not to jump the gun.
h He smelled a rat.
i She thinks she's the bee's knees.
j Tell that to the marines.
k The exam was a piece of cake.
l They get on like a house on fire.

He smelled a rat.

m They're <u>thick as thieves</u>.

n She was sacked because she refused to <u>toe the line</u>.

o This job is <u>right up my street</u>.

p What<u>'s your take on</u> the new evidence?

q Who <u>carries the can</u> for the fiasco?

r You can always <u>beat the rap</u> with a good lawyer.

it won't happen any time soon	das wird nicht so bald passieren
avoid [ə'vɔɪd] **doing something**	es vermeiden, etwas zu tun
become suspicious [sə'spɪʃəs]	misstrauisch werden
whine [waɪn]	jammern
wick [wɪk]	Docht
impress [ɪm'pres]	beeindrucken
sack [sæk] **someone**	jemand rausschmeißen
refuse [rɪ'fjuːz] **to do something**	sich weigern, etwas zu tun
marines [mə'riːnz]	Marineinfanteristen
be in short supply [sə'plaɪ]	Mangelware sein
blame [bleɪm] **someone**	jemand die Schuld geben
evidence ['evɪdəns]	Beweismaterial

78 Jump: Getting jumpy when jumping the queue or a red light

Jump heißt in der Grundbedeutung „springen" oder „Sprung". Bei der Über-setzung der folgenden Sätze helfen Ihnen noch die folgenden Ausdrücke:

> be one jump ahead   take a jump   jump a red light
> jump down someone's throat   jump the gun   jump the queue
> jump to conclusions   jumpy = nervous / anxious / uneasy / worried

a Er sprang auf und rannte weg.

_____

b Sie retteten sich, indem sie aus dem Fenster sprangen.

_____

c Die Leute haben es nicht gern, wenn man sich vordrängelt.

_____

d   Du solltest keine vorschnellen Schlüsse ziehen.

e   Wir haben da wohl ein bisschen voreilig gehandelt.

f   Die Preise für Benzin und Heizöl sind sprunghaft angestiegen.

g   Wir sind der Konkurrenz immer um einen Schritt voraus.

h   Er wurde angehalten, weil er eine rote Ampel überfahren hatte.

i   Ich bin ein bisschen nervös, weil ich morgen eine Operation habe.

j   Als ich sie bat, ihre Entscheidung zu begründen, wurde sie ausfallend.

run away (– ran – run) [rʌn əˈweɪ]	wegrennen; weglaufen
save [seɪv]	retten
queue [kjuː]	(Menschen-)Schlange
conclusions [kənˈkluːʒnz]	Schlussfolgerungen; Schlüsse
jump the gun [gʌn]	(*eigentlich: „loslaufen, bevor der Startschuss ertönt"*) voreilig / vorschnell handeln
petrol [ˈpetrəl] *BE / AE* **gas(oline)** [gæs / ˈgæsəliːn]	Benzin
heating oil [ˈhiːtɪŋ ɔɪl] / **fuel oil** [ˈfjuːəl ɔɪl]	Heizöl
our competitors [kəmˈpetɪtəz]	unsere Konkurrenten / Konkurrenz
stop someone	jemand anhalten
have surgery [ˈsɜːdʒəri] **/ an operation**	eine Operation haben; operiert werden
give reasons for a decision [dɪˈsɪʒn]	eine Entscheidung begründen

▶ *Good advice:*
Don't jump from the frying pan into the fire.
Don't jump into unfamiliar waters.
Better wait and see which way the cat jumps.

79 *You can lose your head only if it's already loose*

Zwei Wörter, die ständig verwechselt werden, sind *lose* [luːz] und *loose* [luːs].
Lose wird mit einem „summenden" (= stimmhaften) *s* gesprochen und ist ein
unregelmäßiges Verb: *lose – lost – lost* (= verlieren – verlor – verloren).
Loose hingegen wird mit einem „zischenden" (= stimmlosen) *s* gesprochen und
ist ein Adjektiv mit der Bedeutung „lose, locker". Von *loose* wird das Adverb
loosely abgeleitet. Außerdem gibt es das Verb *loosen* [ˈluːsn] (= lockern).

Setzen Sie jeweils eines der folgenden Wörter ein.

> lose, loses, lost, losing – loose, loosely, loosen, loosened

a If she _____ her job, she'll have great difficulty finding a new one.
b I've _____ my mobile phone, probably left it in the cab.
c Here's the ticket. Make sure you don't _____ it.
d He spent three days in Las Vegas and _____ all his money.
e What I hate even more than _____ is playing poorly.
f I'm trying to teach my dog how to walk on a _____ leash.
g The stories are _____ connected, but each story could be read
   independently.
h The room was stifling hot, and he _____ his collar.
i The belt is too tight, why don't you _____ it a bit?
j A man who has been linked to 20 bank robberies is still on the _____.
k He was saying such crazy things that I asked myself, "Has he _____
   his mind, does he have a screw _____?"

have difficulty doing something	Schwierigkeiten haben, etw. zu tun
make sure [ʃʊə] **you …**	pass auf, dass du …
on the leash [liːʃ]	an der Leine
independent(ly) [ɪndɪˈpendənt(li)]	unabhängig
stifling hot [staɪflɪŋ ˈhɒt]	stickend heiß
the belt is too tight [taɪt]	der Gürtel ist zu eng
link to a bank robbery [ˈrɒbəri]	mit einem Bankraub in Verbindung bringen
be on the loose [luːs]	auf freiem Fuß sein
lose one's mind [maɪnd]	den Verstand verlieren

80 *Another Antonym Crossword*

Tragen Sie das Antonym (Gegensatzwort) des unterstrichenen Adjektivs in das *Crossword* ein.

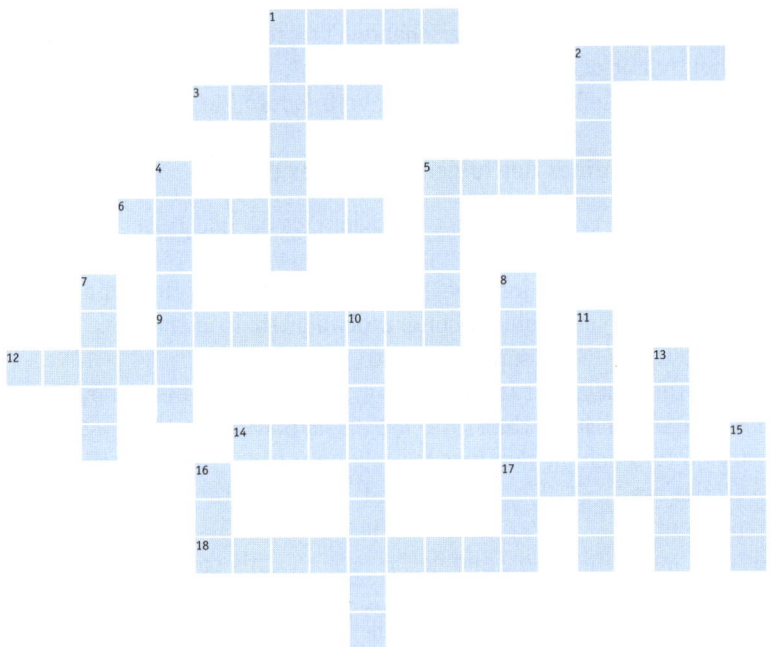

Across

1 a <u>tall</u> woman
2 a <u>plump</u> girl
3 a <u>cowardly</u> act
5 a <u>tight</u> dress
6 a <u>minor</u> accident
9 a <u>guilty</u> man
12 a <u>pretty</u> face
14 a <u>stingy</u> person
17 a <u>sad</u> story
18 an <u>easy</u> task

Down

1 a <u>deep</u> lake
2 a <u>bitter</u> taste
4 a <u>bogus</u> passport
5 a <u>heavy</u> burden
7 a <u>big</u> car
8 a <u>horrible</u> man
10 a <u>cheap</u> hotel
11 an <u>honest</u> official
13 a <u>stationary</u> vehicle
15 a <u>beautiful</u> house
16 a <u>slight</u> cold

81 Präpositionen: *Some more hard nuts to crack*

Setzen Sie passende Präpositionen ein.

a She died _____ a car accident.
b Can't we talk about something else _____ a change?
c He sleeps _____ day and works _____ night.
d Most of the work is done _____ hand.
e Today, playing _____ memory is one of the abilities a professional pianist is expected to have.
f We're a bit short _____ cash _____ the moment.
g We couldn't sleep _____ the noise.
h Lewis won the fight _____ points.
i She heard the concert _____ the radio.
j "I love you," she said _____ a low voice.
k Let's go _____ a walk in the park.

In den folgenden Sätzen geht es um die englischen Entsprechungen für „bis":

l The conference will last _____ 4pm.
m The conference will last from 8am _____ 4pm.
n What have you been doing _____ now?
o We'll have to be there _____ 8 o'clock at the latest.
p She stayed with him _____ the bitter end.
q The book will be finished _____ the end of this year.
r The train went only _____ Dartford.

car accident ['kɑːr æksɪdənt]	Autounfall
talk [tɔːk] **about something**	von / über etwas reden / sprechen
for a change [fər ə 'tʃeɪndʒ]	zur Abwechslung
memory ['meməri]	Gedächtnis
ability [ə'bɪləti]	Fähigkeit
professional pianist ['piːənɪst]	Berufspianist(in)
he's expected [ɪk'spektɪd]	es wird von ihm erwartet,
to have it	dass er sie hat
be short of cash [kæʃ]	knapp bei Kasse sein
noise [nɔɪz]	Lärm
win – won [wʌn] **– won**	gewinnen – gewann – gewonnen

hear [ɪə] – **heard** [ɜː] – **heard**	hören – hörte – gehört
a walk [wɔːk] **in the park**	ein Spaziergang im Park
conference [ˈkɒnfərəns]	Konferenz; Tagung
last [lɑːst]	dauern
at the latest [ət ðə ˈleɪtɪst]	spätestens
she stayed [steɪd] **with him**	sie blieb bei ihm

82 „Wie": *Is as strong as an ox, looks like an ox, but isn't an ox*

Entsprechungen für „wie" sind vor allem *like*, *as* und *how*;
wichtig ist aber auch *what ... like?*
Mit *as ... as* gibt es viele sprichwörtliche Vergleiche, z. B. *as bold as brass*
(= „so kühn wie Messing" / frech wie Oskar), *as busy as a bee* (= emsig wie
eine Biene), *as cold as charity* (= „so kalt wie die Wohlfahrt" / kalt wie
eine Hundeschnauze). Vgl. Übung 50.

Übersetzen Sie.

a   Er sieht aus wie ein Ochse. _____

b   Er isst wie ein Elefant. _____

c   Sie hat blaue Augen wie ihr Vater. _____

d   Er ist so stark wie ein Ochse. _____

e   Sie ist so alt wie ich. _____

f   Komm so schnell(, wie) du kannst. _____

g   Wie groß ist sie? _____

h   Wie stark er (doch) ist! _____

i   Wie geht es ihr? _____

j   Wie war sie angezogen? _____

k   Wie kommt es, dass ich nicht _____
    richtig hören kann, wenn ich eine _____
    Sonnenbrille trage? _____

l   Wie ist der neue Lehrer? _____

m   Wie sind die neuen Schuhe? _____

n   Wie ist das Wetter? _____

o   Wie wäre es mit einem Kaffee? _____

p   Wie heißt du?

q   Wie nennt man diese roten Früchte?

r   Wie spät ist es?

s   Mir gefällt / Ich mag die Art, wie
    sie lächelt.

t   Die Krankheit findet sich oft bei Wild-
    tieren wie Füchsen und Fledermäusen.

look [lʊk]	aussehen
ox [ɒks]	Ochse
elephant ['elɪfənt]	Elefant
strong [strɒŋ]	stark
he was dressed [drest] **in white**	er war weiß gekleidet
I cannot hear properly ['prɒpəli]	ich kann nicht richtig hören
wear [weə] **sunglasses**	eine Sonnenbrille tragen
these red fruits [fruːts]	diese roten Früchte
the disease is often found	die Krankheit findet sich oft
in wild animals	bei Wildtieren
bat [bæt]	Fledermaus

83 „Während": *while* oder *during*?

Das deutsche „während" kann Präposition sein und bezieht sich dann auf ein
Nomen. Die englische Entsprechung ist dann ***during***:
während der Nacht = ***during*** *the night*
während des Fluges = ***during*** *the flight*
während des ganzen Fluges = ***during*** *the entire flight*

„Während" kann aber auch Konjunktion sein und leitet dann einen Nebensatz
oder eine diesen verkürzende Konstruktion ein. Die englische Entsprechung ist
dann ***while***:
während sie im Bett las = ***while*** *(she was) reading in bed*

Auf diesen Unterschied im Gebrauch von *during* und *while* gilt es in den folgenden Sätzen zu achten.

Setzen Sie *during* oder *while* ein.

a These messages came in _____ you were absent.

b These messages came in _____ your absence.

c She lost a lot of weight _____ her illness.

d She lost a lot of weight _____ she was ill.

e You should turn off the TV _____ meals.

f Don't allow your child to watch TV _____ doing homework.

g It's best to leave the television off _____ homework time.

h _____ I'm away I'll write home every day.

i He died from a heart attack _____ on holiday in Peru.

j _____ the war the Queen refused to evacuate to Canada and even learned to use a revolver.

k One British soldier was slightly wounded _____ the fighting.

l He was seriously wounded _____ fighting in France.

m A man robbed a bank _____ he was talking on his cell phone.

n A man robbed a bank _____ talking on his cell phone.

o One should not rob a bank _____ a cell-phone conversation.

p One should not rob a bank _____ carrying on a cell-phone conversation.

q Smith committed a robbery _____ (he was) out of prison.

r Smith committed a robbery _____ which he seriously injured a security guard.

absent ['æbsənt] **– absence**	abwesend – Abwesenheit
die from a heart attack ['hɑːt ətæk]	an einem Herzanfall / Herzinfarkt sterben
refused [rɪ'fjuːzd] **to evacuate** [ɪ'vækjueɪt]	lehnte es ab, sich evakuieren zu lassen
carry on a conversation [kɒnvə'seɪʃn]	eine Unterhaltung führen
commit [kə'mɪt] **a robbery**	einen Raubüberfall begehen

84 „Schnell": *He quickly got a fast car and drove too fast*

Die Unterscheidung zwischen *fast* und *quick* bereitet oft Schwierigkeiten.

Fast betont Geschwindigkeit einer Sache oder einer Person:
Adjektiv: *a **fast** car / train / horse / driver / runner / worker / learner / eater / thinker*
Adverb: *he drives / runs / works / learns / thinks **fast***

Quick betont, dass etwas unverzüglich erfolgt und wenig Zeit erfordert:
Adjektiv: *gave her a **quick** look, walked with **quick** steps, has a **quick** mind, it's **quicker** by train, I had a **quick** shower, we had a **quick** bite to eat*
Adverb: *we got there **quick(ly)**, you get there **quicker / more quickly** by boat, she **quickly** got a job*

Mitunter ist das eine oder das andere möglich:
*the **quickest** way to the airport* (nimmt die wenigste Zeit in Anspruch)
*the **fastest** way to the airport* (das am schnellsten fahrende Transportmittel)

Benutzen Sie bei der Übersetzung das wahrscheinlichere Wort für „schnell".

a   Dein Rechner ist sehr schnell.
_____

b   Sie kann schneller als ich schwimmen.
_____

c   Ich benötige eine schnelle Antwort.
_____

d   Meine Fragen wurden sehr schnell beantwortet.
_____

e   Sie lernte schnell, wie man mit Männern umgeht.
_____

f   Komm schnell!
_____

g   Die Kinder sind so schnell groß geworden.
_____

h   Er wurde schnell gefasst.
_____

i   Schlechte Nachrichten verbreiten sich schnell.
_____

need [niːd]	benötigen
swim – swam –	schwimmen – schwamm –
swum	geschwommen
answer [ˈɑːnsə] **a question**	eine Frage beantworten
how to handle [ˈhændl] **men**	wie man mit Männern umgeht
children grow up (– grew – grown)	Kinder werden groß
catch a criminal (– caught – caught)	einen Verbrecher fassen
bad news [njuːz]	schlechte Nachrichten
travel [ˈtrævl]	reisen; (*Nachrichten, hier:*)
	sich verbreiten

85 *What a worm does in a storm – and other pronunciation problems*

Sie haben es ja bereits leidvoll erfahren: *English is a devil of a language* – nicht zuletzt, was die Aussprache angeht.
Die folgenden Sätze haben es aussprachemäßig in sich.

Sprechen Sie sie laut und: *Enjoy! Have fun!*

a   I must **polish** up my **Polish**.
b   There's a **hovercraft** in the **canal**.
c   The **singer** had his **finger** in the **ginger**.
d   He **lives** his **life** as if it were a **live** show.

The massive bass singer caught a bass.

130

e You **mustn't tear** the **fine linen** to pieces.
f The **massive bass** singer caught a **bass**.
g My **boss grossly** underestimated the **wound**.
h I **admire** what is **admirable** about this **scheme**.
i The **iron industry** generates a lot of **industrial** waste.
j Do all **Arabs** speak **Arabic** and read the **Arabian** Nights?

worm [wɜːm] – **storm** [stɔːm]	Wurm – Sturm
polish ['pɒlɪʃ] **up**	(*Sprachkenntnisse:*) aufpolieren
Polish ['pəʊlɪʃ]	Polnisch
hovercraft ['hɒvəkrɑːft]	Luftkissenfahrzeug
canal [kə'næl]	Kanal (= *Schifffahrtsweg*)
singer ['sɪŋə] – **finger** ['fɪŋgə]	Sänger – Finger
ginger ['dʒɪndʒə]	Ingwer
live [lɪv] – **live** [laɪv]	leben – direkt übertragen
mustn't ['mʌsnt]	darfst / musst / sollst nicht
tear [teə] **the linen** ['lɪnɪn] **to pieces**	das Leinen in Stücke reißen
the massive [æ] **bass** [beɪs] **singer**	der wuchtige Basssänger
bass [bæs]	Barsch
underestimate grossly ['grəʊsli]	grob unterschätzen
wound [wuːnd]	Wunde
admire [əd'maɪə] – **admirable** ['ædmərəbl]	bewundern – bewundernswert
scheme [skiːm]	Plan; Projekt
iron ['aɪən]	Eisen
industry ['ɪndəstri] – **industrial** [ɪn'dʌstriəl]	Industrie – industriell
generate ['dʒenəreɪt] **a lot of waste**	viel Abfall erzeugen
Arab ['ærəb] – **Arabic** ['ærəbɪk]	Araber(in) – Arabisch
the Arabian [ə'reɪbiən] **Nights**	Tausendundeine Nacht

86 „Auch": *There's more to it than "too" and "also"*

Für „auch" hat das Englische eine Vielzahl von – zum Teil mit grammatischen Mitteln ausgedrückten – Entsprechungen.

Übersetzen Sie – und staunen Sie!

a   „Ich liebe dich." – „Ich dich auch."

b   „Ich bin sehr überrascht." – „Ich auch."

c   „Ich bin nicht überrascht." – „Ich auch nicht."

d   „Ich bin überrascht." – „Ich bin auch überrascht."

e   „Ich bin nicht überrascht." – „Ich bin auch nicht überrascht."

f   „Ich weiß es nicht." – „Ich auch nicht."

g   Auch sie war überrascht.

h   Auch überrascht war sie.

i   Sie war überrascht, und ich war es auch.

j   Sie war überhaupt nicht überrascht, und ich war es auch nicht.

k   Wir waren recht überrascht und auch schockiert.

l   Ich war nicht nur überrascht, sondern auch schockiert.

m   Sie ist sehr hübsch. Sie ist auch sehr intelligent.

n   Sie überraschte alle, auch mich.

o   Ich war schockiert, auch wenn ich nicht überrascht war.

p Mir gefällt der Klang des Wortes, auch wenn ich nicht weiß, was es bedeutet.

_____

q Sie gab mir das Geld, ohne auch nur eine Sekunde zu zögern.

_____

surprised [sə'praɪzd]	überrascht
I don't know [nəʊ]	ich weiß es nicht
she wasn't surprised at all	sie war überhaupt nicht überrascht
quite [kwaɪt] **surprised**	recht überrascht
shocked [ʃɒkt]	schockiert
a pretty ['prɪti] **girl**	ein hübsches Mädchen
intelligent [ɪn'telɪdʒənt]	intelligent
surprise [sə'praɪz] **someone**	jemand überraschen
I like [laɪk] **it**	es / er / sie gefällt mir
the sound of the word [wɜːd]	der Klang des Wortes
I don't know [nəʊ] **what it means**	ich weiß nicht, was es bedeutet
give [ɪ] **– gave** [eɪ] **– given** [ɪ]	geben – gab – gegeben
second ['sekənd]	Sekunde
hesitate ['hezɪteɪt]	zögern
without hesitating ['hezɪteɪtɪŋ]	ohne zu zögern

87 *Dual choice: Be sensitive and make a sensible choice*

Welches Wort passt?

a It would be _____ to install a smoke detector.
   sensible · sensitive

b Smoke detectors should not be so _____ that they cause false alarms.
   sensible · sensitive

c An elephant's skin is so _____ that it can feel a fly landing on it.
   sensible · sensitive

d The river forms a natural _____ between Devon and Cornwall.
   boundary · limit

e Where is the _____ between Asia and Europe?
boundary · limit

f It's very important for parents to set _____ for their children.
borders · limits

g Millions of immigrants have crossed America's _____ illegally.
borders · limits

h I _____ him money and never got it back.
borrowed · lent

i When you overdraw, you are _____ money from the bank.
borrowing · lending

j When you put money into your bank account, you're _____ money to the bank.
borrowing · lending

k Burt skilfully _____ us through the winding streets of the old town.
guided · led

l Nelson Mandela _____ his nation to freedom.
guided · led

sensible ['sensəbl]	vernünftig
sensitive ['sensətɪv]	sensibel; empfindlich
install [ɪn'stɔːl] **a smoke detector**	einen Rauchmelder installieren
cause a false alarm [fɔːls ə'lɑːm]	einen Fehlalarm auslösen
boundary ['baʊndəri]	Grenze *(geogr., auch bei Grundstück)*
border ['bɔːdə]	(Landes-)Grenze
borrow money ['mʌni]	(sich) Geld leihen / borgen
lend (– lent – lent) someone money	jemand Geld leihen
overdraw [əʊvə'drɔː]	*(Konto)* überziehen
bank account ['bæŋk əkaʊnt]	Bankkonto
skilful(ly) ['skɪlfəl(i)]	geschickt
guide [gaɪd]	führen *(als [Stadt- etc.]Führer)*
lead [iː] **– led** [e] **– led**	(an)führen – (an)führte – (an)geführt

134

88 „Müssen": Kein Mensch muss müssen

There's no such thing as must: So idiomatisch wollen wir es hier nicht machen, sondern einfach ein paar Grundregeln festhalten:

1. In der Gegenwart nimmt man für „subjektiv empfundenes Müssen" *must*, für „objektiv gegebenes Müssen" *have to*.
2. *Must not / mustn't* ['mʌsnt] drückt eine starke negative Empfehlung aus: *you mustn't show weakness* = du darfst keine Schwäche zeigen, *you mustn't talk such rot* = du musst nicht so einen Quatsch reden.
3. In allen anderen Zeiten als der Gegenwart fahren Sie mit *have to* am besten.

Übersetzen Sie.

a   Wir müssen gegen 10 Uhr am Flughafen sein.

b   Wir müssen nicht alle Antworten wissen.

c   Muss ich an der Versammlung teilnehmen?

d   Du musst nicht unbedingt an der Versammlung teilnehmen.

e   Du musst nicht alles glauben, was sie sagt.

f   Was muss man tun, um Energie zu sparen?

g   Muss das jetzt sein?

h   Sie muss hier gewesen sein.

i   Ich musste fünfmal meinen Pass zeigen.

j   Du hättest das nicht tun müssen, aber ich bin so froh, dass du es getan hast.

k   Du wirst wahrscheinlich lange warten müssen.

l   Wir hätten wahrscheinlich etwa 500 Euro ausgeben müssen.

m Das hätt' ich früher wissen müssen!

n Wir hätten uns kein Geld leihen müssen.

o Ich muss mal.

around ten o'clock [əˈklɒk]	gegen zehn Uhr
at the airport [ˈeəpɔːt]	am Flughafen
attend [əˈtend] **a meeting**	an einer Versammlung teilnehmen
believe [brˈliːv] **everything**	alles glauben
save energy [ˈenədʒi]	Energie sparen
show one's passport [ˈpɑːspɔːt]	seinen Pass zeigen
five times [faɪv ˈtaɪmz]	fünfmal
I'm glad that ...	ich bin froh, dass ...
probably [ˈprɒbəbli]	wahrscheinlich
spend – spent – spent	(*Geld:*) ausgeben – ausgab – ausgegeben
borrow money [ˈmʌni]	sich Geld leihen

89 „Machen": *make, do, take (or drive)?*

Hauptentsprechungen für „machen" sind *make* und *do* (→ Übung 102):
Make betont das „Herstellen, Erzeugen eines Produkts".
Do betont das „Durchführen einer Tätigkeit oder Arbeit".

In manchen Fällen greift diese Regel nicht. Außerdem werden noch andere Verben verwendet, zum Beispiel **take** *an exam,* **pay** *a visit,* **drive** *someone crazy / mad / bonkers.* Solche Kollokationen lernt man am besten als Ganzes. Überhaupt ist es gut, wenn man möglichst zusammengehörige Ausdrücke lernt, nicht einzelne Wörter.

Setzen Sie eine Entsprechung für „machen" in der passenden Form ein.

a We were all cold and wet, so we _____ a fire to warm ourselves and dry our clothes.

b Cornflakes are _____ from corn, which the British call maize.

c We shouldn't _____ the mistake of underestimating him.

d This film has _____ her a star.

e He's often absent from school and never _____ his homework.

f What are you _____ for dinner tonight? One of your delicious pies?

g I _____ the beds and tidied up, _____ the tea for grandma and myself, then _____ the dishes and left for work.

h What are you _____ this weekend?

i Our dog usually _____ his business in the garden.

j Henry Ford _____ a fortune by producing cars cheaply enough to _____ them attractive to everyone.

k When are you _____ your A levels?

l He's _____ his exams in June.

m I _____ a photo of her standing next to the president.

n After supper we _____ a walk in the moonlight – that was really great.

o Let's _____ a break.

p English _____ fun.

q You're _____ me nervous.

r You're _____ me crazy.

maize [meɪz] *BE* / *AE* **corn** [kɔːn]	Mais
underestimate [ʌndərˈestɪmeɪt]	unterschätzen
tidy up [taɪdi ˈʌp]	aufräumen
do the dishes [ˈdɪʃɪz]	das Geschirr machen
business [ˈbɪznəs]	Geschäft (*auch* = „Notdurft")
fortune [ˈfɔːtʃən]	Vermögen
A levels [ˈeɪ levlz]	*BE* ≈ (das) Abitur
break [breɪk]	Pause

90 *False Friend Crossword*

Mit *false friends* beschäftigen wir uns auch anderswo (→ Übungen 48, 61, 128). Hier nun sollen Sie eine gar nicht so einfache Aufgabe lösen: die englischen Wörter finden (und in das *Crossword* eintragen), die durch die Definitionen beschrieben sind. Alle zu findenden Wörter sehen aus wie direkte Übersetzungen deutscher Wörter, haben aber eine ganz andere Bedeutung, sind eben „falsche Freunde".

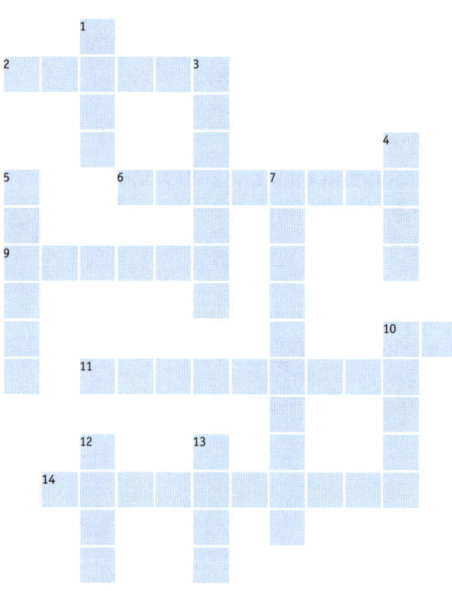

Across

2 a person who writes reviews of books, films, etc.

6 the part of the body you sit on

9 the line that divides two countries

10 a company where you can invest or borrow money

11 a large building in which goods, raw materials, etc. are stored

14 a picture made by means of a camera

Down

1 something you give to someone, a present

3 a reason to worry, or something that causes worry

4 regular payment you make for the right to use a flat or house

5 material made of wool, cotton, silk, or synthetics

7 materials for writing, for example pens and paper

8 a large piece of stone

10 a long, wooden or plastic seat for several people to sit on

12 the most important cook in a restaurant

13 a rounded roof on a building

91 „Liegen" – „legen": Wie man sich bettet, so liegt man ...

... As you make your bed, so you must lie on it.

Den Unterschied zwischen *lie* (= *lie*-gen) und *lay* (= *lay*-gen) kann man sich leicht merken. In den folgenden Sätzen kommen allerdings noch Alternativen vor: für „liegen" vor allem *be* und für „legen" vor allem *put*.

Übersetzen Sie.

a   Er lag auf seinem Bett und las ein Buch.

b   Sie liegt im Krankenhaus.

c   Draußen lag tiefer Schnee.

d   Die Betonung liegt auf der zweiten Silbe.

e   Das Wohnzimmer liegt nach Süden.

f   Die Entscheidung liegt beim Präsidenten.

g   Oxford liegt wie London an der Thames.

h   Aberdeen liegt an der Ostküste Schottlands.

He leaned back and put his feet on the table.

i Du solltest dich 'ne Weile hinlegen.

j Er legte sich auf die Couch.

k Er legte das Kind auf die Couch.

l Er lehnte sich zurück und legte die Füße auf den Tisch.

m Sie legte den Brief hin und ging aus dem Zimmer.

n Ich konnte das Buch einfach nicht aus der Hand legen.

o Sie legte die Steaks in die Pfanne.

in hospital BE / AE **in the hospital**	im Krankenhaus
outside [aʊt'saɪd]	draußen
deep snow [snəʊ]	tiefer Schnee
stress [stres]	Betonung
living room ['lɪvɪŋ rʊm]	Wohnzimmer
face south [feɪs 'saʊθ]	nach Süden liegen
decision [dɪ'sɪʒn]	Entscheidung
the east coast of Scotland ['skɒtlənd]	die Ostküste Schottlands
lie down [laɪ 'daʊn]	sich hinlegen
lean back [liːn 'bæk]	sich zurücklegen
put (– put – put) one's feet on the table	die Füße auf den Tisch legen
put an object ['ɒbdʒekt] **down**	einen Gegenstand hinlegen
leave (– left – left) the room	aus dem Zimmer gehen
put a book down [pʊt 'daʊn]	ein Buch aus der Hand legen (= aufhören zu lesen)
pan [pæn]	Pfanne

92 *Opportunity makes a thief* – „Gelegenheit macht Diebe"

Hier ist eine Meldung aus einer britischen Lokalzeitung. Schreiben Sie sie ab, und setzen Sie dabei die folgenden Verben in der richtigen Form an passender Stelle ein. (Achten Sie auf die zwei unterschiedlichen Verwendungen von *property*.)

> believe   contact   ensure   happen   include   keep   see   steal   watch

THIEVES entered a house in William Street, Upper Kingswood, and ████ an assortment of goods from the kitchen while the occupants ████ television in another room.

The incident ████ between 22.09hrs and 23.09hrs on Tuesday May 30.

Property stolen ████ a brown leather handbag and purse, wallets, keys and mobile phones.

It is ████ that the offenders entered the property from the back garden.

Anyone who ██ any suspicious activity in the vicinity is asked to ████ Upper Kingswood police station on 01726 815000.

Householders are reminded to ████ that all doors and windows are ████ securely locked when rooms are unoccupied. ■

thief [θiːf] **– thieves** [θiːvz]	Dieb – Diebe
steal [iː] **– stole – stolen**	stehlen – stahl – gestohlen
an assortment [əˈsɔːtmənt] **of goods**	eine Reihe von Gegenständen; diverse Sachen
the occupants [ˈɒkjʊpənts]	die Bewohner
incident [ˈɪnsɪdənt]	Vorfall
property [ˈprɒpəti]	Eigentum; Besitz; Grundstück; Haus
purse [pɜːs]	Geldbörse
wallet [ˈwɒlɪt]	Brieftasche
offender [əˈfendə]	Täter(in)
any suspicious [səˈspɪʃəs] **activity in the vicinity** [vəˈsɪnəti]	etwas Verdächtiges in der Umgebung
is asked [ɑːskt]	wird gebeten
contact [ˈkɒntækt] **someone**	sich mit jemand in Verbindung setzen
householder [ˈhaʊshəʊldə]	Hausbesitzer
remind someone to do something	jemand daran erinnern, etwas zu tun
securely [sɪˈkjʊəli] **locked** [lɒkt]	sicher verschlossen
unoccupied [ʌnˈɒkjʊpaɪd] **rooms**	unbewohnte / unbenutzte Zimmer

93 „Sagen" – *There's a lot to be said for "tell"*

Allgemein ist „sagen" = *say*, aber in Verbindung mit einem <u>Personenobjekt</u> ist es *tell*:

He **said** nothing about it.	*Er sagte nichts darüber.*
He **told** <u>me</u> nothing about it.	*Er sagte mir nichts darüber.*

Was Sie also vermeiden müssen, ist:
He said ~~me~~ nothing about it.

Übersetzen Sie.

a   Er sagte, er würde kommen.

b   Er sagte mir, dass er kommen würde.

c   Hat sie das wirklich gesagt?

d   Hat sie dir das wirklich gesagt?

e   Können Sie mir sagen, wie man es installiert?

f   Ich sagte ihr, sie solle es nächstes Mal mitbringen.

g   „Ich kann es gar nicht erwarten, wieder auf Achse zu sein", sagte er.

h   Er sagte, er könne es gar nicht erwarten, wieder auf Achse zu sein.

i   Bitte sag nicht „Opa" zu mir.

j   Was sagst du zu meinem Angebot?

k   Wollen Sie damit sagen, dass ich lüge?

l   „Smith ist ein hoffnungsloser Fall." – „Das kannst du laut sagen."

install [ɪnˈstɔːl]	installieren
I can't wait [weɪt] **to ...**	ich kann es gar nicht erwarten, zu ...
be on the road [rəʊd]	auf Achse sein
grandpa [ˈgrænpɑː]	Opa
offer [ˈɒfə]	Angebot
lie [laɪ] **– lied** [laɪd] **– lying** [ˈlaɪɪŋ]	lügen – log – lügend
a hopeless case [keɪs]	ein hoffnungsloser Fall

 Idioms **mit** *say*

Say cheese!	(*Fotogr.*) Bitte recht freundlich!
It goes without saying that ...	Es versteht sich von selbst, dass ...
There's a lot to be said for it.	Es spricht viel dafür.
to say nothing of the cost(s)	ganz zu schweigen von den Kosten
having said that	davon einmal abgesehen
when all is said and done	letzten Endes
You don't say!	Was du nicht sagst!

94 Euphemismen: *Excuse me, where's the euphemism, please?*

Euphemismen sind verhüllende, beschönigende Umschreibungen. Man gebraucht sie, um Gefühle nicht zu verletzen (*pass away* statt *die*), Peinliches nicht aussprechen zu müssen (*down below / down there* statt *my genitals*), Schlichtes aufzuwerten (*appointment* statt *job*), eine unangenehme Tatsache zu verbrämen (*downsize* statt *fire / dismiss employees*) oder moralisch Anstößiges zu neutralisieren (*pre-emptive strike* statt *unprovoked attack*). Im Gespräch sagt man vielleicht *I'll think about it*, wenn man *no* meint, und euphemistisch ist auch ein Satz wie *I hear what you say*, mit dem man zu verstehen gibt: *I don't agree and I'm not going to do what you suggest*.
Übrigens: Nicht nur im Deutschen, sondern auch im Englischen vermeidet man gern die direkte Frage nach der „Toilette" oder dem „Klo" und benutzt dann Umschreibungen (Euphemismen) wie *cloakroom, bathroom, rest room* oder *the men's / ladies' room*. Daher die Formulierung eines Spaßvogels: *Excuse, where's the euphemism, please?*
Nachstehend finden Sie in der linken Spalte einige häufig gebrauchte *euphemisms*; die Wörter in der rechten Spalte *call a spade a spade*.

KAPITEL 10

Ordnen Sie die Ausdrücke einander zu.

advocacy ['ædvəkəsi]	dead
asleep	die
bathroom	elderly person
collateral [kə'lætərəl] damage	genitals ['dʒenɪtlz]
condition	genocide ['dʒenəsaɪd]
conflict	illness
correctional facility	invade and occupy
enhanced interrogation	killing of innocent bystanders
ethnic cleansing ['klenzɪŋ]	lazy
freedom fighter	lobbying
industrial action	military attack
liberate	political lying
pass away	prison
pre-owned	propaganda
private parts	strike
promotion	tax increase
revenue ['revənju:] enhancement	terrorist
senior citizen [si:niə 'sɪtizn]	toilet
spin	torture ['tɔ:tʃə]
surgical ['sɜ:dʒɪkl] strike	used
unmotivated	war

euphemism ['ju:fəmɪzm]	Euphemismus
call a spade a spade [speɪd]	die Dinge beim Namen nennen
correctional facility [kə'rekʃnl fəsɪləti]	AE Justizvollzugsanstalt
enhanced [ɪn'hɑ:nst] **interrogation**	„verbessertes Verhör"

95 „Zu": *Too good to be true?*

In der Bedeutung „zu etwas hin" und beim Infinitiv wird „zu" mit *to* übersetzt.
Beachten Sie die Schreibung mit Doppel-o, wenn „zu" ein Übermaß ausdrückt:
*Most people use a hairdryer **to** dry their hair.*
*My hair is **too** dry.*

Übersetzen Sie.

a   Warum gehst du nicht zum Arzt?

b   Ich ging zum Bahnhof, um die Fahrkarten zu kaufen.

c   Wollen wir zu mir gehen?

d   Bist du noch zu Hause?

e   Achte darauf, dass die Schuhe zum Kleid passen.

f   Kann man zu Fisch Rotwein trinken?

g   Ich verstehe Leute, die zu Weihnachten deprimiert sind.

h   Was hast du zu Weihnachten bekommen?

i   Wir kauften zwei Karten zu je 50 Dollar.

j   Patienten müssen bis zu sechs Monaten auf eine Operation warten.

k   Für so eine Stellung ist er zu jung.

l   Diese Übung ist zu schwer.

m   Die Fenster sind alle zu.

n   Die Flasche war noch zu.

o   Er ging auf die Soldaten zu.

p   Was beabsichtigst du zu tun?

q   Das war zu erwarten.

doctor ['dɒktə]	Arzt, Ärztin
buy [baɪ] **the tickets**	die Fahrkarten kaufen
make sure ...	achte(n Sie) darauf, dass ...
the shoes go with the dress	die Schuhe passen zum Kleid
Christmas ['krɪsməs]	Weihnachten
depressed [dɪ'prest]	deprimiert
patient ['peɪʃnt]	Patient(in)
wait for an operation [ɒpə'reɪʃn]	auf eine Operation warten
position [pə'zɪʃn] / **job**	Stellung
a difficult exercise ['eksəsaɪz]	eine schwere Übung
soldier ['səʊldʒə]	Soldat(in)
intend [ɪn'tend]	beabsichtigen
expect [ɪk'spekt]	erwarten

96 *Prepositions: You're good at them!*

Hier geht es überwiegend um Adjektiv + Präposition, und zwar Fälle, wo das Englische vom Deutschen abweicht. Ärgern Sie sich also nicht. Merken Sie sich vor allem: *typical of* = „typisch für".

Setzen Sie passende Präpositionen ein.

a He's not afraid _____ expressing his opinion.

b He's an accomplished liar and exceedingly clever _____ covering his tracks.

c As a full-time employee you will be entitled _____ various benefits.

d Many people are frightened _____ losing their jobs.

e This dictionary is particularly good _____ idioms.

f I'm not very good _____ remembering names.

g When their poodle fell ill _____ a throat infection, they sent imme- diately _____ the country's leading ear, nose, and throat specialist.

h Aunty Stella is jealous _____ every woman, old or young, who comes near Uncle Fred.

i He's married _____ a former Miss Universe who is 30 years younger _____ him.

j   He's married _____ two children and three grandchildren.
k   The region is rich _____ natural resources.
l   Police became suspicious _____ the man, stopped him and discovered
    the explosives belt.
m   His reaction is typical _____ someone who does not like to admit
    he's wrong.

express one's opinion [əˈpɪnjən]	seine Meinung äußern
an accomplished [əˈkʌmplɪʃt] **liar** [ˈlaɪə]	ein vollendeter / versierter Lügner
exceedingly [ɪkˈsiːdɪŋli] **clever**	äußerst / ausgesprochen geschickt
cover [ˈkʌvə] **one's tracks**	seine Spuren verwischen
employee [ɪmˈplɔɪiː]	Angestelle(r); Beschäftigte(r)
be entitled [ɪnˈtaɪtld] **to something**	Anspruch auf etwas haben
various [ˈværiəs] **(fringe) benefits**	diverse zusätzliche Leistungen
be frightened [ˈfraɪtnd]	Angst haben
particularly [pəˈtɪkjələli] **good**	besonders gut
remember [rɪˈmembə] **names**	sich Namen merken (→ Übung 102)
throat infection [ˈθrəʊt ɪnfekʃn]	Halsentzündung
be jealous [ˈdʒeləs] **of someone**	auf jemand eifersüchtig sein
natural resources [rɪˈsɔːsɪz]	natürliche Ressourcen; Naturschätze
become suspicious [səˈspɪʃəs]	Verdacht schöpfen
explosives [ɪkˈspləʊsɪvz] **belt**	Sprengstoffgürtel

97 „Sie": *she, her, they, them, it, you*

Das kleine Wörtchen „sie" hat tatsächlich mindestens sechs Entsprechungen im Englischen, weshalb es Lernenden häufig Schwierigkeiten bereitet:

	Subjekt	Objekt
Weiblich:	**she** is here	I see **her**
Sächlich:	**it** is here	I see **it**
Plural:	**they** are here	I see **them**
Anrede:	**you** are here	I see **you**

Übersetzen Sie.

a   Warum will sie ihn heiraten?

b   Warum will er sie heiraten?

c   Warum wollen sie heiraten?

d   Wenn ich sie wäre, würde ich ihn nicht heiraten.

e   Wenn sie nicht gewesen wäre, hätte ich bestimmt den Verstand verloren.

f   Sie war es, die ihn umgebracht hat.

g   Sie waren es, die den Krieg angefangen haben.

h   Mir gefällt die Lampe, sie ist sehr hübsch, aber ich würde sie nicht kaufen.

i   Mir gefallen die Schuhe, sie sind sehr modisch, aber ich könnte sie nicht tragen.

j   Würden Sie bitte dieses Formular ausfüllen.

k   Darf ich Sie bitten, dieses Formular auszufüllen?

I wouldn't ['wʊdnt] **marry him**	ich würde ihn nicht heiraten
if I were / was so-and-so	wenn ich Soundso wäre
if it hadn't been for X [eks]	wenn X nicht gewesen wäre
go mad / lose [luːz] **one's mind**	den Verstand verlieren
it was X who ...	X war es, der ...
kill [kɪl] **someone**	jemand umbringen
start a war [wɔː]	einen Krieg anfangen
I like the lamp [læmp]	mir gefällt die Lampe
buy [baɪ] **something**	etwas kaufen
wear [weə] **trendy shoes** [ʃuːz]	modische Schuhe tragen
fill in a form [fɔːm]	ein Formular ausfüllen

98 *Dual choice: A live coward is better than a dead hero*

Beachten Sie den Aussspracheunterschied zwischen dem Verb *live* [ɪ] und dem Adjektiv *live* [aɪ]. Auch *alive* [əˈlaɪv] ist ein Adjektiv, das aber im Gegensatz zu *live* [aɪ] nicht vor dem Nomen stehen kann: *a live* [aɪ] *fish is alive*.

„Schatten" als „schattige Stelle" ist *shade*, als „Umriss eines nicht lichtdurch-lässigen Körpers" dagegen *shadow*.

„Küche" als Raum ist *kitchen*, als „Art des Kochens" dagegen *cooking* oder (im Test nicht vorkommend) *cuisine* [kwɪˈziːn].

Welches Wort passt?

a   A _____ dog is better than a dead lion.
    life · live

b   Luckily the fish was still _____ and we were able to get it back in the pond quickly.
    alive · live

c   Most people prefer a _____ performance to a recorded one.
    life · live

d   When Beethoven wrote his Fifth Symphony, Haydn was still _____.
    alive · live

e   This CD was recorded _____ at the Royal Festival Hall, London, in the late 1980s.
    alive · live

f   As a banker he has to wear a jacket and tie, even if it's 40 degrees in the _____.
    shade · shadow

g   Peter Schlemihl is "The Man Who Sold His _____" in the famous story by Adelbert von Chamisso.
    shade · shadow

h   I'm a huge fan of Indian _____.
    cooking · kitchen

i   Curry is an important spice in an Indian _____.
    cooking · kitchen

get the fish back in (to) the pond [pɒnd]	den Fisch zurück in den Teich schaffen
wear [weə] **a jacket** ['dʒækɪt]	ein Jackett tragen
even if it's 40 degrees [dɪ'griːz]	auch wenn es 40 Grad sind
an important [ɪm'pɔːtənt] **spice**	ein wichtiges Gewürz

99 „Kommen": *Coming down is easier than going up*

Come (←) ist in seiner Grundbedeutung das Gegenteil von *go* (→). Sie können also *come* nicht (entsprechend dem Deutschen) benutzen, wenn die Bewegung weg vom Ort des Sprechens geht (vgl. die Sätze i und j).

„Kommen" in der Bedeutung „gelangen" ist häufig *get* (vgl. die Sätze d, e, f, h). Ansonsten wird „kommen" mitunter auch durch eine Form von *be* ausgedrückt (vgl. die Sätze b und n).

Übersetzen Sie.

a   Ich komme gerade von einer Beerdigung.

b   Ich kam zu spät zur Sitzung.

c   Wenn sie aus der Schule kommt, steht ihr Essen auf dem Tisch.

d   Als wir nach Hause kamen, war es Mitternacht.

e   Wie seid ihr hergekommen – mit dem Auto?

f   Wie komme ich zum Rathaus?

g   Wir kamen durch ein Städtchen namens Rogersville.

h   Ich bin nur bis Seite 50 gekommen.

i   Kommen gute Menschen in den Himmel?

j   Er wurde erwischt und kam ins Gefängnis.

k   Wir mussten den Arzt kommen lassen.

l   Mir kam der Gedanke, dass irgendetwas schiefgegangen sein musste.

m   Was auch immer kommen mag, wir werden immer einen Weg finden.

n   Wo kommen (= stammen) Sie her?

o   Wie kommt es, dass du so elegant angezogen bist?

p   Sie kommt nach ihrer Mutter.

q   Es kam alles ganz anders.

funeral ['fjuːnərəl]	Beerdigung
meeting ['miːtɪŋ]	Sitzung
her lunch [lʌntʃ] **/ dinner**	ihr Essen
midnight ['mɪdnaɪt]	Mitternacht
by car [baɪ 'kɑː]	mit dem Auto
town hall / city hall [sɪti 'hɔːl]	Rathaus
a little town called Rogersville	ein Städtchen namens Rogersville
page [peɪdʒ] **50**	Seite 50
good people ['piːpl]	gute Menschen
heaven ['hevn]	(der) Himmel
catch [æ] **– caught** [ɔː] **– caught**	erwischen – erwischte – erwischt
prison ['prɪzn]	Gefängnis
dressed smart(ly) / elegantly ['elɪgəntli]	elegant angezogen

100 „Rand" Crossword

Das deutsche Wort „Rand" hat im Englischen eine erstaunliche Vielzahl von Entsprechungen. In den *clues* zum *Crossword* fehlt jeweils das Wort für „Rand" oder „Ränder". Setzen Sie es in das *Crossword* ein. *Have fun!*

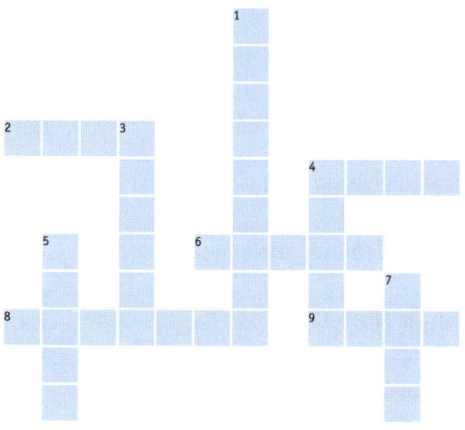

Across

2 She filled the cup to the _____ with boiling hot tea.

4 I could tell by the red _____ around his eyes that he had been working through the night.

6 Humans have pushed orang-utans to the _____ of extinction.

8 In the USA, there are vast numbers of undocumented immigrants living on the _____ of society.

9 You must never dive off the _____ of the pool unless you know for sure that the water is deep enough.

Down

1 Cheaper hotels and motels are to be found on the _____ of the city.

3 Please write clearly and leave a wide _____ for corrections.

4 He was pale and had dark _____ round his eyes.

5 He was obviously on the _____ of a nervous breakdown.

7 The hotel is beautifully situated at the _____ of a forest.

101 Deutsch: Adverb – Englisch: Verb

Übersetzen Sie die deutsche Adverbkonstruktion mit einer englischen Verbkonstruktion.

a **Zufällig** kenne ich die Geschichte. (*happen*)

b Der Angeklagte erschien **nicht** vor Gericht. (*fail*)

c **Hoffentlich** hast du recht. (*hope*)

d **Wahrscheinlich** bin ich eifersüchtig. (*guess / suppose*)

e Ich bin **gern** hier. (*like*)

f Ich bin **sehr gern** mit dir zusammen. (*enjoy*)

g Ich würde **liebend gern** kommen, aber ich glaube nicht, dass ich es schaffen kann. (*love*)

h Ich würde **lieber** mit dem Zug fahren. (*prefer*)

i **Vielleicht** ist es ein Druckfehler. (*may*)

j Wir haben **früher** hier gewohnt. (*used to*)

k Wo sie **wohl** ist? (*wonder*)

l Es war **wohl** nur ein Gerücht. (*suppose*)

m Die Preise steigen **weiter**. (*continue*)

n Lesen Sie bitte **weiter**. (*go on*)

o Ich sage **immer wieder** das Falsche. (*keep*)

p Ich sagte ihr, sie solle aufhören, aber sie schimpfte immer **weiter**. (*keep on*)

I know [nəʊ] **the story**	ich kenne die Geschichte
the defendant / accused [ə'kjuːzd]	der / die Angeklagte
appear [ə'pɪə] **in court**	vor Gericht erscheinen
you're right [jɔː 'raɪt]	du hast recht
jealous ['dʒeləs]	eifersüchtig
I can't make it [kɑːnt 'meɪk]	ich kann es nicht schaffen
go by train [treɪn]	mit dem Zug fahren
misprint ['mɪsprɪnt]	Druckfehler
rumour ['ruːmə]	Gerücht
rise [aɪ] **– rose** [əʊ] **– risen** [ɪ]	(*Preise:*) steigen – stieg – gestiegen
say the wrong thing(s)	das Falsche sagen
stop [stɒp]	aufhören
moan [məʊn]	jammern; schimpfen

102 *I remember reminding you to make tea before doing your homework*

In dieser Übung zwei *notorious troublemakers*: die Unterscheidung
zwischen *make* und *do* (→ Übung 89) und zwischen den häufig verwechselten
Verben *remember* und *remind*.

Make oder do?
Setzen Sie die passende Form von *make* oder *do* ein.

a   Have you _____ your homework?
b   Praise your dog when it _____ something right, but do not punish it
    harshly when it _____ something wrong.
c   Shall I _____ you some coffee?
d   She hardly ever _____ mistakes.
e   She _____ a delicious pie and we sat and chatted.
f   What do you _____ for a living?
g   What have you _____ with your hair? I liked it the way it was before.
h   You don't save money if you _____ your own dresses.
i   You have _____ an excellent choice.

Remember **oder** *remind*?
Ergänzen Sie die passende Form von *remember* **oder** *remind*, **und übersetzen Sie die Sätze.**

j I can't _____ what I did today.
k I think I _____ seeing his name on the list.
l He wrote to _____ me to put his name on the list.
m Please _____ me to call Tony.
n I must _____ to call Tony.
o This photo _____ me of my childhood.
p This photo makes me _____ my childhood.

notorious [nəʊˈtɔːriəs]	notorisch; berüchtigt
troublemaker [ˈtrʌblmeɪkə]	Unruhestifter(in); Störenfried
praise [preɪz] **your dog**	lobe deinen Hund
punish [ˈpʌnɪʃ] **someone harshly**	jemand streng bestrafen
a delicious pie [dɪˈlɪʃəs ˈpaɪ]	eine leckere Pastete
for a living [ˈlɪvɪŋ]	als Lebensunterhalt
the way it was before	wie es vorher war
an excellent [ˈeksələnt] **choice**	eine ausgezeichnete Wahl
remind [rɪˈmaɪnd] **someone** to do sth	jemand daran erinnern, etw. zu tun

103 So ist es nun mal – *That's the way it is*

Dem deutschen „so" entsprechen im Englischen eine Reihe von Wörtern und Wortgruppen: *so, such, like that, (that's) the way, as, that, this.*

Benutzen Sie diese Ausdrücke beim Übersetzen der folgenden Sätze.

a Sie ist ja so klug.

_____

b Es ist ja so schade.

_____

c Warum bist du denn so aggressiv?

_____

155

d   Ich liebe dich ja so sehr.

_____

e   Er ist so ein Idiot.

_____

f   Er ist so ein fantastischer Liebhaber.

_____

g   So einen Hund habe ich noch nie gesehen.

_____

h   So ist das Leben.

_____

i   Du musst die Flasche (*zeigt:*) so öffnen.

_____

j   So ist er nun mal.

_____

k   Sie behandelt ihn so, wie ein Lehrer ein ungezogenes Kind behandeln würde.

_____

l   Ihr Haar war so schwarz wie Ebenholz.

_____

m   Du bist fast so gut wie ich.

_____

n   Sie kümmerte sich um ihn so gut sie konnte.

_____

o   Ich gebe dir so bald wie möglich Bescheid.

_____

p   Wären Sie wohl so freundlich, mir das Buch zu signieren?

_____

q   So einfach ist es nun auch wieder nicht.

_____

r   Ich ahnte nicht, dass es so teuer sein würde.

_____

s   Der Stein war etwa (*zeigt:*) so groß.

_____

t   Du musst es (*zeigt:*) so machen.

_____

u   Hast du es so gemacht, wie ich dir gesagt habe?

_____

it's a pity ['pɪti]	es ist schade
a fantastic [fən'tæstɪk] **lover**	ein fantastischer Liebhaber
a naughty ['nɔːti] **child**	ein ungezogenes Kind
ebony ['ebəni]	Ebenholz
take (– took – taken) care	sich um jemand
of someone	kümmern
I'll let you know [nəʊ]	ich werde dir Bescheid geben
autograph ['ɔːtəgrɑːf] **a book**	ein Buch signieren
I didn't think [θɪŋk]	ich ahnte nicht

104 „Ärger", „Ärgernis", „ärgerlich", „verärgert", „böse", „wütend"

Setzen Sie jeweils ein passendes Wort aus der folgenden Liste ein.

bother	angry	furious	furiously	evil
nuisance	annoyed	irritated	annoying	wicked
trouble	cross	angrily	irritating	

a   I had a lot of _____ at the office.

b   The new law has caused us a lot of _____.

c   There goes our bus. What a _____!

d   Cell phones in restaurants are a bloody _____.

e   Are you _____ with me?

f   It's _____ when someone's mobile phone rings in class.

g   In Sweden, people get extremely _____ when the bus is two minutes late.

h   While the amplified sounds of a rock concert are music to some ears, they are _____ noise to others.

i   Shoppers and traders have reacted _____ to the news that one of Dursley's busiest car parks could be sold.

j   The athlete _____ denied the allegation that he used performance-enhancing drugs.

k   She was absolutely _____ when he accused her of lying.

l   A lot of _____ things have been done in the name of religion.

m   Snow White had a(n) _____ stepmother.

trouble ['trʌbl] / **bother** ['bɒðə]	Ärger
nuisance ['njuːsns]	Ärgernis
angry ['æŋgri]	böse; verärgert; wütend
annoyed [ə'nɔɪd]	verärgert
cross [krɒs]	böse; ärgerlich
furious ['fjʊəriəs]	wütend
annoying [ə'nɔɪɪŋ] / **irritating**	ärgerlich; lästig
evil ['iːvl] / **wicked** ['wɪkɪd]	(*moralisch*) böse, schlecht
cause [kɔːz]	verursachen; bereiten
bloody ['blʌdi]	verdammt
amplify ['æmplɪfaɪ]	verstärken
noise [nɔɪz]	Lärm
a busy ['bɪzi] **car park**	ein stark benutzter Parkplatz
deny [di'naɪ] **an allegation** [ælə'geɪʃn]	sich gegen eine Behauptung wehren
performance-enhancing [ɪn'hɑːnsɪŋ] **drugs** (→ Übung 69)	leistungssteigernde Mittel
accuse [ə'kjuːz] **someone of lying**	jemand der Lüge bezichtigen

105 „Brauchen": *Do you have what it takes?*

Bei „brauchen" sind im Wesentlichen vier Entsprechungen zu unterscheiden:
1. = „benötigen": *How much money will you **need**?*
2. = „Zeit in Anspruch nehmen": *How much time will it **take** (you)?*
3. = „verbrauchen": *A big car **uses** too much petrol.*
4. = Gegenteil von *must / have to*: *You **needn't** come / don't **need to** come.*

Übersetzen Sie.

a   Was wir brauchen, sind Menschen mit neuen Ideen.

b   Wir brauchen noch weitere 10 000 Euro.

c   Werden Sie ein Wörterbuch brauchen?

d   Wie lange werden Sie für das Buch brauchen?

e   Wie lange braucht man zum Flughafen?

f   Er brauchte eine Stunde, um eine Parklücke zu finden.

g   Energiesparlampen brauchen viel weniger Strom und halten viel länger.

h   Man braucht kein Genie zu sein, um Einsteins berühmte Gleichung zu verstehen.

i   Du wirst nicht zu warten brauchen.

j   Ich brauchte nicht zu warten.

k   Du hättest nicht zu warten brauchen.

people with new ideas [aɪˈdɪəz]	Menschen mit neuen Ideen
another 10,000 euros [ˈjʊərəʊz]	weitere 10 000 Euro
dictionary [ˈdɪkʃənri]	Wörterbuch
get to the airport [ˈeəpɔːt]	zum Flughafen kommen / gelangen
parking space [ˈpɑːkɪŋ speɪs]	Parklücke
energy-saving light bulb	Energiesparlampe
less electricity [ɪlekˈtrɪsəti]	weniger Strom
they last longer [lɑːst ˈlɒŋgə]	sie halten länger
a genius [ˈdʒiːnɪəs]	ein Genie
famous [ˈfeɪməs]	berühmt
equation [ɪˈkweɪʒn]	Gleichung
wait [weɪt]	warten

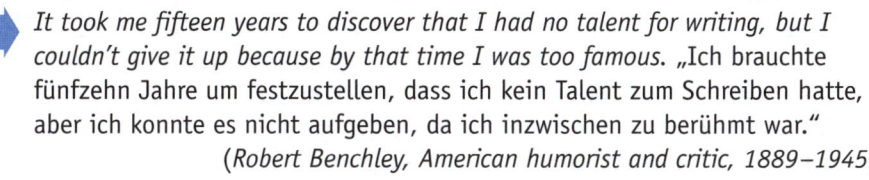

It took me fifteen years to discover that I had no talent for writing, but I couldn't give it up because by that time I was too famous. „Ich brauchte fünfzehn Jahre um festzustellen, dass ich kein Talent zum Schreiben hatte, aber ich konnte es nicht aufgeben, da ich inzwischen zu berühmt war."
(*Robert Benchley, American humorist and critic, 1889–1945*)

106 *Multiple choice: If the shoe doesn't fit, don't wear it*

Which word fits?

a   The ride was smooth and we reached our _____ in two hours.
    aim · destination · target

b   He fired six bullets, and missed the _____ every time.
    aim · goal · target

c   Our _____ is to create an environment which makes criminal activity
    as difficult as possible.
    aim · destination · target

d   Mountaineers witnessing the incident described how the soldiers took
    careful _____ and fired repeatedly at the civilians.
    aim · goal · target

e   We'll have to be creative and flexible to achieve our _____.
    destinations · goals · targets

f   The man who sacrifices his life to save another is _____ as a hero.
    esteemed · estimated · guessed

g   The number of servers Google runs is unknown but is _____ to be
    in the hundreds of thousands.
    esteemed · estimated · guessed

h   You might have _____ from the name that the restaurant doesn't
    serve traditional English fare.
    esteemed · estimated · guessed

ride [raɪd]	Fahrt
smooth [smuːð]	ruhig; reibungslos
aim [eɪm] / **goal** [gəʊl]	Ziel (*das man anstrebt*)
destination [destɪ'neɪʃn]	(Reise-, Fahrt-)Ziel; Bestimmungsort
target ['tɑːgɪt]	Ziel(scheibe); (*z. B. Produktions-*)Ziel
bullet ['bʊlɪt] ⚠	(*z. B. Pistolen-*)Kugel
environment [ɪn'vaɪrənmənt]	Umfeld; Milieu
mountaineer [maʊntɪ'nɪə]	Bergsteiger(in)
witness an incident ['ɪnsɪdənt]	Zeuge eines Vorfalls sein

fire repeatedly [rɪ'piːtɪdli] at	wiederholt feuern / schießen auf
achieve [ə'tʃiːv] an aim / a goal	ein Ziel erreichen
sacrifice ['sækrɪfaɪs]	opfern
esteem [ɪ'stiːm]	(hoch) schätzen
estimate ['estɪmeɪt]	(*Preis, Größe, Anzahl etc.*) schätzen
guess [ges]	schätzen; erraten; vermuten
traditional [trə'dɪʃnəl] English fare	traditionelle englische Kost

107 „Bringen": *Bring it here and take it there*

Die (allerdings auch von Muttersprachlern nicht immer beachtete) Regel ist:
bring = hin zum Sprecher oder zusammen mit dem Sprecher
take = weg vom Sprecher bzw. vom Ort des Sprechens
In dem Märchen von *Little Red Riding Hood* sagt die Mutter zu Rotkäppchen:
*Here is a piece of cake and a bottle of wine. **Take** them to your grandmother.*
Hätte die Oma Rotkäppchen um diese Dinge gebeten, so hätte sie das so ausgedrückt:
*Could you please **bring** me a piece of cake and a bottle of wine?*
Außer *bring* und *take* kommen in den folgenden Sätzen noch folgende Entsprechungen für „bringen" vor: *carry, get, give, make, put*.

Übersetzen Sie.

a   Er bringt mir jeden Tag Blumen.

b   Sie ließ für uns alle Pizzen bringen.

c   Warum habt ihr die Kinder nicht mitgebracht?

d   Kannst du das Auto in die Werkstatt bringen?

e   Ich bringe dich zum Flughafen.

f   Ihr solltet ihn sofort ins Krankenhaus bringen.

g Wir gingen früh nach Hause, um die Kinder ins Bett zu bringen.

h Dieses Auto hat uns nichts als Ärger gebracht.

i Sie brachte ihn dazu, den Vertrag zu unterschreiben.

j Es ist sehr schwierig, ihn zum Lachen zu bringen.

k Ich konnte es nicht über mich bringen, ihr die Wahrheit zu sagen.

l Wir müssen es schnell hinter uns bringen.

m Kennedy war einer der wenigen Senatoren, die es bis zum Präsidenten gebracht haben.

n Alle Zeitungen brachten die Geschichte.

*She got him to sign
the contract.*

flower ['flaʊə]	Blume
pizza ['piːtsə] ⚠	Pizza
garage ['gærɑːʒ]	(Autoreparatur-)Werkstatt
immediately [ɪ'miːdiətli] / **straight away**	sofort
hospital ['hɒspɪtl]	Krankenhaus
trouble ['trʌbl]	Ärger (→ Übung 104)
sign [saɪn] **a contract** ['kɒntrækt]	einen Vertrag unterschreiben

difficult ['dɪfɪkəlt]	schwierig
tell someone the truth [tru:θ]	jemand die Wahrheit sagen
few [fju:]	wenige
senator ['senətə]	Senator(in)

108 *Translating „sein" – not always easy to achieve*

Wörter, die „sein" ausdrücken.
Setzen Sie die passende Entsprechung für „sein" ein.

a Where will we _____ tomorrow?

b The wine has lost _____ flavour.

c He is a well-educated man and he certainly knows _____ subject.

d Everyone has _____ share of bad luck, don't they?

e One shouldn't overestimate _____ own strength.

f That must _____ been in Glasgow in 1995.

g _____ strong means overcoming the fear to do what you know is right.

h Oh, _____ on the Riviera now that winter's here! Wouldn't that be terrific!

Die fett gedruckten Nomen in den folgenden Sätzen bezeichnen alle etwas, das man erreichen, erzielen, erringen möchte. Das zu den Nomen passende Verb ist immer das gleiche.

Setzen Sie das Verb jeweils in der richtigen Form ein.

i They could have _____ their **aims** by choosing negotiation instead of violence.

j Persistence is one of the qualities you need to _____ an **end**.

k Alcohol Prohibition in the United States (1920–33) didn't _____ its **goals**.

l The dictator _____ his **objectives** by suppressing his opponents, censoring the press, and manipulating elections.

m He's written a book that tells you how to _____ **success** in whatever you do.

n The general said he needed more troops to _____ **victory**.

flavour ['fleɪvə]	Aroma
know one's subject ['sʌbdʒɪkt]	sein Fach beherrschen
one's share [ʃeər] **of bad luck**	seine Portion Pech
he overestimates his strength [streŋθ]	er überschätzt seine Kraft
negotiation [nɪɡəʊʃi'eɪʃn]	Verhandlung(en)
violence ['vaɪələns]	Gewalt(tätigkeit)
persistence [pə'sɪstəns]	Hartnäckigkeit; Beharrlichkeit
prohibition [prəʊɪ'bɪʃn]	Verbot
suppress [sə'pres] **opponents** [ə'pəʊnənts]	Gegner unterdrücken

109 „Aus": *Out of sight, out of mind*

Für „aus" als Präposition sind *out of* und *from* die häufigsten Entsprechungen. Nur die Sätze j bis p erfordern andere Übersetzungen.

Übersetzen Sie.

The magician pulled a rabbit out of the hat.

a Sie tat es aus Liebe.

b Der Zauberer zog ein Kaninchen aus dem Hut.

c Das kleine Mädchen fiel aus dem Fenster, aber ein Mann konnte es auffangen.

d Ich bin ein bisschen aus der Übung.

e Sie schrieb uns aus Paris.

f   Der beste Whisky kommt aus Schottland.

g   Du musst nicht aus der Bratpfanne ins Feuer springen.

h   Wir müssen aus unseren Fehlern lernen.

i   Hierzulande wird die Butter aus Kuhmilch hergestellt.

j   Die Griffe sind aus Plastik.

k   Ich bin aus folgenden Gründen gegen den Gesetzentwurf.

l   Die Datei wurde aus Versehen gelöscht.

m   Was ist aus unseren Idealen geworden?

n   (*Tennis:*) Der Ball war aus.

o   Die Schule ist aus.

p   Das Spiel ist aus.

magician [məˈdʒɪʃn]	Zauberer(in)
rabbit [ˈræbɪt]	Kaninchen
out of practice [ˈpræktɪs]	aus der Übung
write [raɪt] **– wrote – written**	schreiben – schrieb – geschrieben
frying pan [ˈfraɪŋ pæn]	Bratpfanne
mistake [mɪˈsteɪk]	Fehler (→ Übung 67)
in this country [ˈkʌntri]	hierzulande
cow's milk [ˈkaʊz mɪlk]	Kuhmilch
handle [ˈhændl]	Griff
plastic [ˈplæstɪk]	Plastik; Kunststoff
reason [ˈriːzn]	(*logischer*) Grund
bill [bɪl]	Gesetzentwurf
delete [dɪˈliːt] **a file**	eine Datei löschen

110 *Advanced Learner's Crossword*

Dieses *Crossword* enthält Wörter, die schwer zu unterscheiden sind und bei deren Gebrauch deshalb häufig Fehler gemacht werden.

Tragen Sie die englische Übersetzung des deutschen Worts in das *Crossword* ein – es ist immer ein Wort.

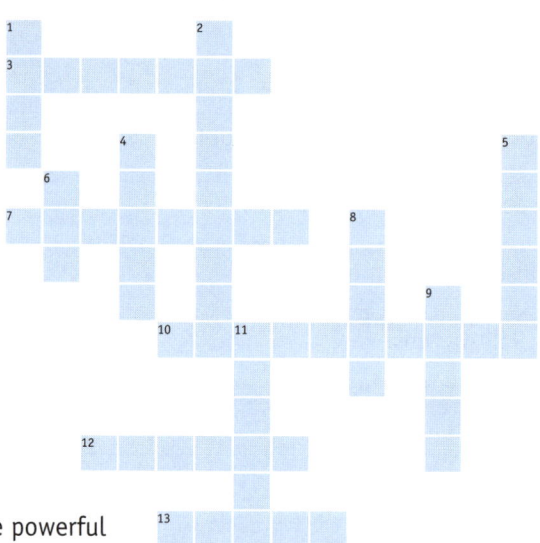

Across

3 Sports cars usually have powerful (*Motoren*).

7 A week is a long time in (*der Politik*).

10 I am interested in everything to do with (*Technik*).

12 A (*Punkt*) is used to end a sentence that is not a question or an exclamation. (Use the American word for *Punkt*.)

13 She doesn't like to (*tragen*) a lot of luggage.

Down

1 She doesn't like to (*tragen*) skirts.

2 In the 19th century, a Belgian mathematician developed a (*Technik*) for measuring the amount of fat in the human body.

4 The green (*Farbe*) on the walls was peeling badly.

5 He criticized the government's health (*Politik*).

6 For further information go to our website www.englishmaster.(*Punkt*)de

8 The pump is driven by an electric (*Motor*).

9 That's a (*Punkt*) we'll return to later.

11 Green is my favourite (*Farbe*).

111 Andersartige Konstruktionen im Deutschen und Englischen

In den Beispielen auf dieser Seite entspricht dem deutschen Satz im Englischen eine ganz andere Konstruktion.

Übersetzen Sie entsprechend der jeweiligen Überschrift.

Deutsch: Nomen – Englisch: Verb-Konstruktion

a   Das soll wohl ein **Witz** sein.   _____

b   Er wird bestimmt **Erfolg** haben.   _____

c   Schnelles **Handeln** war erforderlich.   _____

d   Ich kann deinen **Ärger** gut verstehen.   _____

e   Ich habe gerade mit der **Lektüre** seines neuesten Romans begonnen.   _____

f   Sie hat mich nie um **Entschuldigung** gebeten.   _____

g   Vom Augenblick unserer **Ankunft** an wurden wir verwöhnt.   _____

Deutsch: „mir"-Konstruktion – Englisch: *I*-Konstruktion

h   **Mir** ist kalt.   _____

i   **Mir** ist schlecht.   _____

j   **Mir** ist es egal.   _____

k   **Mir** ist egal, was die Leute sagen.   _____

l   **Mir** ist so komisch zumute.   _____

m   Sie tut **mir** so leid.   _____

n   **Mir** wurde klar, dass ich mich ändern musste.   _____

o   **Mir** macht es nichts aus.   _____

p   **Mir** gefällt die Musik nicht.   _____

Deutsch: „mich"-Konstruktion – Englisch: *I*-Konstruktion

q   Geld interessiert **mich** nicht.   _____

r   **Mich** wundert, dass er noch immer frei herumläuft.   _____

s   Es hat **mich** nicht sonderlich beeindruckt.   _____

t   Es freut **mich**, dass es dir gefallen hat.   _____

his latest novel ['nɒvl]	sein neuester Roman
spoil [spɔɪl] **someone**	jemand verwöhnen
I had to change [tʃeɪndʒ]	ich musste mich ändern
music ['mjuːzɪk]	Musik
money ['mʌni]	Geld
he's still at large [ət 'lɑːdʒ]	er läuft immer noch frei herum
not particularly [pə'tɪkjələli]	nicht sonderlich
impress [ɪm'pres] **someone**	jemand beeindrucken

112 „Groß": *Big fish eat little fish*

Setzen Sie eine passende Entsprechung für „groß" in der richtigen Form ein.

a It was quite a _____ room, about 20 square metres.

b D'you see that _____ house down there in the trees?

c It was a _____ mistake to go there.

d I'd hesitate to spend such a _____ amount of money.

e Albert Einstein was one of the _____ scientists of all time.

f The Annual Ball is always a _____ occasion.

g The storms caused _____ delays for commuters.

h You're a _____ boy now. You can get to school on your own.

i My _____ sister is so bossy.

j He's 1.85 metres _____.

k He's only fourteen but already _____ than his father.

l Higher incomes do not mean _____ happiness.

m This coat is at least two sizes too _____.

n The store offers a _____ selection of high-quality fashions.

o She looked as if she was in _____ pain.

p Of the Latin poets he studied Ovid with the _____ pleasure.

q A _____ coalition might be the best solution.

r One of Lincoln's _____ skills was his talent as a cross-examiner.

s Her 90th birthday was celebrated in a _____ way.

t The wedding of the two megastars was a very _____ occasion.

u What the world needs is a _____ strategy for fighting poverty.

square metre [skweə 'miːtə]	Quadratmeter
hesitate ['hezıteıt]	zögern
amount [ə'maʊnt] **of money**	Geldbetrag
scientist ['saıəntıst]	Naturwissenschaftler(in)
annual ['ænjuəl]	alljährlich
occasion [ə'keıʒn]	Anlass
cause [kɔːz]	verursachen
delay [dı'leı]	Verspätung
commuter [kə'mjuːtə]	Pendler(in)
on your own [ɒn jɔːr 'əʊn]	allein
size [saız]	(Konfektions-)Größe, Nummer
high-quality ['kwɒləti] **fashion**	Qualitätsmode
the Latin ['lætın] **poets** ['pəʊıts]	die lateinischen Dichter
skills [skılz]	Fähigkeiten
cross-examine [krɒsıg'zæmın] **someone**	jemand ins Kreuzverhör nehmen
celebrate ['seləbreıt] **a birthday**	einen Geburtstag feiern
fight poverty ['pɒvəti]	die Armut bekämpfen

113 „Gern": „Der kann mich mal gern haben!"

Zum Ausdruck des deutschen „gern" gibt es im Englischen verschiedene idiomatische Möglichkeiten.

Beachten Sie bei der Übersetzung die eingeklammerten Hilfen.

a Sie hat ihn sehr gern. (*like*)

_____

b Ich bin gern mit Freunden zusammen. (*like*)

_____

c Ich lasse mich nicht gern anbrüllen. (*like*)

_____

d Ich hätte gern einen Kaffee. (*like*)

_____

e Ich würde ja liebend gern kommen, aber ich kann leider nicht. (*love*)

_____

f   Ich würde gern den Rest meines Lebens hier verbringen. (*gladly*)
_____

g   Gern sieht sie den Kindern beim Spielen zu. (*enjoy*)
_____

h   Ich habe die Goldfische richtig gern. (*fond*)
_____

i   Ich will Ihnen gern helfen. (*happy*)
_____

j   Sie sind bei uns immer gern gesehen. (*welcome*)
_____

k   Sie können gern unser Telefon benutzen. (*welcome*)
_____

l   Sie können die Liste gern haben. (*welcome*)
_____

m   Was, beschwert er sich schon wieder? Der kann mich mal. (*get stuffed*)
_____

be with friends [frendz]	mit Freunden zusammen sein
shout [ʃaʊt] **at someone**	jemand anbrüllen
unfortunately [ʌnˈfɔːtʃənətli]	unglücklicherweise; leider
spend the rest of my life here	den Rest meines Lebens hier verbringen
watch [wɒtʃ] **the children play**	den Kindern beim Spielen zusehen
goldfish [ˈgəʊldfɪʃ]	Goldfisch(e)
use [juːz] **the phone** [fəʊn]	das Telefon benutzen
complain [kəmˈpleɪn]	sich beschweren
get stuffed! [get ˈstʌft]	du kannst mich mal (am Arsch lecken)!

 Stuff (eigentlich = „stopfen") ist britischer Slang und wird in Ausdrücken wie diesen gebraucht:

Stuff it! What do I care?	Scheiß drauf! Ist mir doch wurscht!
(You can) Stuff your money!	Ich scheiß auf dein Geld!
I couldn't give a stuff what they think.	Ist mir doch scheißegal, was die denken! (→ Übung 116)

114 *Dual choice: The jury was convinced and convicted the defendant*

Welches Wort passt?

a I warned them again and again, but no one _____.
heard · listened

b Am I _____ what you are saying? I mean, do you mean what you say?
hearing · listening

c D'you know the Randy Raiders? I'm just _____ their latest album.
hearing · listening to

d I have no time for TV, but I _____ the radio a lot.
hear · listen to

e He was _____ of robbery and sentenced to 18 years in prison.
convicted · convinced

f He was _____ of the need for social change.
convicted · convinced

g Would it be _____ wrong to clone a human being?
ethically · ethnically

h They live in a racially, culturally, and _____ diverse neighbourhood.
ethically · ethnically

i We watched the film several times and were able to see where _____ strong and weak points are.
it's · its

j You have to see a film several times to see where _____ strong and where _____ weak.
it's · its

k That's a decision only you can _____.
do · make

l The airline is currently _____ talks with Boeing and Airbus to purchase aircraft.
holding · leading

again and again [ə'gen]	immer wieder
sentence to 18 years in prison ['prɪzn]	zu 18 Jahren Gefängnis verurteilen
convict [kən'vɪkt] **someone**	jemand schuldig befinden / verurteilen
convince [kən'vɪns]	überzeugen
social change [səʊʃl 'tʃeɪndʒ]	soziale Veränderungen
clone a human being [hjuːmən 'biːɪŋ]	einen Menschen klonen
ethical(ly) ['eθɪkəl(i)]	ethisch; moralisch einwandfrei
ethnic(ally) ['eθnɪk(əli)]	ethnisch
a culturally diverse [daɪ'vɜːs] **neighbourhood**	ein multikultureller Kiez
currently ['kʌrəntli]	zur Zeit
purchase ['pɜːtʃəs] **aircraft** ['eəkrɑːft]	Flugzeuge kaufen

115 „Besuchen" – „Besuch": *Short visits make long friends*

Das allgemeinste Wort für „besuchen" ist *visit*. Umgangssprachlich und sehr häufig sind auch *call on (someone)*, *come and see (someone)*, *come to see (someone / a place)*, *go to see (someone / a place)*.

„Besuchen" im Sinne von „teilnehmen" ist *go to* oder *attend (a school / a lecture / a meeting etc.)*.

Beim Nomen ist die nachfolgende Präposition *to* zu beachten: *a visit **to** London* = „ein Besuch **in** London".

Übersetzen Sie.

a   Sie besucht eine Schule in Oldham, wohnt aber nicht in Oldham.

_____

b   Die Königin besucht regelmäßig Schulen.

_____

c   Unsere Vertreter besuchen täglich bis zu zehn Kunden.

_____

d Wenn sie in Schottland ist, besucht die Königin regelmäßig den Gottesdienst in der Crathie Church.

e Kommen Sie uns doch mal besuchen!

f Gestern kam uns ein alter Bekannter besuchen.

g Wir haben sie in Glasgow besucht, als wir das letzte Mal in Schottland waren.

h Wir haben gestern die Monet-Ausstellung in der Königlichen Akademie besucht.

i Die Versammlung war gut besucht.

j Zur Zeit besucht sie einen Englischkurs in Folkestone.

k Sie starb während eines Besuches in Kanada vor fünf Jahren.

l Im Dezember 1970 stattete Elvis Presley der Stadt einen Besuch ab.

m Bei einem kürzlichen Besuch konnte ich einige sehr schöne Bilder von dem Dorf machen.

regularly attend [ə'tend] **services**	regelmäßig den Gottesdienst besuchen
our sales reps ['seɪlz reps]	unsere Vertreter
up to ten customers ['kʌstəməz]	bis zu zehn Kunden
an old friend [frend]	ein(e) alte(r) Bekannte(r)
exhibition [eksɪ'bɪʃn]	Ausstellung
meeting ['miːtɪŋ]	Versammlung
currently ['kʌrəntli] **/ at the moment**	zur Zeit
pay a visit to someone / a place	jem. / einem Ort einen Besuch abstatten
on a recent ['riːsnt] **visit**	bei einem kürzlichen Besuch
take pictures ['pɪktʃəz] **of something**	Bilder von etwas machen

116 *The F-word*

Das Wort *fuck* kommt in der Alltagssprache zu oft vor, als dass man es in einem Buch über die am häufigsten gebrauchten Wörter ignorieren dürfte.

Zunächst: *Fuck* bezeichnet ursprünglich den Geschlechtsakt (*sexual intercourse*) und wird auch heute noch (nicht nur vulgär) in diesem Sinn gebraucht. Diese „biologische" Verwendung interessiert uns hier nicht. Was uns interessieren muss, ist der Gebrauch des Wortes als Kraftausdruck, nämlich:

1. als Verstärker,
2. als Ausdruck von Ärger oder Verachtung.

Häufige deutsche Entsprechungen sind „Scheiß(-)" oder „verdammt".

Besonders häufig vorkommende Verwendungen des Wortes:

a	**Fuck you!**	Leck mich (doch am Arsch)!
b	**Fuck him!**	Der kann mich mal (...)!
c	**Fuck what you think!**	Ich scheiß auf deine Meinung!
d	**Where the fuck is Jack?**	Wo zum Teufel ist Jack?
e	**Fuck off!**	Verpiss dich!
f	**I fucked up my maths exam.**	Ich hab die Mathe-Klausur in den Sand gesetzt.
g	**You know fuck all about football.**	Du hast keinen Schimmer von Fußball.
h	**I had fuck all to do with it.**	Ich hatte nicht das Leiseste damit zu tun.
i	**The fucking computer / car!**	Der Scheißcomputer / Das Scheißauto!
j	**I don't fucking care.**	Es ist mir scheißegal.
k	**Fucking hell!**	Verdammte Scheiße!
l	**It was fucking boring.**	Es war scheißlangweilig.
m	**Shut the fuck up!**	Halt doch bloß die Schnauze!
n	**There's been a fuck-up.**	Da hat jemand Scheiße gebaut.
o	**That really fucks me off.**	Das geht mir voll auf den Sack.

Als Nichtmuttersprachler sollte man *fuck* eher nicht benutzen.

Ersetzen Sie die *fuck*-Ausdrücke in den obigen Beispielen durch standard-sprachliche bzw. „mildere" Formulierungen aus der folgenden Liste.

> a bad mistake has been made   annoys me tremendously   be quiet
> bloody   damn(ed)   extremely   flunked   get lost   give a damn
> I don't care   leave me alone   let him go to hell   nothing at all
> oh damn   on earth   shut up   very

117 „Sprechen", „reden": *Talk less, listen more*

Übersetzen Sie.

a   Er spricht Spanisch, aber kein Französisch.

b   Sie ist fast vier, aber kann noch nicht sprechen.

c   Ach, da bist du ja, Emily, wir haben gerade von dir gesprochen.

d   Wenn man vom Teufel spricht, dann ist er nicht weit.

e   Darüber werden wir reden müssen.

f   Wir reden nie über Politik.

g   Ich muss mit Ihnen reden.

h   Könnte ich Sie mal kurz sprechen?

i   Mit ihr kann man einfach nicht reden.

j   Wir reden nicht mehr miteinander.

k   Klar, er sagt nicht viel, aber wenn er redet, dann ist man ganz Ohr.

l   Du hast gut reden.

m   Kann ich den Chef sprechen?

n   Ich werde morgen mit deiner Lehrerin reden – vielleicht gibt sie dir einen Tag frei.

o   Ich musste mir das von der Seele reden.

p   Er sprach vor beiden Häusern des Kongresses.

He was all ears.

Spanish [ˈspænɪʃ]	Spanisch
French [frentʃ]	Französisch
she's almost [ˈɔːlməʊst] **four**	sie ist fast vier
talk [tɔːk] **about something**	über / von etwas reden
speak of the devil [ˈdevl]	vom Teufel reden
talk (about) politics [ˈpɒlətɪks]	über Politik reden
have a word with someone	(kurz) mit jemand sprechen
talk to each other / one another	miteinander reden
I'm all ears [ɪəz]	ich bin ganz Ohr
speak / talk to the boss [bɒs]	mit dem Chef / der Chefin sprechen
give someone a day off	jemand einen Tag frei geben
get something off one's chest	sich etwas von der Seele reden
address [əˈdres] **both houses of Congress**	vor beiden Häusern des Kongresses sprechen

To make enemies, talk; to make friends, listen.
Actions speak louder than words.
Never trust a man who speaks well of everybody.

118 Ein deutsches Wort – mehrere englische Entsprechungen

Setzen Sie jeweils ein Wort für „unter" ein.

a   The people living _____ me have got used to me jumping up and
down during my workouts.
b   _____ other things he wrote a book about the effects of globalization.
c   I think we're _____ friends here.
d   He's at his best when he's _____ pressure.
e   Temperatures were _____ zero most of the time.
f   She suffered _____ insomnia all her life.

Setzen Sie jeweils ein Wort für „Stelle" ein.

g   I'm looking for a _____ to park my car.
h   It's a good _____ for a picnic.
i   This is the _____ where they met their death.
j   Let me go in your _____.
k   I wouldn't like to be in your _____.
l   That's a weak _____ in the system.
m   She quoted a _____ from the Bible.

Setzen Sie jeweils ein Wort für „Null" / „null" ein.

n   Four minus four is _____.
o   3.06 is read as _____.
p   There are three _____ in 1,000.
q   There is no year _____ in the Christian calendar.
r   The year 1905 is read as _____.
s   The car accelerates from _____ to 60 mph in 4 seconds.
t   The temperature was ten degrees below _____.
u   Leeds United won three–_____.
v   My room number is seven _____ three.

get used [juːst] **to something**	sich an etwas gewöhnen
workout(s) [ˈwɜːkaʊt(s)]	Fitnesstraining
the effects [ɪˈfekts] **of**	die Auswirkungen der
globalization	Globalisierung
pressure [ˈpreʃə]	Druck
insomnia [ɪnˈsɒmniə]	Schlaflosigkeit
look for something	etwas suchen
meet (– met – met) one's death	den Tod finden; zu Tode kommen
quote [kwəʊt]	zitieren
accelerate [əkˈseləreɪt]	beschleunigen
60 mph [em piː ˈeɪtʃ]	(= 97 km/h)
(= miles per hour)	

119 *Idioms* mit *know*: *Knowing which side your bread is buttered*

Wie lassen sich die folgenden Sätze auf Deutsch ausdrücken?

a   He knows the town like the back of his hand.

b   He knows his stuff / his onions.

c   She knows which side her bread is buttered.

d   She doesn't know the first thing about computers.

e   I know the irregular verbs back to front.

f   He thinks he knows all the answers.

g   The shopkeeper didn't know me from Adam but he treated me as if I was his best customer.

h   If a kid doesn't know right from wrong, their parents are doing something wrong.

i   He doesn't know his arse from his elbow.

j   She knows the ropes of the music business.

k   The first time I fell in love I didn't know what hit me.

l   He knows better than to call us after 10pm – unless something is wrong.

m   You know full well that I'm right.

n   She doesn't know her own mind.

o   Our teacher knows what he's talking about, and makes the class fun and interesting.

p   Of course he's making mistakes, but he's young and doesn't know any better.

q   I had so much to do yesterday that I didn't know whether I was coming or going.

r   There's no knowing how long it'll take.

s   What's great about this job is that you never know what's going to happen next.

treated ['tri:tɪd] **me as if I …**	behandelte mich, als ob ich …
his best customer	sein bester Kunde / seine
['kʌstəmə]	beste Kundin
arse [ɑːs] **– elbow** ['elbəʊ]	Arsch – Ell(en)bogen
rope [rəʊp]	Seil; Tau; Strick
fall in love [lʌv]	sich verlieben
call [kɔːl] **someone**	jemand anrufen
10pm ['ten piː 'em]	22 Uhr
unless [ən'les]	es sei denn, dass; wenn nicht
mind [maɪnd]	Gedanken; Verstand; Geist

120 *Proverb Crossword*

Setzen Sie jeweils das letzte Wort des Sprichworts in das *Crossword* ein.

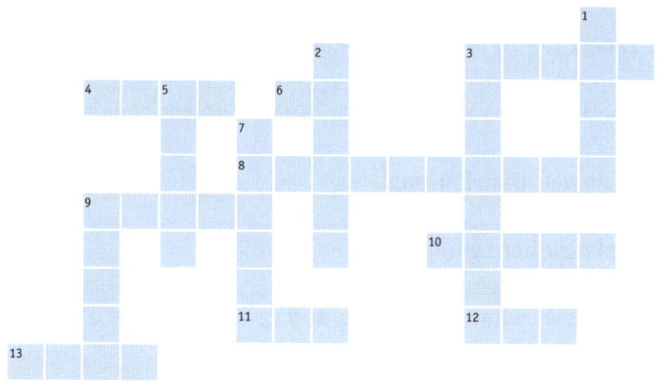

Across

3 New brooms sweep _____.

4 Pride comes before the

_____.

6 Quickly come, quickly

_____.

8 Good fences make good

_____.

9 It's a small _____.

10 The end justifies the _____.

11 Rome was not built in a

_____.

12 Once bitten, twice _____.

13 To the pure all things are

_____.

Down

1 Dead men tell no _____.

2 Honesty is the best _____.

3 Beggars can't be _____.

5 It is never too late to

_____.

7 A friend in need is a friend

_____.

9 Blood is thicker than _____.

Good fences make good neighbours.

121 „Erst": Oft anders zu übersetzen, als man denkt

Bei „erst(e)" denken wir immer zuerst an *first* als englische Entsprechung.
Leider stimmt diese Vokabelgleichung häufig nicht. Beachten Sie in den folgenden Sätzen vor allem die Fälle, wo nicht *first*, sondern **only** oder **not until** die
einzig sinnvollen Übersetzungen sind.

Übersetzen Sie.

a Das erste Jahr war das schwierigste

_____.

b Papa ist immer der Erste, der morgens aufsteht.

_____

c Mach erst mal deine Hausaufgaben fertig.

_____

d Erst mal machen wir eine Pause.

_____

e Ich glaube, wir sollten erst den Chef fragen.

_____

f Wir werden das morgen gleich als Erstes erledigen.

_____

g Es ist erst halb sieben.

_____

h Sie ist erst gestern hier gewesen.

_____

i Erst gestern hat es wieder einen Zwischenfall gegeben.

_____

j Er war erst sechzehn, als ich ihn kennenlernte.

_____

k Erst da wurde ihm klar, was eigentlich passiert war.

_____

l Sie ist eben erst angekommen.

_____

m Das Hotel ist erst vor kurzem renoviert worden.

_____

n Wir bekommen die Ergebnisse erst Anfang nächster Woche.

_____

o Wir werden erst Freitag Genaueres wissen.

p Meinen ersten wirklichen Kuss bekam ich erst, als ich 17 war.

q Wenn wir das erst mal geschafft haben, können wir uns den anderen Problemen zuwenden.

get up in the morning (– got – got)	morgens aufstehen
have a break [breɪk]	Pause machen
incident ['ɪnsɪdənt]	Zwischenfall
first meet (– met – met) someone	jemand kennenlernen
he realized ['rɪəlaɪzd]	ihm wurde klar
what had actually happened	was eigentlich passiert war
renovate / refurbish a building	ein Gebäude renovieren
something / anything more	etwas Genaueres
definite ['defɪnət]	
achieve [əˈtʃiːv] / **do something**	etwas schaffen (→ Übung 108)
address [əˈdres] **other issues**	sich anderen Problemen zuwenden
['ɪʃuːz]	(→ Übung 22)

122 *A good run is better than a bad stand*

Das Nomen *run* (= Lauf) wird in zahlreichen idiomatischen Fügungen benutzt, für die Sie hier einige typische Beispiele finden.

Versuchen Sie die Sätze zu verstehen bzw. zu übersetzen.
Im Zweifel schauen Sie bitte im Schlüssel (→ S. 215) nach.

a OK they won, but we **gave them a good run for their money**.

b The suspect is still **on the run**.

c My family sure **keeps** me **on the run**.

d   We have enough troops to **keep** the insurgents **on the run**.

e   Canberra's **run of** hot weather is starting to take its toll on the surrounding landscape.

f   Well, my **run of** good luck had to end some time.

g   The company has had a long **run of** success.

h   Artists are different from **the common run** of people.

i   While we're away you can have **the run of** the house.

j   He jumped the next train, but was quickly spotted and **made a run for it**.

k   This system costs more to begin with but is cheaper **in the long run**.

l   The show has had an extremely long **run**.

the suspect ['sʌspekt]	der mutmaßliche Täter
the insurgents [ɪnˈsɜːdʒənts]	die Aufständischen
it takes its toll [təʊl]	es fordert seinen Tribut
surround [səˈraʊnd]	umgeben
the surrounding landscape ['lændskeɪp]	die landschaftliche Umgebung
good luck – bad luck	Glück – Pech
company ['kʌmpəni]	Gesellschaft; Firma
success [səkˈses]	Erfolg
artist ['ɑːtɪst]	Künstler(in)
different ['dɪfrənt] **from**	anders als
jump [dʒʌmp] **a train**	auf einen Zug aufspringen
spot [spɒt] **someone**	jemand entdecken
cost [kɒst] ⚠	kosten
to begin with [tə bɪˈgɪn wɪð]	zunächst
cheap(er) [tʃiːp(ə)]	billig(er)

123 „In": *Are you in the picture?*

Are you in the picture? – eine zweideutige Frage: „Bist du auf dem Bild, also zum Beispiel dem Foto?" oder „Bist du im Bilde, d. h. informiert?"

Deutsch „in" ist auch im Englischen häufig *in*. Wo „in" nicht mit *in* übersetzbar ist, lauern die Fehler – wie in den folgenden Sätzen, wo „in" meistens **nicht** *in* ist.

Übersetzen Sie (und passen Sie auf wie ein Habicht – *like a hawk!*).

a   Sind Sie schon mal in Australien gewesen?

b   Die Kinder sind in der Schule.

c   Die meisten Leute hier gehen jeden Sonntag in die Kirche.

d   Der Schulbus bringt die Kinder in die Schule.

e   Seine Mutter ging in die Schule, um mit der Lehrerin zu sprechen.

f   Leider haben wir im Moment keine Stellen frei.

g   Er hat sich in eine Frau aus dem Internet verliebt.

h   Ihre Eltern würden nie in die Heirat einwilligen.

i   Meine Eltern fahren in Urlaub in die Schweiz.

j   Wir gehen heute Abend in ein Konzert.

k   Wussten Sie, dass auch Fontane *Hamlet* ins Deutsche übersetzt hat?

l   Er warf den Brief ins Feuer.

m Er ging in die Küche, um Tee zu machen.

n Wir sprangen alle ins Wasser.

o Du kannst dein Fahrrad in die Garage stellen.

Australia [ɒ'streɪliə]	Australien
I'm afraid [ə'freɪd]	leider
no vacancies ['veɪkənsiz]	keine Stellen frei
parents ['peərənts]	Eltern
consent [kən'sent] **to a marriage**	in eine Heirat einwilligen
go on holiday ['hɒlədeɪ]	in Urlaub fahren
Switzerland ['swɪtsələnd]	die Schweiz
concert ['kɒnsət]	Konzert
translate [træns'leɪt]	übersetzen
throw [əʊ] **– threw** [u:] **– thrown**	werfen – warf – geworfen
jump [dʒʌmp]	springen (→ Übung 78)
bike [baɪk]	Fahrrad
garage ['gærɑ:ʒ]	Garage

124 *Dual choice: The age of miracles is past*

Welches Wort passt?

a He has written an extremely _____, yet readable, book on English grammar.
comprehensible · comprehensive

b His book makes grammar _____ without sending you to sleep.
comprehensible · comprehensive

c The Great Pyramid of Giza was one of the Seven _____ of the Ancient World.
Miracles · Wonders

d Christians believe that Jesus performed many _____.
miracles · wonders

e Is it any _____ that I'm tired?
miracle · wonder

f They're in big trouble and only a _____ can save them.
miracle · wonder

g People were _____ to her for the happiness she gave them.
grateful · thankful

h _____, no one was near the oven at the time of the explosion.
Gratefully · Thankfully

i Candidates for membership have to _____ certain conditions.
fill · meet

j It's very important to take _____ in class.
notes · notices

k It's important to read the _____ about fire, first aid and other
emergencies in the school building.
notes · notices

comprehensible [kɒmprɪ'hensəbl]	verständlich; fassbar
comprehensive [kɒmprɪ'hensɪv]	umfassend
the Ancient ['eɪnʃənt] **World**	die antike Welt
perform [pə'fɔːm] **miracles**	Wunder vollbringen
win the election [ɪ'lekʃn]	die Wahl gewinnen
be in big trouble ['trʌbl]	in großen Schwierigkeiten stecken
save [seɪv]	retten
near the oven ['ʌvn]	in der Nähe des (Back-)Ofens
membership ['membəʃɪp]	(die) Mitgliedschaft
certain conditions [kən'dɪʃnz]	bestimmte Bedingungen
notes [nəʊts]	Notizen
notice ['nəʊtɪs]	Anschlag; Aushang

125 „Gehen", „fahren": *If you want a thing done, go; if not, send*

„Gehen" und „fahren" sind extrem häufig gebrauchte Wörter; bei der Wahl ihrer Entsprechungen im Englischen werden oft Fehler gemacht. Auf „fahren" sind wir schon einmal eingegangen (→ Übung 57).

Hilfreich ist vielleicht diese Beobachtung:
-   „Gehen" und „fahren" sind im allgemeinen Sinn = **go**;
-   bei Betonung des Zufußgehens ist „gehen" = **walk**;
-   bei Betonung des Tätigseins als Fahrer ist „fahren" = **drive**.

Übersetzen Sie.

a   Gehst du zum Bahnhof?
b   Gehst du oder fährst du?
c   Da können Sie zu Fuß hingehen.
d   Wer fuhr das Fahrzeug?
e   Sie fährt Motorrad und spielt
    gut Fußball.
f   Das Auto fährt sich gut und
    lässt sich auch gut parken.
g   Er fiel hin, als er mit dem Hund ging.
h   Meistens fahre ich mit dem Bus.
i   Die Busse fahren alle 20 Minuten.
j   Wir hatten viel Schnee und
    die Busse fuhren nicht.

k   Wir fahren diesen Sommer an die See.   _____

l   Fährst du immer so langsam?   _____

m   Ein Freund fuhr ihn ins Krankenhaus.   _____

n   Er ging vor dem Haus auf und ab.   _____

o   Wir gehen heute schwimmen.   _____

p   Ich gehe heute Nachmittag
    zu meiner Oma.   _____

q   Sie geht noch zur Schule.   _____

r   Unser Flugzeug geht um Viertel
    nach fünf.   _____

s   Es ging alles nach Plan.   _____

t   Also, das geht denn doch wirklich
    zu weit.   _____

u   Wie geht es Ihnen?   _____

v   Er will Jura studieren und dann
    in die Politik gehen.   _____

w   Wohin geht diese Straße?   _____

x   Mein Fenster geht nach Osten.   _____

motorcycle [ˈməʊtəsaɪkl]	Motorrad
go to the seaside [ˈsiːsaɪd]	an die See fahren
my nan / gran(ny) / grandma	meine Oma
according [əˈkɔːdɪŋ] **to plan**	nach Plan
study law [lɔː] **/ go to law school**	Jura studieren

126   *No news is good news*

Beachten Sie, dass *news* anders als im Deutschen (= „Nachrichten") im Englischen Einzahl ist und dass „eine Nachricht" mit *a news item* übersetzt werden kann.

Hier haben wir einige recht typische *news headlines* (= Kurznachrichten) für Sie zusammengestellt. Auf sie bezieht sich der nachstehende Text.

Füllen Sie die Lücken mit Wörtern aus der folgenden Liste in der passenden Form.

able	enjoy	kill	possible	task
be	face	kind	problem	threaten
cheer	fault	overcome	shoot	watch
destroy	item	play	take	

Teenager _____ teacher
Bomb _____ 33 in market
Gunman _____ woman hostage
Global warming _____ billions
World _____ water crisis
Coastal cities _____ by hurricane

"There should _____ more good news on TV," said a prominent English clergyman yesterday. "I've given up _____ the TV news at night. Earlier in the day I might be _____ to take it, but at night it's altogether too much for me."
In the clergyman's view the news was an endless repetition of violence, aggression, disasters, and social _____.
He added, "I wish there _____ always at least one _____ in the news to _____ people up, such as children _____ happily together, people _____ the beauties of nature, or someone _____ adversity."
A television news editor said he didn't understand this _____ of criticism. "Our _____ is to select and summarize the news as fairly as _____, and it isn't our _____ if so much of the news these days is gloomy."

cheer up [tʃɪər ˈʌp]	aufheitern
destroy [dɪˈstrɔɪ]	zerstören
face a crisis [ˈkraɪsɪs]	mit einer Krise rechnen müssen
it isn't my fault [fɔːlt]	es ist nicht meine Schuld
overcome adversity [ədˈvɜːsəti]	mit Widrigkeiten fertig werden
select [sɪˈlekt] **and summarize**	auswählen und zusammenfassen

127 Präpositionen: *Surprises never cease*

„Überraschungen hören nie auf" – *cease* [siːs] ist eine förmlichere Ausdrucksweise für *stop, end, come to an end*.
In den folgenden Sätzen fehlen die Präpositionen, und es sind eigentlich alles Fälle, wo man vom Deutschen her versucht ist, eine falsche Präposition zu wählen.

Setzen Sie – wo notwendig – Präpositionen aus der folgenden Liste ein.

> at   by   for   of   to   without

a She was driving _____ a steady 80kph in the fast lane, oblivious to the huge queue behind.
b I went _____ train this time.
c She was the first of seventeen children, most of whom died _____ an early age.
d Were you _____ the concert too?
e She's a professor _____ English _____ Duke University.
f I went over to a girl who was sitting _____ herself and asked her if she would like to dance.
g My roommate's going home _____ Easter, so I'll have the room all _____ myself _____ the weekend.
h His body was never found, and he was declared _____ dead in 1999.
i We discussed the proposals point _____ point and suggested a number of changes.
j It was typical _____ her that she left the door of her office open _____ all times so that students could walk in _____ much ceremony.
k We know that a woman soldier was killed _____ the Battle _____ Gettysburg in 1863.

kph (= kilometres per hour)	km/h (= Stundenkilometer)
be oblivious [ə'blɪvɪəs] **to something**	etwas gar nicht bemerken
declare [dɪ'kleə] **someone dead**	jemand für tot erklären
discuss proposals [dɪ'skʌs prə'pəʊzlz]	Vorschläge diskutieren
without much ceremony ['serəməni]	ohne große Umstände

128 *Let me see that tattoo on your backside*

Mit den leidigen *false friends* haben wir uns bereits ausführlicher beschäftigt
(→ Übungen 48, 61, 90). Hier nun diesmal eine listige kleine Übung, in der
sich englische mit deutschen Sätzen abwechseln. In beiden Sprachen begegnen
Sie dem falschen Freund.

**Übersetzen Sie ins Deutsche bzw. Englische, damit Sie gegen die Fehler-
versuchung immun werden.**

a   He has a tattoo on his **backside**.

b   Er hat eine Tätowierung auf der **Rückseite** des Halses.

c   Don't **blame** me!

d   **Blamiere** mich nicht vor anderen!

e   He's a **brave** boy.

f   Er ist ein **braver** Junge.

g   He will **eventually** come back.

h   Er wird **eventuell** zurückkommen.

i   This remark **irritated** me.

j   Lange Sätze **irritieren** den Leser.

k   She asked me the **meaning** of the word.

l   Sie fragte mich nach meiner **Meinung**.

m   It's a **personal** matter.

n   Es ist eine **Personal**angelegenheit.

o   Das **Personal** war sehr hilfsbereit und freundlich.

_____

p   They **spend** too much money on restaurant food.

_____

q   Sie **spendierten** mir eine Pizza.

_____

r   Sie **spendeten** das Geld an eine wohltätige Einrichtung.

_____

tattoo [tæ'tuː]	Tätowierung
the back [æ] **of the neck** [e]	die Rückseite des Halses
blame [bleɪm] **someone**	jemand die Schuld geben
make a fool [fuːl] **of someone**	jemand blamieren
brave [breɪv] ⚠	tapfer
eventually [ɪ'ventʃuəli]	schließlich
irritate ['ɪrɪteɪt]	ärgern
confuse [kən'fjuːz]	irritieren
staff [stɑːf] **/ personnel** [pɜːsə'nel]	Personal
treat [triːt] **someone to something**	jemand etwas spendieren
donate [dəʊ'neɪt] **money (to)**	Geld spenden (an)
charity ['tʃærəti]	wohltätige Einrichtung

129 *Make your choice: How good is your grammar?*

Jetzt geht es mal nicht um Wortschatz, sondern um Grammatik.

Hier sind 15 Sätze, die es in sich haben. Bis 12 Richtige können Sie Ihre Eng-
lischkenntnisse als „sehr gut" ansehen; haben Sie weniger als 6 richtig, sollten
Sie vielleicht etwas an Ihrer Grammatik tun.
Good luck, and enjoy yourself!

a   _____ shown lots of photos but didn't recognize anyone in them.
    I was · Me were

b   It _____ people like her that give our industry a bad name.
    are · is

192

c If you are arrested, the police _____ the right to take your fingerprints and photographs.
has · have

d He's written an interesting book about the everyday life of British soldiers in the 18th and 19th _____.
centuries · century

e I _____ a few days ago and haven't received any confirmation yet.
booked · have booked

f I _____ him for a long time and have a lot of confidence in him.
have known · know

g When Haydn wrote his last symphony, Mozart _____ dead for four years.
had been · was

h Oh Amanda, I've loved you ever _____ I first saw you.
for · since

i Oh Michelle, I've loved you _____ as long as I can remember.
for · since

j He's such an interesting man; I really enjoyed _____ with him.
talking · to talk

k There are mistakes you can hardly avoid _____ because of your upbringing, your character, and your mentality.
doing · making · to do · to make

l Her teacher suggested _____ some research online.
her to do · that she do

m It was a nice hotel and I wouldn't mind _____ there again.
staying · to stay

n By the way, did I remind you _____ Grandma on her birthday?
of calling · to call

o Our committee discussed _____ the matter long and hard.
about · –

130 *Superpower Crossword: The United States of America*

Die *clues* zu diesem *Crossword* bilden einen zu-
sammenhängenden Text. Sie stehen allerdings
nicht in der logischen Reihenfolge. Stellen Sie
diese zunächst her, dann ist das *Crossword*
leichter zu lösen.

Goodbye and all the best!
Besuchen Sie unsere Website
www.englishmaster.de.
Von dort aus können
Sie uns per E-Mail Ihre
Kommentare und
Fragen übermitteln.

Across

3 It lies between the Atlantic and
Pacific _____.
6 The United States has a
_____ of over 300 million.
11 Each of the 50 states has its
_____ government and
legislative system.
12 The US is the world's most
_____ industrial nation.
13 13 colonies under British rule
_____ their independence
in 1776.
14 It's one of the richest countries
_____.

Down

1 It's the world's _____ military
superpower.
2 The country was colonized mainly
in the 17th _____.
4 The _____ is Washington.
5 It _____ 50 states.
7 In the Civil War (1861–65) the
northern states _____ the
southern states.
8 The national government
_____ of the President and
the Congress.
9 It shares _____ with Canada
and Mexico.
10 The United States is a _____
in North America.

Übung 1
a When
b when
c as / when
d as
e as
f than
g than
h than
i than
j from / to / than
k as
l but
m as

Übung 2
a Everyone / Everybody loves him.
b We all love him
c I don't know them all / all of them.
d I don't know any of them.
e There isn't enough for everyone / everybody.
f This book is for anyone / anybody / everyone / everybody who wants to improve their English.
g She's an example to/for us all / for/to all of us.
h As we all know, the customer is always right.
i All children are entitled to education / have the right to an education.
j All the children in the village were vaccinated.
k She knows all the students, and all the students know her.
l All citizens are equal before the law.
m She spelled / spelt all the words right.
n All cats are grey in the dark / by night / at night.
o All roads lead to Rome.
p He comes every two weeks.
q He comes every six months.

Übung 3
a Have you forgotten everything?
b I told her all / everything I knew.
c Money isn't everything.
d There's a time for everything.
e Everything / All she says is true.
f I've told you all / everything I know.
g That's all I know.
h Is that all the luggage you have? / Is that all you have in the way of luggage?
i You can buy or sell anything on eBay.
j I'd do anything for you.
k These people are capable of anything.
l I love you more than anything in the world.
m He's anything but a hero.
n All in all, I'm very pleased with the quality of this printer.
o All that glitters is not gold.

Übung 4
a–k c–j e–a g–f i–h k–g
b–e d–b f–c h–d j–i

Übung 5
a convicted
b convinced
c took
d catch
e caught
f took
g talked / spoke
h adopt
i affect
j effect

Übung 6
a Where did you get it / that?
b I got / had a letter from her the other day.
c What did you get for your birthday?
d Work is hard / difficult to get here.
e I can't get him to eat something / anything in the morning.
f We had to get him out of the water.
g She's going to have a baby.
h You'll catch (a) cold sitting there.
i I owe you 50 euros.
j I'm getting hungry. / I'm beginning to get hungry.
k The children got / became scared / frightened and ran away.
l Eventually they got / became homesick and returned to Ireland.
m Milk doesn't agree with me.

Übung 7
a visits
b like
c happened to find
d obtain
e reduce
f is about
g returned
h rising
i discovered
j invented
k bullied
l extinguished
m tolerated
n overcharging
o addressed

Übung 8
a roads
b road
c street
d street
e road
f street
g streets
h street
i road
j road

Übung 9

a	by	i	by
b	from	j	at
c	on	k	by
d	on	l	with
e	for / with	m	on
f	for	n	in
g	at	o	on
h	from	p	on

Übung 10

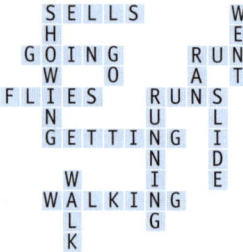

Übung 11

a It was my own fault.
b He's a victim of his own success.
c I prefer to sleep / I prefer sleeping in my own bed.
d Mind your own business.
e We saw with our own eyes what was happening (there).
f They paid for everything out of their own pocket.
g This is my own computer.
h I have a computer of my own.
i She has her own talents.
j She has talents of her own.
k She lived in her own flat / apartment up to / until / till the age of 105.
l She had saved enough money to move into a flat / an apartment of her own.
m Our cat is very particular / fussy about her/his food.

Übung 12

a a light bag
b an easy task
c light reading
d a slight delay
e a slight headache
f light rain
g easy to understand

h easily done
i easier said than done
j slightly injured
k scantily clad / dressed
l a heavy bag
m a difficult / hard task
n difficult / hard times
o a serious illness
p a serious / grave mistake
q a serious / severe / heavy blow
r hard / difficult to say
s work hard
t heavily armed
u seriously injured

Übung 13

a	have / take	g	makes
b	make	h	keep
c	take out	i	running
d	took	j	had
e	give	k	suffers
f	play		

Übung 14

Dustmen remove / take bride's presents
Bride Emily Bell was shattered when her wedding presents were taken away – by dustmen.
Emily, 23, and her husband, Oliver, had stored the gifts in their yard while they renovated their new home. They had carefully packed about £2,000 worth of cutlery, crockery and glasses in cartons.
But when they went out to bring them back in, the boxes had disappeared.
Heartbroken, Emily said last night: "A neighbour told us she saw the refuse collectors removing / loading them. We made a claim for compensation, but the council's insurers more or less informed us the cartons shouldn't have been deposited near the dustbin."

Übung 15

a Her / Their son became a famous musician.
b What are you going to be when you grow up?
c He became / got very angry.
d I could see that he was getting / becoming / growing angry.
e We('d) better be going / We('d) better go. / We'd better be off. It's getting late.
f The economic situation has become very difficult.
g Your tea is getting cold.

h Things are getting / growing / becoming worse by the day.
i All the systems are checked twice a year.
j The man is (currently) being questioned by the police.
k The book was translated into several languages.
l He has been sentenced to five months in prison.
m I'm (slowly) getting tired.
n Have you gone mad / crazy?
o She'll be 80 next year.
p She('s) just turned 20.
q I'm not going to get / fall / become ill.

Übung 16

1–2	6–12	10-4	14–13
2–7	7–17	11–5	15–3
3–9	8–8	12–15	16–14
4–6	9–10	13–16	17–1
5–11			

Übung 17

a You have / You've got 60 minutes to answer the questions.
b Things have developed in a completely unexpected way.
c What was decided?
d That doesn't explain his behaviour.
e I think that this is a misunderstanding.
f We have found that many customers welcome / appreciate this kind of service.
g These chemicals are often used to build bombs.
h The authorities are working to solve this problem.
i These buildings cannot be used to house prisoners.
j We immediately contacted the bank / got in touch with the bank.
k It is often difficult to communicate with these patients.
l He said how important it was to negotiate.

Übung 18

a sole
b alone
c single
d lonely
e heavy
f difficult
g serious
h sensible
i sensitive

Übung 19

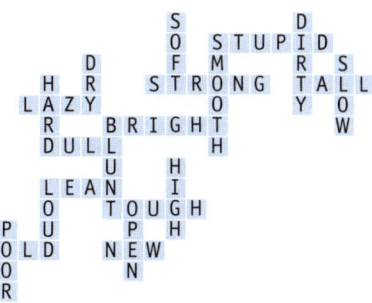

Übung 20

a Eric was her / their only child.
b Eric was an only child.
c Eric has always been a loner.
d Money isn't our only worry.
e It's the only thing we can do.
f We're not the only ones who / to think so / that.
g There was not a single piece missing.
h I remember every single word.
i The children came in one by one / singly.
j The individual is powerless.
k I'd like to talk to/with each member individually.
l Parts / Components of the package cannot be sold separately.
m He spent more than 11 years in solitary confinement.
n Unfortunately, this is not an isolated case.
o We look at each individual case.
p We look at each case individually.

Übung 21

a certain
b sure
c sure
d certain
e certain / sure
f Surely
g certainly
h safe / secure
i safe
j safe
k safely
l secure
m secure(ly) / safe(ly)
n secure; secure / safe

Übung 22

a address an issue / a problem
b address the issue / problem of domestic violence
c make an issue of corruption / make corruption an issue

d solve / resolve a problem, resolve / solve an issue
e a solution to / of the problem / to the issue
f money isn't an issue, money is no problem
g a controversial issue
h a big / major / great problem / issue
i. a burning issue / problem
j. a crucial issue / question / problem
k an unresolved issue / problem / question
l a global problem / issue
m environmental issues / problems

Übung 23

a The furniture is nice.
b The evening news was depressing.
c This information is very valuable.
d The progress we have made is most encouraging.
e Much of / A lot of his advice is good.
f Some of the homework was rather difficult.
g My knowledge of French has improved.
h The United States is a country of contrasts.
i The stairs are rather steep.
j These are my best glasses.
k These trousers are a bit tight.
l The surroundings are beautiful.
m The contents of this box are worth a fortune.
n The police are on the right track.
o The American people are very religious.

Übung 24

a real
b really
c obviously
d obvious
e obviously; slowly / slow
f frequent
g frequently
h seriously; serious
i Unfortunately
j Unfortunately; extremely
k normally
l normal
m extremely dangerous
n dangerously extreme
o quickly / (sehr viel seltener:) quick
p quickly
q Quick

Übung 25

a Can you play chess?
b We can play a game of chess(, if you like). / We might as well play a game of chess.
c I (can) speak English.
d I can't help you.
e We won't be able to help these people.
f There wasn't much the president could do. (Durch das wasn't ist klar, dass could hier past ist.)
g I was able to repair the damage myself.
h Mozart could play / was able to play the piano at the age of four.
i It must be wonderful to be able to play the piano.
j That may be the right method.
k That can't be the right method.
l There may be a civil war.
m There could / might be difficulties.
n Can I help you?
o Can / May I have another copy?

Übung 26

a	holding	i	stopped
b	hold	j	saved
c	hold / last	k	lasts
d	keep	l	lasts
e	keep	m	consider
f	keeps	n	take
g	keep	o	stick / keep
h	gave / made		

Übung 27

a He spoke / talked quietly.
b The guy at the next table was talking loudly about a video game he was playing.
c He spoke in a low / quiet voice.
d Could you speak a bit more quietly / quieter, please? / Could you please lower your voice a bit?
e Could you speak up a bit, please. / Could you speak a bit louder / more loudly, please?
f I hear you loud and clear.
g She complained loudly that everything was so expensive / about how expensive everything was.
h I think she should sing this a bit more softly / quietly.

i There was soft music coming from the house next door.
j We heard the gentle murmur of a brook.
k The hotel is in / on a very noisy street.
l What I hate most is noisy neighbours.
m Can't you turn the radio down / up a bit?
n There was a faint smell of perfume in the air.
o I didn't have the slightest / faintest idea.
p Could you read the poem out loud / aloud to us, please?
q "This place is just a rip-off. / They just rip you off here." – "You can say that again!"

Übung 28

a humane
b humanly
c humanitarian
d human
e humanely
f industrial
g industrially
h industrious
i industriously

Übung 29

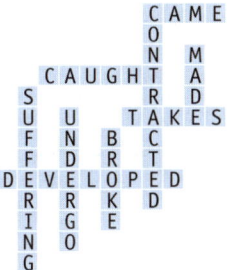

Übung 30

a Shall we take a taxi? / (*Wenn nach dem Willen des andern gefragt wird:*) Do you want us to take a taxi?
b Shall I feed / Do you want me to feed the dog?
c What shall I do – give her a piece of my mind or just ignore her?
d You mustn't think that I don't love you.
e You mustn't / shouldn't spoil me so (much).
f We're (supposed) to wait outside the station / in front of the station.
g Are we (supposed) to translate all (of) these sentences? (Shall we ... *hier unwahrscheinlich, da es sich um einen „übergeordneten Willen", eine Anordnung handelt.*)

h You know that you're not supposed to do that.
i Is that supposed to be funny / to be a joke?
j What's that supposed to mean?
k The president is supposed / said to have known nothing about it.
l He's said to be very rich.
m He's said to have been rich once.
n You should learn Chinese – that's where the future is / lies.
o You ought to / should be grateful to these people.
p I should have taken notes.
q I wish I'd known that before / earlier.
r They told me / I was told to come again in a week's time / a week later.
s (*Biblisch:*) Thou shalt not steal. / You shall not steal.

Übung 31

a The food was nothing to write home about.
b I know it's not cricket to attack an opponent from behind.
c He's as thick as two short planks.
d She can act and she's easy on the eye.
e The driver was clearly under the influence.
f Well, you've really made a hash of it, haven't you?
g What's happened is unacceptable, and the culprits must be brought to book.
h Does she know he's carrying a torch for her?
i Gee, what's happened? You look like something the cat brought in.
j The old men just sat there chewing the fat.

Übung 32

a Do you really want to go home?
b Do you really want me to go home?
c She wanted to tell the truth.
d She wanted me to tell the truth.
e She wanted to be told the truth.
f She wanted the truth to be told.
g I don't want to make coffee.
h I don't want you to make / you making coffee.
i I don't want you to watch / don't want you watching this film / movie.
j Don't you think your hair wants cutting? / (*Häufiger:*) Don't you think you need a haircut?
k I don't want you to cut / you cutting my hair.
l I want my hair cut short.
m My mother wants my hair (to be) cut really short.

n I don't want you to be disappointed.
o I don't want you to disappoint me.
p I know you don't want me to make / me making jokes about it.
q She could have stayed if she had wanted to.
r I asked her to stay, but she didn't want to.

Übung 34

a	raise	f	literate
b	rise	g	literal
c	economic	h	literally
d	historic	i	literary
e	historical		

Übung 35

a	on	m	at
b	by; at	n	in the way of
c	by	o	on / in; at; by
d	in	p	in
e	on / in	q	in
f	of / from	r	in
g	from / of	s	on
h	of	t	to
i	on	u	until / till
j	by	v	for
k	at / by	w	up
l	on		

Übung 36

a Can she do that?
b I can't go on.
c I don't / can't speak French.
d I have to go / must go / be going / be off (now).
e I need to go to the toilet / loo *BE* / *AE* bathroom.
f You're not supposed to do that.
g What's that supposed to mean?
h When can we go in the water?
i "Is he allowed to do that?" – "He is."
j We don't want to go home yet.
k I want to go to the station.
l We want to get / go in there.

Übung 37

a She wants to be an architect.
b She wants to learn Chinese.
c She wants me to learn Chinese.
d She insists on paying the bill.
e The car wouldn't start / refused to start.

f She claims to have seen him take / taking the money.
g The president claims to have known nothing about it.
h I'd prefer to stay / I'd rather stay at home.
i We were (just) about to leave / were on the point of leaving.
j Won't you sit down?
k Shall we go to my place?

Übung 38

a completed / finished / written / read
b written / completed
c produced / written
d produced / directed
e rendered
f getting on / along
g took
h suffice / be enough
i decorated / painted
j cheated / tricked / ripped off
k cheated / swindled
l abolished
m played
n abandoned / discarded / given up
o serve as
p manage / get along
q ruined / finished / broke / out of business
r wore me out / exhausted me
s renovating

Übung 39

Two men hurt in car crash
Two men were <u>treated</u> at St. Francis Medical Center Monday for injuries they <u>suffered</u> in a collision at the junction of Illinois Route 89 and Rutland Road in Marshall County. Both were <u>released</u> after treatment.
Terry Hufford, 35, of Toluca, was <u>driving</u> north on Route 89 when his car was <u>hit</u> by a camper <u>driven</u> by Byron Jenkins, 73, of Texas. Jenkins, who was headed south, <u>realized</u> too late that a car in front of him had <u>stopped</u> to make a left turn. Jenkins <u>lost</u> control when he braked and <u>swerved</u> into the northbound lane, state police said.
Hufford was ticketed for not <u>wearing</u> his seat belt. Jenkins was ticketed for failure to <u>reduce</u> speed and using the wrong lane, state police said.

Übung 40

```
        S K E P T
        H       I
    C L O C K W O R K
    T   T       A   E
  C R Y T       A   D
  E     T   B U C K
  E     L       H
  S T R A N G E D
        R       D
        G
      L E G
```

Übung 41

a at / in
b –
c in
d of / from
e –
f die of natural causes than in / die from
  natural causes than from / in
g by
h by
i –
j (over)
k with
l off
m on
n by
o by

Übung 42

a Ich habe eine Stunde gebraucht.
b Man hoffte, dass sich ein Kompromiss
  erreichen ließe.
c Wie sich erwies, war das Material nicht
  wasserdicht.
d So eine Frechheit!
e Wer ist da? – Frank.
f Wir waren es nicht, die andern waren es.
g Leiden werden darunter die Armen.
h Um deinetwillen bin ich zurückgekommen.
i Warum muss ausgerechnet ich immer die
  Drecksarbeit machen?
j Wenn du nicht gewesen wärest, wäre ich
  gestorben.
k Das Auto ist im Eimer.
l Unsere Ehe ist kaputt.
m Wenn ich nicht zahle, bin ich geliefert.
n Gib ihm Saures! / Gib's ihm!
o Es geht das Gerücht, dass die beiden Banken
  fusionieren werden.

p Ich meine, wir sollten uns darüber
  aussprechen.
q Ich gehe davon aus, dass Sie heute fertig
  werden.
r Die Alte ist immer noch schwer auf Zack.
s Er denkt, er ist der Größte.

Übung 43

a The people are starving – they need help.
b There are many / lots of people who can't
  help themselves.
c There's someone at the door.
d Once upon a time there was a king /
  There was once a king who had a beautiful
  daughter.
e Long live the Queen!
f You like it here, don't you?
g I'm sorry I can't help you.
h I'm glad to see you're so well.
i This castle is haunted.
j I mean well by you.
k "Will he recover?" – "I hope so."
l "Does she still live there? / Is she still living
  there?" – "I don't know."

Übung 44

a Can I get you a drink? – Maybe some water.
b Can I help you? – No thanks. I'm just having
  a look round.
c Did you have a good trip? – Yes, not too bad,
  thanks.
d He says he loves her. – Men say a lot of
  things.
e Hello, is that Lucy Tyler? – Yes, speaking.
f Hello. May I join you? – Yes, please do.
g How are you? – Fine, thanks.
h I'm afraid I can't come. – Oh, what a pity!
i Lovely day, isn't it? – Well, let's hope it lasts.
j New bike, Jack? – Thought I'd cycle to the
  gym. Not much point in driving there.
k Sorry I'm late. – That's all right.
l Take care. – I will.
m Well, I must be off now. – Cheerio, then.
  Have a good trip.
n What are you doing tonight? – Nothing much.
o What does she do? – She's an architect.
p What time do you finish work? – I should be
  through by five.
q What took you so long? – Had to go to the
  loo.
r Why don't you have a car? – Can't afford one.
s You own this house, do you? – No, it's rented.

Übung 45

a	insured	g	robbed
b	ensured	h	stole
c	found	i	stay
d	founded	j	remains
e	stole	k	remains
f	robbed	l	stay

Übung 46

a Where's the nearest internet café?

b I'm getting off at the next stop.

c Who will be the next president of the United States?

d The nearest star is 4.2 light years away.

e Next please!

f In Australia, your nearest neighbour may be 50 miles away.

g Energy costs will rise / are going to rise enormously in the next few years.

h A lot has happened in the last few weeks.

i During the last few months, Venus has been steadily increasing its distance from / to the Sun.

j We just made the / just managed to catch the last bus.

k They fought to the last man.

l She gave him the last of her money.

m We were the last (ones) to arrive.

n The captain was the last (person / man) to leave the ship / vessel.

o The latest news isn't very encouraging.

p He has improved a lot recently.

Übung 47

ache – cake, air – heir, aren't – aunt, berry – bury, blood – mud, Britain – written, bury – berry, busy – dizzy, cake – ache, choose – lose, climber – timer, comb – home, cough – off, dizzy – busy, done – run, doubt – out, fez – says, food – mood, foot – put, front – hunt, gone – on, got – yacht, heart – start, height – right, heir – air, hen – men, home – comb, hunt – front, juice – loose, limb – slim, loose – juice, lord – sword, lose – choose, meant – rent, men – hen, mood – food, mud – blood, off – cough, on – gone, out – doubt, put – foot, red – said, rent – meant, right – height, run – done, said – red, says – fez, sicker – vicar, slim – limb, start – heart, sword – lord, timer – climber, vicar – sicker, written – Britain, yacht – got.

Übung 48

a in the current / present situation

b the current / latest fashion

c a subject of topical interest

d use a data projector / digital projector

e have a baby

f I don't want to make a fool of myself

g be a good boy / girl!

h the boss of Airbus

i the shops in the city centre

j a crafty businessman

k Cologne Cathedral

l a committed / dedicated environmentalist

m politically active citizens

n a possible successor

o a chocolate factory

p a great guy

q a vivid imagination

r a famous photographer

s a brilliant move

t chocolate is poison for dogs

u where's my mobile (phone) BE / AE my cell phone?

v it wouldn't be humane

w the sign confuses drivers / motorists

x a consistent approach

y act consistently

z inspect tickets

aa multinational corporations

bb take criticism seriously

cc it's interesting to read / it's an interesting read

Übung 49

a–g	c–a	e–i	g–j	i–c	k–l
b–b	d–f	f–k	h–h	j–d	l–e

Übung 50

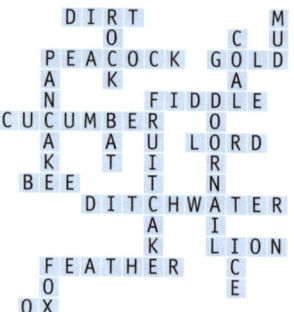

Übung 51

a	to	j	with
b	in	k	on; for
c	in	l	for
d	with	m	by
e	at	n	with
f	with; on	o	of; of
g	of	p	to
h	from	q	in
i	by		

Übung 52

a Our parents love us unconditionally.
b The Bible tells us to love others as we love ourselves.
c We love each other / one another, but we fight / quarrel / argue a lot too.
d Let us / Let's not kid / delude ourselves.
e A (woman) friend of ours is a doctor.
f By harming others we harm ourselves.
g We'll buy / We're going to buy (ourselves) an island in the South Pacific.
h We are afraid of ourselves.
i We were both cold.
j We have all changed.
k We meet every two weeks.
l We should apologize / ought to apologize to her.
m We cannot afford to spend too little on education.

Übung 53

a May/Can we use / Are we allowed to use a dictionary?
b Yes, you may / can use / you're allowed to use a dictionary.
c Will we be allowed to use a dictionary?
d Unfortunately we weren't allowed to use a dictionary.
e I don't know if I would have been allowed to visit him.
f You mustn't eat so much sugar.
g You mustn't lose hope.
h The dog knows that he mustn't bark / isn't allowed to bark here.
i That's something a teacher shouldn't say. / A teacher shouldn't say such a thing / something like that. / (*Mit etwas anderem Sinn:*) A teacher wouldn't be allowed to say such a thing / something like that.

j You shouldn't have said that. / That's something you shouldn't have said.
k These changes should be easy to make.
l It shouldn't be too difficult to find a room.
m That shouldn't really make a difference.

Übung 54

a took
b took
c went for / took
d suffers from
e enjoyed / met with
f enjoys
g know
h got / received
i tolerate / put up with
j tricked / deceived / fooled / duped / conned / taken for a ride
k drunk / downed
l got it copied / arranged for it to be copied
m gave birth to
n play
o carrying on / conducting
p showed no mercy to / for

Übung 55

a	incredulous	e	except
b	incredulously	f	expect
c	incredibly	g	accept
d	incredible	h	excess

Übung 56

a Fares have been increased / raised / put up.
b Air fares have risen / increased by 12 per cent.
c We're unable to reduce / lower our prices.
d We've been able to reduce / lower our costs.
e Oil prices are falling / dropping / going down / decreasing at the moment.
f The music heightens / increases the tension.
g The Titanic sank / went down on April 15, 1912.
h He's 85 but still climbs trees.
i As / When temperatures fall, heating costs go up / rise.
j He fell to his knees.
k Make sure / Mind you don't drop the plates.

Übung 57

a	going	g	drive
b	going	h	drive
c	go	i	driving
d	take / ride	j	ride
e	going / doing	k	runs
f	drives / runs	l	go / leave

Übung 58

a When we arrived the show had already started.
b We've already booked for next year.
c Do you really have to go? / Do you have to go just yet?
d She could read and write when she was only four.
e Chimps used tools as early as the Stone Age.
f Maybe things will look brighter tomorrow.
g Are you being served / (gehoben:) attended to?
h What woman would want to marry me?
i We're an odd pair, aren't we?
j The mere thought of it makes me feel sick.
k How long have you known Judy?
l Have you ever been to Australia?
m I've seen this film before.
n I've always been a pessimist.
o Has she left yet? / Did she leave yet?
p She('s) already told me.
q I've been looking for you for half an hour.

Übung 59

a Are you afraid of me?
b You were / You've been lucky.
c We were unlucky with the weather.
d The children / kids were very hungry.
e I'm not thirsty.
f He's successful with women.
g These efforts were unsuccessful.
h You must be patient with him.
i She's furious with him / hopping mad at him.
j I'm / I feel frustrated and angry at / with myself.
k We're very worried.
l These forms are available online.
m These measures were not effective.

Übung 60

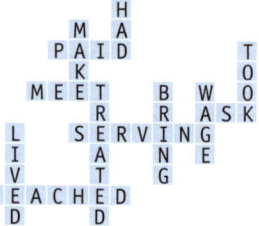

Übung 61

a harassment in the workplace
b catch the murderer
c take notes
d a novella by Hemingway
e the second TV / television channel
f a commission of 20 per cent
g check someone's documents
h test / examine a student
i pay the last instalment
j receive / draw / get a pension
k available on prescription only
l wear a short skirt
m the back of the house
n Finland's countless lakes
o his self-confident manner / behaviour / bearing / demeanour
p broadcast radio programmes
q a sensitive person
r a respectable gentleman
s a reputable company
t wear a dinner jacket BE / AE tuxedo
u save money
v donate money
w an amiable / a pleasant / a likeable woman
x change the subject
y a topic of conversation
z ignore a remark
aa overlook a mistake
bb go hiking / walking
cc (department) stores like Harrods in London
dd a spa (hotel)
ee who is the best player?
ff where are the keys?

Übung 62

a the wisdom that comes with age
b do something about unemployment
c the fight / struggle against poverty
d more money for education
e we must fight / combat evil
f the advantages of democracy
g sex before marriage
h die for freedom
i what we can learn from history
j the role of women / women's role in society
k the increase in violence
l who benefits from globalization?
m work in industry
n traumatic experiences in childhood
o go to war
p dogs in art and literature
q subsidize agriculture
r she loved life
s what people say about us
t anything / everything is possible in love
u women in power
v fight for freedom of speech / expression
w go out of fashion
x the joys of music
y the beauties of nature
z what happens in politics
aa his interest in religion
bb the dangers of technology
cc save someone from death
dd fight for independence
ee promote economic growth
ff how time flies!

Übung 63

a	calm	g	hardly
b	quiet	h	rare
c	calmly	i	adapt
d	quietly	j	abide
e	hard	k	adept
f	hard	l	adopt

Übung 64

a Ruth is a friend of hers.
b Do you have / Have you got a photo of her?
c She's a woman of character.
d It was very nice of her.
e The ring is a present from him.
f He comes / is from the coast.
g They moved from Montrose to Aberdeen.

h Montrose is south of Aberdeen.
i It's a distance of about 40 miles.
j Here's a report from our correspondent in Moscow.
k He calls from time to time.
l From here on it gets easier.
m They were both tired from working.
n I saw him jump off the bridge.
o He lost his balance and fell off the ladder.
p He borrowed money from / off her.
q I bought it with my pocket money.
r She was deceived by him.
s Who was the radio invented by?
t I('ve) just read a novel by Steinbeck.
u She has a child by him.
v She's a psychologist by profession.

Übung 65

a	to	i	for / with
b	–	j	with.
c	for	k	for
d	in; at	l	in
e	with	m	On
f	on	n	by
g	in	o	under
h	for	p	In; as

Übung 66

a Treat yourself to a night at the Ritz.
b Please restrict yourselves to one piece of luggage per person.
c He introduced himself.
d She regards herself as / considers herself extremely generous.
e Fortunately the animal managed to free itself.
f And these people call themselves democrats.
g One must be honest with oneself.
h They love each other / one another and want to get married.
i The children told each other / one another stories and teased each other / one another.
j You should / You ought to apologize to her.
k She behaved very well.
l The world is changing.
m She complained to the manager.
n They avoided looking at each other.
o They met in a pub near the station.
p She worries about him.
q She's afraid of dogs.

r Would you please close / shut the door behind you.
s She has a great career in front of / ahead of her.
t She broke her right arm.
u Several prisoners took their own lives.

Übung 67

a a false
b falsely / wrongly
c a false
d false
e wrong
f incorrectly / wrongly
g incorrectly / wrong
h an incorrect
i a false
j wrong
k wrong
l errors / mistakes
m faults
n flaw / fault
o error
p an error
q fault
r failure
s fallacy

Übung 68

a The Statue of Liberty has stood at the entrance to New York harbour since 1886.
b I've been standing here for half an hour.
c The piano is in the living room.
d On the table stands an empty wine glass. / There's an empty wine glass on the table.
e There's nothing about it in the paper.
f The sign says VACANCIES.
g What's the score? – One-nil to Arsenal.
h That dress doesn't suit you.
i How are you doing in / at school?
j And what about pay(ment)?
k Put the wine glasses on the table, will you?
l We can put this lamp in the living room.
m May / Can I ask you a few questions?
n How do you / does one set the clock?
o Let's set the alarm for five thirty.

Übung 69

a improved
b deteriorated / worsened
c enhanced
d exacerbated / aggravated
e aggravated / exacerbated

Übung 70

Übung 71

a Let me go!
b Let the children have their fun / enjoy themselves.
c Let's take a taxi, shall we?
d You shouldn't have let him in / into the house.
e You should have left the dog in the house.
f You can leave everything as it is.
g Leave me alone / in peace!
h She didn't dare (to) leave the sick child alone.
i Unfortunately I'd left my mobile at home.
j I have / get my hair cut every six weeks.
k She had the book bound in red leather.
l I've had three copies made.
m You can get / have your car washed while you shop or have lunch.
n Can't you have / get it dry-cleaned?
o They kept me waiting for over an hour.
p The guards made the prisoners march for hours in the scorching / burning heat.
q We had to call the doctor / send for / call for the doctor.
r He's divorcing his wife.

Übung 72

a This is a good place to park.
b Everyone / Everybody wants a place in the sun.
c Such a method would be out of place here.
d In this case, an apology is called for.
e Our team finished in third place.
f There's plenty of room / space in the wardrobe.

g There isn't enough room / space for books.
h There's no room / space left in the boot *BE* / *AE* trunk.
i This stuff takes up a lot of space / room.
j Berlin's Gendarmenmarkt is one of the finest / most beautiful squares in Germany.
k (The) Place de la Concorde is the largest square in Paris.
l He spends most of his time on the tennis court.
m Two players were sent off.
n A young man offered me his seat.
o I (have) booked / reserved two seats at the Piccadilly Theatre.
p Is this seat taken?
q Please sit down. / Please be seated. / Please take a seat.
r There's a large car park *BE* / *AE* parking lot right next to the hotel.
s Natural reproduction is (slowly) giving way to artificial reproduction.

Übung 73

a	price	h	costs
b	prize	i	cost
c	price	j	expense
d	charge; fee / charge	k	prize; expenses
e	fees	l	fares
f	charges	m	sum
g	cost	n	amount

Übung 74

a	at / for	g	to
b	at	h	on; in
c	on	i	For; in
d	on; in	j	of; for
e	of; of	k	for; in
f	of	l	of; by; about; of

Übung 75

a The film / movie got many bad reviews.
b That's bad news.
c The fear of pain is much worse than the pain itself.
d I've heard nothing but bad things about him.
e Many successful people had bad / poor marks / grades in / at school.
f I'm bad at maths *BE* / *AE* math.
g He's said to be in poor / (*seltener:*) bad health.
h Maybe I picked a bad / poor example.
i The service was rather poor.

j These stones are of inferior quality.
k The milk has gone bad / off again.
l My Spanish is good, but my French is rather poor.
m Things are getting worse by the day.
n I felt sick afterwards.
o She was obviously in bad shape / in a bad way.
p Even a bad person / an evil person doesn't always do bad / evil things.
q She behaved badly to you.
r The afternoon performance / The matinee was poorly attended.
s That'll be difficult to arrange.
t He finds it difficult to express his feelings.

Übung 76

a	wear	h	bear
b	wear	i	bore
c	carries	j	bear (*auch* carry
d	wears		*kommt vor; sehr*
e	wears		*häufig:* support)
f	carried	k	carry
g	carried	l	bears

Übung 77

a I'm sure it won't happen
b in short supply
c doesn't impress
d annoys me
e don't like
f exactly what I need
g be too hasty
h became suspicious
i the greatest
j I don't believe you
k very easy
l enjoy each other's company
m very close
n do what was expected of her
o very suitable for me
p do you think of
q is to blame
r avoid being punished

Übung 78

a He jumped up and ran away.
b They saved themselves by jumping out of / by jumping from the window.
c People don't like you to jump the queue.
d You shouldn't jump to conclusions.
e We rather jumped the gun there, didn't we?

f   The prices of petrol *BE* / *AE* gas(oline) and heating oil / fuel oil have taken a jump.
g   We're always one jump ahead of our competitors.
h   He was stopped for jumping a red light.
i   I'm a bit jumpy because I'm having surgery / an operation tomorrow.
j   When I asked her to give reasons for her decision, she jumped down my throat.

Übung 79

a	loses	g	loosely
b	lost	h	loosened
c	lose	i	loosen
d	lost	j	loose
e	losing	k	lost; loose
f	loose		

Übung 80

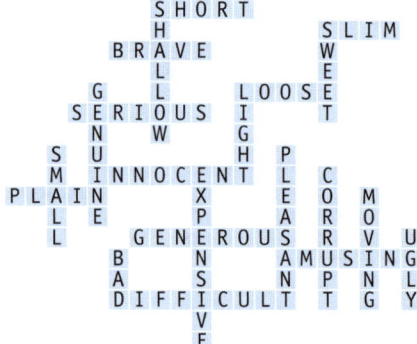

Übung 81

a	in	j	in
b	for	k	for
c	by; by	l	until / till
d	by	m	to
e	from	n	up to
f	of; at	o	by
g	for	p	to
h	on	q	by
i	on	r	to D / as far as D

Übung 82

a   He looks like an ox.
b   He eats like an elephant.
c   She has blue eyes like her father.
d   He's as strong as an ox.
e   She's as old as I am. / She's as old as me.

f   Come as fast / quick(ly) as you can.
g   How tall is she?
h   How strong he is!
i   How is she (doing)?
j   How was she dressed?
k   How is it that I cannot hear properly when I wear / I'm wearing sunglasses?

l   What's the new teacher like?
m   What are the new shoes like?
n   How's the weather? / What's the weather like?
o   How about a coffee?
p   What's your name?
q   What are these red fruits called?
r   What time is it?
s   I like the way she smiles.
t   The disease is often / frequently found in wild animals such as foxes and bats.

Übung 83

a	while	j	During
b	during	k	during
c	during	l	while
d	while	m	while
e	during	n	while
f	while	o	during
g	during	p	while
h	While	q	while
i	while	r	during

Übung 84

a   Your computer is very fast.
b   She can swim faster than me.
c   I need a quick answer.
d   My questions were answered very quickly.
e   She quickly learned how to handle men.
f   Come quick!
g   The children / kids have grown up so quickly.
h   He was quickly caught.
i   Bad news travels fast.

Übung 86

a   "I love you." – "I love you too."
b   "I'm very surprised." – "So am I. / Me too."
c   "I'm not surprised." – "Nor / Neither am I. / Nor me."
d   "I'm surprised." – "I'm suprised too. / Me too."
e   "I'm not surprised." – "I'm not surprised either."
f   "I don't know." – "I don't know either."
g   She, too, was surprised.

h She was surprised, too. / She was also surprised.

i She was surprised, and so was I / and I was, too.

j She wasn't surprised at all / at all surprised, and neither was I.

k We were quite surprised and also shocked.

l I was not only surprised but also shocked.

m She's very pretty. She's very intelligent too / as well. / She's also very intelligent.

n She surprised everyone / everybody, even me / me too / me as well.

o I was shocked, even if / even though I wasn't surprised.

p I like the sound of the word, even if / even though I don't know what it means.

q She gave me the money without even hesitating (for) a second.

Übung 87

a sensible	g borders
b sensitive	h lent
c sensitive	i borrowing
d boundary	j lending
e boundary	k guided
f limits	l led

Übung 88

a We (*objektiv:*) have to be / (*subjektiv:*) must be at the airport around / at about ten o'clock.

b We don't have to know all the answers.

c Do I have to / (*situativ wesentlich seltener:*) Must I attend the meeting?

d You don't really have to attend the meeting. / It isn't absolutely necessary that you attend / for you to attend ...

e You mustn't believe / don't have to believe everything she says.

f What do you have to do to save energy?

g Does it have to be now?

h She must have been here.

i I had to show my passport five times.

j You didn't have to do that, but I'm so glad you did.

k You'll probably have to wait a long time.

l We probably would have had / We would probably have had to spend about 500 euros.

m I should have known that earlier.

n We wouldn't have had to borrow money.

o I have to go to the toilet / loo / lavatory / *AE* bathroom.

Übung 89

a made	k doing / taking
b made	l taking / doing / sitting
c make	
d made	m took
e does	n took
f making	o have
g made; made; did	p is
h doing	q making
i does	r driving
j made; make	

Übung 90

Übung 91

a He was lying / He lay on his bed reading a book.

b She is in hospital (*AE* in the hospital).

c There was deep snow outside.

d The stress is on the second syllable.

e The living room faces south.

f The decision rests / lies with the president.

g Oxford, like London, is on the Thames.

h Aberdeen is (situated) / lies on the east coast of Scotland.

i You should lie down for a while.

j He lay down (*von* lie!) on the couch.

k He laid (*von* lay!) the child on the couch.

l He leaned back and put his feet on the table.

m She put the letter down and left the room.

n I just couldn't put the book down.

o She put the steaks in the pan.

Übung 92

Thieves entered a house in William Street, Upper Kingswood, and <u>stole</u> an assortment of goods from the kitchen while the occupants <u>watched / were watching</u> television in another room.

The incident <u>happened</u> between 22.09hrs and 23.09hrs on Tuesday May 30.

Property stolen <u>included</u> a brown leather handbag and purse, wallets, keys and mobile phones.

It is <u>believed</u> that the offenders entered the property from the back garden.

Anyone who <u>saw</u> any suspicious activity in the vicinity is asked to <u>contact</u> Upper Kingswood police station on 01726 815000.

Householders are reminded to <u>ensure</u> that all doors and windows are <u>kept</u> securely locked when rooms are unoccupied.

Übung 93

a He said he would come.
b He told me that he would come.
c Did she really say that?
d Did she really tell you that?
e Can you tell me how to install it?
f I told her to bring it next time.
g "I can't wait to be back on the road / to be on the road again," he said.
h He said he couldn't wait to be back on the road / to be on the road again.
i Please don't call me grandpa.
j What do you think of / say to my offer?
k Do you mean to say that I'm lying?
l "Smith is a hopeless case / a dead loss." – "You can say that again."

Übung 94

advocacy	lobbying
asleep	dead
bathroom	toilet
collateral damage	killing of innocent bystanders
condition	illness
conflict	war
correctional facility	prison
enhanced interrogation	torture
ethnic cleansing	genocide
freedom fighter	terrorist
industrial action	strike
liberate	invade and occupy
pass away	die
pre-owned	used
private parts	genitals
promotion	propaganda
revenue enhancement	tax increase
senior citizen	elderly person
spin	political lying
surgical strike	military attack
unmotivated	lazy

Übung 95

a Why don't you go to the doctor?
b I went to the station to buy the tickets.
c Shall we go to my place?
d Are you still at home?
e Make sure the shoes go with / match the dress.
f Can you drink red wine with fish?
g I understand people who are depressed at Christmas.
h What did you get for Christmas?
i We bought two tickets at 50 dollars each.
j Patients have to wait up to six months for an operation.
k He's too young for such a position / job.
l This exercise is too difficult.
m The windows are all shut.
n The bottle was unopened.
o He walked towards the soldiers.
p What do you intend to do?
q That was to be expected.

Übung 96

a	of	h	of
b	at	i	to; than
c	to	j	with
d	of	k	in
e	on	l	of
f	at	m	of
g	with; for		

Übung 97

a Why does she want to marry him?
b Why does he want to marry her?
c Why do they want to get married?
d If I were / was her, I wouldn't marry him.
e If it hadn't been for her I'm sure I would have gone mad / I would have lost my mind.
f It was she / her who killed him.
g It was they / them who started the war.

210

h I like the lamp, it's very pretty / nice, but I wouldn't buy it.
i I like the shoes, they're very trendy, but I couldn't wear them.
j Would you please fill in this form.
k May I ask you to fill in this form?

Übung 98

a	live [laɪv]	f	shade
b	alive	g	Shadow
c	live [laɪv]	h	cooking
d	alive	i	kitchen
e	live [laɪv]		

Übung 99

a I've just come from a funeral.
b I was late for the meeting.
c When she comes home from school, her lunch / dinner is on the table.
d It was midnight when we got home. / By the time we got home, it was midnight.
e How did you get / come here – by car?
f How do I get to the town/city hall *BE / AE* to city hall?
g We passed through a little town called Rogersville.
h I only got as far as page 50.
i Do good people go to heaven?
j He was caught and went to prison.
k We had to send for / call the doctor.
l It occurred to me that something must have gone wrong.
m Come what may, we'll always find a way.
n Where are you from?
o How come / How is it you're dressed so smart(ly) / elegantly?
p She takes after her mother.
q Everything / It all turned out quite differently.

Übung 100

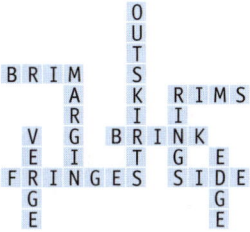

Übung 101

a I happen to know the story.
b The accused / defendant failed to appear in court.
c I hope you're right.
d I guess / suppose I'm jealous. / I'm jealous I guess / suppose
e I like to be / like being here.
f I enjoy being with you.
g I'd love to come, but I don't think I can make it.
h I'd prefer to go by train.
i It may be a misprint.
j We used to live here.
k I wonder where she is.
l It was just a rumour I suppose.
m Prices continue to rise.
n Go on reading, please.
o I keep saying the wrong thing(s).
p I told her to stop, but she kept on moaning.

Übung 102

a	done	i	made
b	does; does	j	remember
c	make	k	remember
d	makes	l	remind
e	made	m	remind
f	do	n	remember
g	done	o	reminds
h	make	p	remember

Übersetzung der Sätze j bis p:
j Ich kann mich nicht erinnern, was ich heute gemacht / getan habe.
k Ich glaube, ich erinnere mich, seinen Namen auf der Liste gesehen zu haben.
l Er schrieb, um mich (daran) zu erinnern, dass ich seinen Namen auf die Liste setzen soll(t)e.
m Erinnere mich bitte (daran), dass ich Tony anrufe.
n Ich muss daran denken, Tony anzurufen.
o Dieses Foto erinnert mich an meine Kindheit.
p Dieses Foto lässt mich an meine Kindheit zurückdenken.

Übung 103

a She's so clever.
b It's such a pity.
c Why are you so aggressive?
d I (do) love you so much.
e He's such a fool / such an idiot.
f He's such a fantastic lover.

g I've never seen a dog like that (before).
h That's life. / Such is life.
i You must open the bottle like this.
j That's (just) the way he is.
k She treats him the way a teacher would treat a naughty child.
l Her hair was as black as ebony.
m You're almost as good as me.
n She took care of him / looked after him as best she could.
o I'll let you know as soon as I can / as soon as possible.
p Would you be so kind as to autograph the book for me?
q It isn't as simple / easy as (all) that.
r I didn't think / I never dreamed/dreamt it would be that expensive / it would be as expensive as that.
s The stone was about this big.
t You must do it like this.
u Did you do it as I told you / like I said?

Übung 104

a trouble / bother
b trouble
c nuisance / bother
d nuisance
e angry / cross / annoyed
f annoying / irritating
g annoyed / irritated
h annoying / irritating
i angrily / furiously
j angrily
k furious
l evil
m a wicked / an evil

Übung 105

a What we need is people with new ideas.
b We need another 10,000 euros.
c Will you need / Will you be needing / Are you going to need a dictionary?
d How long will it take you to read / write the book?
e How long does it take to get to the airport?
f He took an hour / It took him an hour to find a parking space.
g Energy-saving light bulbs use much less electricity and last much longer.
h You don't have to / need to be a genius to understand Einstein's famous equation.

i You won't have to / need to wait.
j I didn't have to wait.
k You needn't have waited.

Übung 106

a destination
b target
c aim
d aim
e goals / targets
f esteemed
g estimated
h guessed

Übung 107

a He brings me flowers every day.
b She had pizzas brought for all of us.
c Why didn't you bring the children (along / with you)?
d Can you take the car to the garage?
e I'll take you to the airport.
f You ought to / should take / get him to hospital immediately / straight away.
g We went home early to put the kids / children to bed.
h This car has given us nothing but trouble.
i She got him to sign the contract.
j It's very difficult to make him laugh / to get him to laugh.
k I couldn't bring myself to tell her the truth.
l We must get it over with quickly.
m Kennedy was one of the few senators who made it to President.
n All the papers carried the story.

Übung 108

a be
b its
c his
d their
e one's
f have
g Being
h to be
i achieved
j achieve
k achieve
l achieved / achieves
m achieve
n achieve

Übung 109

a She did it out of love.
b The magician pulled a rabbit out of the hat.
c The little girl fell out of the window but a man was able to catch her.
d I'm a bit out of practice.
e She wrote to us from Paris.
f The best whisky comes from Scotland.
g You mustn't jump out of / from the frying pan into the fire.
h We must learn from our mistakes.

i   In this country, butter is made from cow's milk.
j   The handles are made of plastic.
k   I'm against the bill / I'm opposed to the bill for the following reasons.
l   The file was deleted by mistake.
m   What has become of our ideals?
n   The ball was out.
o   School is out / over. / School has finished.
p   The game / match is over / has finished.

Übung 110

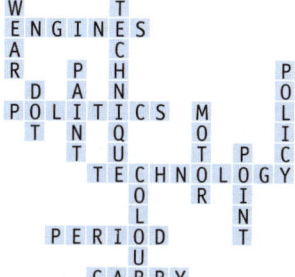

```
W           T
E N G I N E S
A         C
R     P   H           P
  D   A   N           O
P O L I T I C S   M   L
  T   N   Q   O   I
      T   U   T   P   C
      T E C H N O L O G Y
          O   R   I   N
          L       N   T
  P E R I O D     T
          U
      C A R R Y
```

Übung 111

a   You must be joking.
b   He's sure / bound to succeed.
c   Something had to be done quickly.
d   I can see why you're annoyed.
e   I have just started reading his latest novel.
f   She (has) never apologized to me.
g   We were spoiled / spoilt from the moment we arrived.
h   I'm cold.
i   I don't feel well.
j   I don't care / couldn't care less.
k   I don't care what people say.
l   I'm feeling kind of strange / funny.
m   I feel so sorry for her.
n   I realized that I had to change.
o   I don't mind.
p   I don't like the music.
q   I'm not interested in money.
r   I'm surprised that he's still at large.
s   I wasn't particularly impressed.
t   I'm glad you liked it.

Übung 112

a	big / large	l	greater
b	big	m	big / large
c	big / great	n	wide / broad
d	large	o	great
e	greatest	p	greatest
f	great / big / grand	q	grand
g	long / big / great	r	greatest
h	big	s	big
i	big	t	big / grand
j	tall	u	grand

k   (*Körpergröße:*) taller / (*wenn er auch kräftiger gebaut ist:*) bigger

Übung 113

a   She likes him a lot / likes him very much.
b   I like being with friends.
c   I don't like being shouted at.
d   I'd like a coffee.
e   I'd really love to come, but unfortunately I can't.
f   I'd gladly spend the rest of my life here.
g   She enjoys watching the children play.
h   I'm really fond of the goldfish.
i   I'll be happy to help you.
j   You're always welcome here.
k   You're welcome to use our phone.
l   You're welcome to the list.
m   What, is he complaining again? He can get stuffed! (→ Übung 116)

Übung 114

a	listened	g	ethically
b	hearing	h	ethnically
c	listening to	i	its
d	listen to	j	it's; it's
e	convicted	k	make
f	convinced	l	holding

Übung 115

a   She goes to / attends a school in Oldham, but does not live in Oldham.
b   The Queen regularly visits schools.
c   Our sales reps call on up to ten customers a day.
d   When in Scotland, the Queen regularly attends services at Crathie Church.
e   Come and see us some time.
f   Yesterday an old friend came to see us.

g We went to see them in Glasgow the last time we were in Scotland.

h We went to see the Monet exhibition at the Royal Academy yesterday.

i The meeting was well attended.

j She's currently attending / doing an English course in Folkestone. / She's attending / doing an English course in Folkestone at the moment.

k She died during a visit / while on a visit to Canada five years ago.

l In December 1970 Elvis Presley paid a visit to the city.

m On a recent visit I was able to take some very beautiful pictures of the village.

Übung 116

a Leave me alone!

b He can go / Let him go to hell!

c I don't care what you think.

d Where on earth is Jack?

e Get lost!

f I flunked my maths exam.

g You know nothing at all about football.

h I had nothing at all to do with it.

i The bloody / damn / (sehr viel seltener:) damned computer / car!

j I don't give a damn.

k Oh damn!

l It was extremely / very boring.

m Be quiet! / Shut up!

n A bad mistake has been made. / There's been a bad mistake.

o That (really) annoys me tremendously.

Übung 117

a He speaks Spanish but not French / but doesn't speak French.

b She's almost four but can't talk yet.

c Ah, there you are, Emily, we were just talking about you.

d Speak / Talk of the devil and he'll appear.

e We'll have to talk about that. / That's something we'll have to talk about.

f We never talk (about) politics. / We never discuss politics.

g I have to talk to you.

h Could I have a word with you?

i You just / simply can't talk to her.

j We don't talk to each other any more. / We're no longer on speaking terms.

k Sure he doesn't say / talk much, but when he does speak, you're all ears.

l It's easy for you to say that / for you to talk.

m Can I speak / talk to the boss?

n I'll have a word with your teacher tomorrow – perhaps she'll give you a day off.

o I had to get that off my chest.

p He addressed both houses of Congress.

Übung 118

a below

b Among

c among

d under

e below

f from

g place

h place

i spot

j place

k position / shoes

l spot

m passage

n zero / (BE auch:) nought

o three point zero / (BE auch:) nought six

p zeros / (BE auch:) noughts

q zero

r nineteen oh five

s zero / (BE auch:) nought

t zero

u three nil

v oh / zero

Übung 119

a Er kennt die Stadt wie seine Westentasche.

b Er versteht sein Handwerk.

c Sie weiß, wo ihr Vorteil liegt.

d Sie hat keine Ahnung von Computern.

e Die unregelmäßigen Verben kann ich aus dem Effeff.

f Er denkt, dass er alles weiß.

g Der Ladenbesitzer hatte keine Ahnung, wer ich war, aber er behandelte mich, als ob ich sein bester Kunde wäre.

h Wenn ein Kind nicht zwischen Recht und Unrecht unterscheiden kann, machen die Eltern etwas falsch.

i Er ist zum Scheißen zu blöd.

j Sie kennt sich im Musikgeschäft aus.

k Als ich mich das erste Mal verliebte, wusste ich nicht, wie mir geschah.

l Er wird sich hüten, uns nach 22 Uhr anzurufen – es sei denn, es ist was passiert.

m Du weißt nur zu gut, dass ich recht habe.

n Sie weiß nicht, was sie will.

o Unsere Lehrerin weiß, wovon sie redet, und sie macht den Unterricht lustig und interessant.

p Natürlich macht er Fehler, aber er ist jung und weiß es nicht besser.

q Ich hatte gestern so viel zu tun, dass ich nicht wusste, wo mir der Kopf stand.

r Kein Mensch weiß, wie lange es dauern wird.

s Das Tolle an dieser Arbeit ist, dass man nie weiß, was als Nächstes passiert.

Übung 120

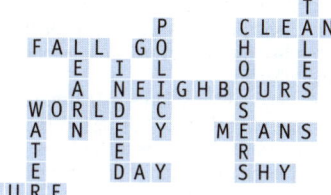

Übung 121

a The first year was the most difficult / the hardest / the toughest.

b Dad is always the first to get up in the morning.

c Finish your homework first.

d We'll have a break first.

e I think we should ask / we ought to ask the boss first.

f We'll do that first thing tomorrow (morning).

g It's only half past six.

h She was here only yesterday.

i There was another incident only yesterday.

j He was only sixteen when I first met him.

k Only then did he realize what had actually happened.

l She has only just arrived.

m The hotel was renovated / refurbished only recently / only a short time/while ago.

n We won't get the results until the beginning of next week / until early next week.

o We won't know anything more definite until Friday.

p I didn't get my first real kiss until I was 17.

q Once we have achieved / done that, we can address the other issues / deal with the other issues. (→ Übung 22)

Übung 122

a Gut, sie haben gewonnen, aber wir haben es ihnen nicht leicht gemacht.

b Der mutmaßliche Täter ist immer noch auf der Flucht.

c Meine Familie hält mich ganz schön auf Trab.

d Wir haben genug Truppen, um die Aufständischen nicht zur Ruhe kommen zu lassen.

e Canberras Hitzeperiode beginnt sich auf die landschaftliche Umgebung auszuwirken.

f Nun, meine Glückssträhne musste ja irgendwann enden.

g Die Firma blickt auf eine lange Erfolgsperiode zurück.

h Künstler sind anders als gewöhnliche Menschen / sind keine gewöhnlichen Menschen.

i Während wir weg sind, steht euch das ganze Haus zur Verfügung.

j Er sprang auf den nächsten Zug, wurde aber schnell entdeckt und rannte davon.

k Dieses System kostet zunächst mehr, ist aber auf die Dauer billiger.

l Die Show läuft schon sehr lange.

Übung 123

a Have you ever been to Australia?

b The children are at school.

c Most of the people here go to church every Sunday.

d The school bus takes the children to school.

e His mother went to the school to talk to the teacher.

f I'm afraid we have no vacancies at the moment.

g He's fallen in love with a woman from the Internet.

h Her parents would never consent to the marriage.

i My parents are going on holiday to Switzerland.

j We're going to a concert tonight.

k Did you know that Fontane, too, translated *Hamlet* into German?

l   He threw the letter into the fire.
m   He went into / to the kitchen to make tea.
n   We all jumped into / in the water.
o   You can put your bike in / into the garage.

Übung 124

a	comprehensive	g	grateful
b	comprehensible	h	Thankfully
c	Wonders	i	meet.
d	miracles	j	notes
e	wonder	k	notices
f	miracle		

Übung 125

a   Are you going to the station?
b   Are you walking or driving / or going by car / bus / etc.?
c   You can walk there.
d   Who was driving the vehicle?
e   She rides a motorcycle and plays soccer / football well.
f   The car is easy to drive, and easy to park as well.
g   He fell while walking his/the dog.
h   I usually go by bus.
i   The buses run / go every 20 minutes.
j   There was lots of snow and the buses didn't run.
k   We're going to the seaside this summer.
l   Do you always drive so slow(ly)?
m   A friend drove him (als Patienten:) to hospital BE / AE to the hospital / (als Nichtpatienten:) BE & AE to the hospital.
n   He was walking up and down outside the house / in front of the house.
o   We're going (to go) swimming today.
p   I'm going to see my nan / gran(ny) / grandma this afternoon.
q   She's still at school.
r   Our plane leaves at (a) quarter past five.
s   Everything went according to plan.
t   Now, that's really going too far.
u   How are you (doing)?
v   He wants to study law / go to law school and then go into politics.
w   Where does this road go / lead (to)?
x   My window faces east.

Übung 126

Teenager shoots / kills teacher
Bomb kills 33 in market
Gunman takes woman hostage
Global warming threatens billions
World faces water crisis
Coastal cities destroyed / threatened by hurricane
"There should be more good news on TV," a prominent English clergyman said yesterday. "I've given up watching the TV news at night. Earlier in the day I might be able to take it, but at night it's altogether too much for me." In the clergyman's view the news was an endless repetition of violence, aggression, disasters, and social problems.
He added, "I wish there was always at least one item in the news to cheer people up, such as children playing happily together, people enjoying the beauties of nature, or someone overcoming adversity."
A television news editor said he didn't understand this kind of criticism. "Our task is to select and summarize the news as fairly as possible, and it isn't our fault if so much of the news these days is gloomy."

Übung 127

a	at	g	at/for; to; for
b	by	h	–
c	at	i	by
d	at	j	of; at; without
e	of; at	k	at; of
f	by		

Übung 128

a   Er hat eine Tätowierung auf dem **Hintern**.
b   He has a tattoo on the **back** of his neck.
c   **Gib** nicht mir **die Schuld**!
d   Don't **make a fool of** me in front of others.
e   Er ist ein **tapferer** Junge.
f   He's a **good** boy.
g   Er wird **schließlich / letzten Endes** zurückkommen.
h   He **may (possibly)** come back.
i   Diese Bemerkung **ärgerte** mich.
j   Long sentences **confuse** the reader.
k   Sie fragte mich nach der **Bedeutung** des Wortes.

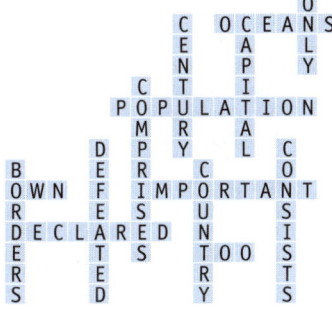

l   She asked me (for) my **opinion**.
m   Es ist eine **persönliche** Angelegenheit.
n   It's a **personnel** matter.
o   The **staff** was / were very helpful and friendly.
p   Sie **geben** zu viel Geld für Restaurantessen **aus**.
q   They **treated** me **to** a pizza.
r   They **donated** the money to a charity.

Übung 129

a   I was
b   is
c   have
d   centuries
e   booked
f   have known
g   had been
h   since
i   for
j   talking
k   making
l   that she do
m   staying
n   to call
o   –

Übung 130

The United States is a <u>country</u> in North America.
It lies between the Atlantic and Pacific <u>oceans</u>.
It shares <u>borders</u> with Canada and Mexico.
It <u>comprises</u> 50 states.
The <u>capital</u> is Washington.
The national government <u>consists</u> of the President and the Congress.
Each of the 50 states has its <u>own</u> government and legislative system.
The US is the world's most <u>important</u> industrial nation.
It's one of the richest countries <u>too</u>.
It's the world's <u>only</u> military superpower.
The country was colonized mainly in the 17th <u>century</u>.
13 colonies under British rule <u>declared</u> their independence in 1776.
In the Civil War (1861–65) the northern states <u>defeated</u> the southern states.
The United States has a <u>population</u> of over 300 million.

Die Zahlen beziehen sich auf die durchnummerierten Übungen.

A

a far cry from   40
A levels: do / take one's A.
  13, 89
abide   63
able to   25
accept   55
account: in an a.   65
achieve   108
Adam: doesn't know him
  from A.   119
adapt   63
address   117
address an issue   22
adept   63
Adjektiv – Adverb   24, 28
adopt   5, 63
Adverb – Adjektiv   24, 28
advice   23
affect   5
afraid of   96
aggravate   69
agree: doesn't a. with sb   6
aim   106, 108
aktuell   48
alive   98
all   2, 3
alle   2
allein(ig)   18
alles   3
allowed to   53
alone   18
aloud   27
already   58
als   1
also   86
am   35
ameliorate   69
amount   73
an   35
angrily   104
angry   104
Angst haben   59
Ankunft   111
annoyed   104
annoying   104
Antonyme   19, 80
anything   3
Ärger   111
Ärger(nis)   104

ärgerlich   104
arse: doesn't know his a.
  from his elbow   119
Artikel: Nichtgebrauch   62
as   1, 82, 103
as ... as   50
as far as   81
ask questions   60, 68
at   9
at an age   127
at length   9
at night   9
at school   123
at the moment   56, 65, 115,
  123
attend   115
auch   86
auf   35
aus   109
Aussprache   33, 47, 85
avoid   129

B

back to front   119
backside   90, 128
bacon: bring home the b.   4
bad(ly)   75
ball is in sb's court   49
bank   90
bark up the wrong tree   49
bathroom   44, 94
be   15, 59, 68, 91, 99
be able to   25
be all at sea   49
be allowed to   53
be on about sth   49
be said to   30
be sick and tired of   40
be (supposed) to   30
be told to   30
be used to sth   49
Beamer   48
Beantwortung   17
bear   76
beat the rap   77
become   6, 15
bedfellows: make strange b.   40
bee's knees   77
bekommen   6, 48
bench   90
Berufe   70

best thing since sliced bread   49
Besuch   115
besuchen   115
big   112
bis   81
blame   128
blamieren   48, 128
bleiben   45
blühend   48
book: bring to b.   31
border   87, 90
borgen   87
borrow   87
böse   104
bother   104
boundary   87
brauchen   105
brav   48, 128
brave   128
bread: which side her b. is
  buttered   119
break out in a rash   29
break: have a b.   89
brim   100
bring happiness   60
bring home the bacon   4
bring to book   31
bringen   107
brink   100
broad   112
buck: make a fast b.   40
but   1, 9, 64, 81
by accident   9
by and large   40
by herself   127
by mistake   109
by nature   9
by profession   9
by train   127

C

cake: piece of c.   77
call on   7, 115
calm(ly)   63
can   25, 53
can: carry the c.   77
care for   7
carry   76, 107
carry a torch for   31
carry the can   77

cat: like sth the c. brought in
 31
catch a bus 5
catch (a) cold 5, 7, 29
catch a glimpse of 74
cease 127
certain(ly) 21
chance: fat c. 77
change: for a c. 81
charge(s) 73
cheese: say c. 93
chef 90
Chef 48
cheque for 65
chew the fat 31
City 48
clear out 7
clever 48
clever at 96
climb 56
clockwork. run like c. 40
come 99
come across 7
come and see 115
come by 7
come down with 29
come to see 115
common run 122
comprehensible 124
comprehensive 124
concern 90
condition: on c. 65
conditions: meet c. 124
confess to 51
consent to 123
contents 23
continue 101
contract AIDS 29
convict 5, 114
convince 5, 114
cooking 98
cost(s) 73
could 25
counsel: keep one's own c. 4
court: ball is in sb's c. 49
cricket: not c. 31
critic 90
cross (Adj.) 104
cry: a far c. from 40
cuisine 98
cut back on 7
cut no ice 77

D
dankbar 124
dead loss 93
deal in / with 51
deal with 7
declare sb dead 127
decrease 56
destination 106
deteriorate 69
develop heart trouble 29
die for sb to 49
die of / from / by 41
difficult 12, 18
discuss 129
divorce sb 71
do 38, 57, 89
do – make 102, 114
do away with 38
do for 38
do in 38
do up 38
do well 38
do without 38
doctor: what the d. ordered 77
Dom 48
dome 90
done for 38
down below 94
downsize 94
drive 57, 89, 125
drive sb crazy 89
drop 56
drop by 7
dual choice 45, 87, 98, 114,
 124, 129
dürfen 36, 53
dürfte 53
during 83
Durst haben 59

E
each other 52, 66
easier said than done 12
easily 12
easy 12
easy on the eye 31
economic(al) 34
edge 100
effect 5
eigen 11
Einzel- 20
einzeln 20
einzig 20

*elbow: doesn't know his arse
 from his e.* 119
end 108
engagiert 48
enhance 69
enhanced interrogation 94
enjoy 101, 113, 129
ensure 45, 92
entitled to 96
Entscheidung 17
Entschuldigung 111
Entwicklung 17
envy 41
Erfahrung 17
Erfolg 111
erhöhen 56
erinnern 102
Erklärung 17
erreichen 106, 108
erringen 108
error 67
erst 121
erzielen 108
es 42, 43
esteem 106
estimate 106
ethically 114
ethnic cleansing 94
ethnically 114
Euphemismen 94
eventually 6, 128
eventuell 48, 128
every 2
everybody 2
everyone 2
everything 3
evil 75, 104
exacerbate 69
except 55
excess 55
expect 55
expense(s) 73
eye: easy on the e. 31

F
fabric 90
Fabrik 48
face (Verb) 91, 125, 127
fahren 57, 125
fail to 101
failure 67
faint 27
fall 56

fall in love with   123
fallacy   67
fallen   56
falsch   67
falsche Freunde   48, 61, 90,
   128
false friends   48, 61, 90, 128
false(ly)   67
famos   48
Fantasie   48
Farbe   110
fare(s)   73
fast   84
fat chance   77
fat: chew the f.   31
fault   67
fear: for f. of   65
fear: in f. of   65
fee(s)   73
*feet: have both f. on the
   ground*   4
Fehler   67
few   46
fire: get on like a house on f.
   77
first   121
first thing   121
first: not know the f. thing   119
flaw   68
fly off the handle   4
fond of   74, 113
for   9, 109
for – since   129
for lack of   9
Fotograf   48
found – founded   45
Frage   22
fringe   100
from   1, 9, 64, 109
from experience   9
from memory   9
früher   101
fruitcake   50
fuck   116
fuck all   116
fuck off   116
fuck up   116
fuck-up   116
fucking   116
führen   87
für sich   20

furious(ly)   104
furniture   23
F-word   116

G
Gebühr   73
gehen   125
genial   48
gentle   27
gern   101, 113
get   6, 15, 99, 107
get (= „lassen")   71
get homesick   6
get hungry   6
get on like a house on fire   77
get on sb's wick   77
get on top of sth   49
get scared   6
get stuffed   113
gift   90
Gift   48
give a jump   78
give a speech   26
gladly   113
glasses   23
glimpse: catch a g. of   74
Glück haben   59
go   10, 57, 99, 125
go back   7
go crazy   15
go down   56
go mad   15
go on   101
go to   115
go to see   115, 125
go up   7, 56
goal   106, 108
goes without saying   93
good at / on   96
Grammatik   129
grand   112
grateful   124
grave   12
great   112
Grenze   87
groß   112
ground: thin on the g.   77
grow   15
guess   101, 106
guide   87
gun: jump the g.   77

H
halten   26
Handeln   111
handle: fly off the h.   4
Handy   48
happen   101
happy   113
hard   12
hard(ly)   63
hash: make a h. of sth   31
have   54
have (= „lassen")   71
have a baby   6
have a break   13
have a talk   60
have both feet on the ground   4
have no time for   77
have to   88
have to oneself   127
having said that   93
hear   114
heavily   12
heavy   12, 18
heighten   56
her   97
Herstellung   17
historic(al)   34
hit on   7
hit: didn't know what h. me
   119
hoffentlich   101
hold   26
hold talks   114
holiday: on h.   123
homework   23
homework: do one's h.   89
how   82
how come   82, 99
human   48
human(ly)   28
humane(ly)   28
humanitarian   28
Hunger haben   59
*hymn sheet: sing from the
   same h. s.*   31

I
ice: cut no i.   77
idioms   4, 31, 40, 49,
   77,119,122
illness   29
image: be the spitting i. of   49
immer wieder   101

improve 69
in 123
in 9, 123
in a low voice 9
in power 9
in the long run 122
incorrect(ly) 67
increase 56
incredible 55
incredibly 55
incredulous(ly) 55
individual(ly) 20
industrial(ly) 28
industrious(ly) 28
inferior 75
influence: under the i. 31
information 23
insure 45
into 123
irritate 128
irritated 104
irritating 104
irritieren 48, 128
isolated 20
issue 22
it 42, 97
item 126
its – it's 114

J
jealous of 96
jedes x-beliebige 3
jump (idioms) 78
jump the gun 77, 78
jump: one j. ahead 78
jumpy 78
jury is still out on 49

K
keep 26, 92
keep (on) + -ing 101
keep a low profile 4
keep one's mouth shut 40
keep one's own counsel 4
keep sb on the run 122
keep to 26
-keit-Wörter 17
kitchen 98
knees: bee's k. 77
know 119
know all the answers 119
know better than 119
know full well 119

know right from wrong 119
know the ropes 119
know: didn't k. whether I was
  coming or going 119
know: not k. any better 119
knowing: there's no k. 119
knowledge 23
Kollokationen 12, 13, 29, 54,
  60, 89
kommen 99
können 25, 36
konnte 25
könnte 25
konsequent 48
kontrollieren 48
Konzern 48
Kosten 73
Kritik 48
Küche 98

L
lack: for l. of 65
Landeskunde 130
large 112
lassen 71
last 26, 46
latest 46
laufen 10
laut 27
lay 91
lead 87, 125
leave 57, 71, 125
leg: not have a l. to stand on
  4, 40
legen 91
leicht – schwer 12
leihen 87
leise 27
Lektüre 48, 111
lend 87
let 71
letzte 46
lie 91
lie down 91
lieber 101
liegen 91
light(ly) 12
like (= „wie") 82
like (Verb) 101, 113
like sth the cat brought in 31
like that 103
like the back of his hand 119
limit 87

line: toe the l. 77
listen 114
literal(ly) 34
literary 34
literate 34
live (Adj.) 98
live (Verb) 41, 98
live a life of 60
lonely 18
loner 20
long 112
loose(ly) 79
loosen 79
lose 79
lose 79
Lösung 17
lot to be said for 93
loud(ly) 27
love to 101, 113
low 27
lower 27, 56
lunatic 50
-ly 24, 28

M
machen 89, 102
mad as a hatter 50
mad as a March hare 50
made from / of 51
madman 50
madwoman 50
make 89
make – do 102, 114
make (= „veranlassen") 71
make a fast buck 40
make a good recovery 29
make a hash of 31
make a living 13
make a promise 60
make a run for it 122
make a speech 26
make strange bedfellows 40
make up 7
margin 100
marines: tell it to the m. 77
married to / with 96
may 25, 53, 101
mean: didn't mean to 93
meaning 128
meet conditions 124
meet demands 60
meet with 51
Meinung 17, 128

221

mich 111
might 25
mind (Verb) 129
Minidialoge 44
mir 111
miracle 124
mistake 67
mistake: make a m. 89
Mobbing 61
möglich 25
moment: at the m. 65, 81, 123
Mörder 61
morning: in the m. 65
morning: on the m. 65
Motor 110
mouth: keep one's m. shut 40
multiple choice 5, 18, 28, 34, 55, 63, 76, 106
müssen 36, 88
mustn't 30, 53, 88

N

nächste 46
name: by / under the n. of 65
nearest 46
need (to) 105
needn't 105
news 23, 126
next 46
nil 118
noisy 27
Nomen ohne Artikel 62
not by a long shot 40
not cricket 31
not have a leg to stand on 4, 40
not know any better 119
not know the first thing 119
not see the wood for the trees 40
not set the world on fire 4
not until 121
notes 124
nothing: think n. of doing sth 49
nothing to write home about 31
notices 124
Notizen 61
nought 118
Novelle 61
nuisance 104
null 118
nutty as a fruitcake 50

O

objective 108
occupations 70
of 64, 109
oh 118
on 9
on fire 9
on holiday 9, 123
on purpose 9
on schedule 9
on the run 122
one another 52, 66
onions: knows his o. 119
only 20, 121
operate on sb 51
opinion: in my o. 65
ordered: what the doctor o. 77
ought to 30
ours 52
ourselves 52
out 109
out of 109
out to lunch 50
outskirts 100
over 109
own 11

P

pass 99
pass away 94
pay (for) 51
pay a visit 60, 89
Pech haben 59
people 23
Perfekt 58
personal 128
Personal 128
photograph 90
phrasal verbs 7
piece of cake 77
place 72, 118
planks: thick as two short p. 31
Platz 72
Plural oder Singular? 23
point by point 127
points: win on p. 81
police 5, 23
Politik 110
poor(ly) 75
position 118
pot: a watched p. never boils 40

Präpositionen 9, 35, 41, 51, 64, 65, 74, 81, 96, 118, 123, 127
prefer 101
Preis 73
present perfect 58
price 73
prize 73
problem 22
Problem 22
profile: keep a low profile 4
profit: at a p. 74
Programm 61
progress 23
progressive form 58
property 92
proverbs 3, 8, 16, 43, 78, 117, 120
Provision 61
prüfen 61
Punkt 110
push around 7
put 66, 89, 107
put off 7
put out 7
put up 56
put up with 7

Q

quick(ly) 84
quiet(ly) 27, 63

R

radio: on the r. 81
raise 34, 56
Rand 100
rap: beat the r. 77
rare 63
rat: smell a r. 77
Rate 61
reach a conclusion 60
recently 46
reden 117
reduce 56
remain 45
remember 102
remind 102, 129
rent 90
Rente 61
resolve – solve 22
Rezept 61
rich in 96
ride 57, 125

right up sb's street 77
ring 100
ring: throw one's hat in the r. 4
rings: run r. around sb 4
rip off 7
rise 34, 56
road – street 8
rob 45
rock 90
Rock 61
room 72
ropes: know the r. 119
round the bend 50
rub sb up the wrong way 4
Rückseite 61, 128
ruhig 27, 63
run 10, 57, 122, 125
run a tight ship 4
run like clockwork 40
run of 122
run rings around sb 4
run: good run for 122
run: in the long r. 122

S
safe(ly) 21
sagen 93
said to 30
said: a lot to be s. for 93
save 26
say 68, 93
say cheese 93
say: you can s. that again 93
saying: goes without s. 93
scantily 12
scanty 12
Schatten 98
schätzen 106
Scheiß- 116
schlecht 75
schlimm 75
schnell 84
schon 58
schwer 18
schwer – leicht 12
scream with pain 9, 51
sea: be all at s. 49
seat 72
seat: take a s. 72
secure(ly) 21
See 61
sein 108
selbstbewusst 61

-self 66
send for 71, 96, 99
senden 61
senken 56
sensibel 18, 61, 87
sensible 18, 87
sensitive 18, 87
separately 20
seriös 61
serious 18
serious(ly) 12
serve a prison term 60
set 68
set: not s. the world on fire 4
severe(ly) 12
shade 98
shadow 98
shall 30
shalt 30
she 97
ship: run a tight s. 4
short of sth 81
shot: not by a long s. 40
should 30, 88
should(n't) 53
sich 66
sicher 21
sick and tired of 40
side 100
sie 97
silly season 14
similes 50
since – for 129
sing from the same hymn sheet 31
single 18, 20
Singular oder Plural? 23
sink 56
sinken 56
sliced bread: best thing since s. b. 49
slight(ly) 12
smell a rat 77
smell of 51
Smoking 61
so 103
so 103
soft(ly) 27
sole 18
solitary 20
sollen 30, 36
solution 22

solve – resolve 22
sort out 7
space 72
sparen 61
speak up 27
speaking terms: on s. t. 117
specialize in 51
speed: at a s. of 74
spend 128
spenden 61, 128
spendieren 128
spin 94
spitting image 49
spot 118
sprechen 117
Sprichwörter 3, 8, 16, 43, 78, 117, 120
square 72
stairs 23
stand 68
stationery 90
stay 45
steal 45, 92
stehen 68
steigen 56
Stelle 118
stellen 68
stick to 26
stop 26
street – road 8
street: right up sb's s. 77
stuff (it) 113
stuff: knows his s. 119
stuffed: get s. 113
success 108
such 103
suffer a heart attack 29
suggest 129
suit 68
sum 73
suppose 101
supposed to 30
sure(ly) 21
surroundings 23
suspicion: on s. of 74
suspicious of 96
sympathisch 61

T
take 26, 57, 89, 105
take (= „bringen") 107
take a break 13
take a jump 78

take a photo   60
take a walk   5
take after   99
take A-levels   13, 89
take medication   29
take out insurance   13
take the view   5
take: what's your take on   77
talk about   5
talk to   123
tall   112
target   106
Technik   110
tell   93
tell it to the marines   77
tell sb to   30
than   1
thankfully   124
that   103
them   97
Thema   22, 61
they   97
thick as thieves   77
thick as two short planks   31
thieves: thick as t.   77
thin on the ground   77
think nothing of doing sth   49
think of   74
this   103
throw one's hat in the ring   4
till   81
time: have no t. for   77
time: on/in t.   74
to   81, 95
to say nothing of   93
toe the line   77
too (= „auch")   86
too (= „zu")   95
top: get on t. of sth   49
topic   22
torch; carry a t. for   31
tour of   74
towards   95
tragen   76, 110
treat sb to a meal   60
trouble   104
trousers   23
turn   15
turn down / up   27
turn out   99
typical of   96, 127

U
überhören   61
übersehen   61
under the influence   31
undergo surgery   29
-ung-Wörter   17
United States   23, 130
uns   52
unter   118
Unterbringung   17
until   81
until: not u.   121
up to   81, 95
us   52
use (Verb)   105
used to   101
used: be u. to sth   49

V
veranlassen   71
verärgert   101
verbessern   69
Verbindung   17
verdammt   116
Verfügung   17
verge   100
Vergleiche   50
Verlaufsform   58
verlieren   79
verrückt   50
verschlechtern   69
Verständigung   17
Verwendung   17
victory   108
vielleicht   101
view of   74
visit   115
visit to   74
voice   27
voice: in a low v.   81
von   64

W
wage war   60
während   83
wahrscheinlich   101
walk   10, 125
walk out on sb   49
walk: go for a w.   81
wandern   61
want   32
warehouse   90

Warenhaus   61
watch   92
watched pot never boils   40
way: give w. to   72
way: that's the w.   103
wear   76
weep for joy   9, 65
weiter   101
welcome   41, 65, 113
Wellness   61
wer   61
werden   15
what ... like   82
when   9
when all is said and done   93
while   83
Wichtigkeit   17
wick: get on sb's w.   77
wicked   104
wide   112
wie   82
with   9
Witz   111
wo   61
wohl   101
wollen   32, 36, 37
wonder   101, 124
wood: not see the w. for the
   trees   40
word: have a word   117
world: in / of the w.   74
worsen   69
wrong(ly)   67
Wunder   124
wütend   104

Y
yet   58
you   97
you don't say   93

Z
zero   118
Ziel   106, 108
zu   95
zufällig   101
zulassen   71